Essays in Medieval History

Companion Volume

Essays in Modern History

EDITED BY IAN R. CHRISTIE

Essays in Medieval History

SELECTED FROM
THE TRANSACTIONS OF
THE ROYAL HISTORICAL SOCIETY
ON THE OCCASION OF
ITS CENTENARY

Edited by R. W. Southern

MACMILLAN
London · Melbourne · Toronto
ST MARTIN'S PRESS
New York
1968

© The Royal Historical Society 1968

Published by
MACMILLAN & COMPANY LTD
Little Essex Street London WC2
and also at Bombay Calcutta and Madras
Macmillan South Africa (Publishers) Pty Ltd Johannesburg
The Macmillan Company of Australia Pty Ltd Melbourne
The Macmillan Company of Canada Ltd Toronto
St Martin's Press Inc New York

Library of Congress catalog card no. 68 – 14233

Printed in Great Britain by
RICHARD CLAY (THE CHAUCER PRESS) LTD
Bungay, Suffolk

Contents

Contents

Preface

The essays printed in this volume have been selected from the first four series of the *Transactions* of the Royal Historical Society, beginning in 1871 and ending in 1950. The choice has been limited to essays which have not previously been reprinted. They have been revised and the bibliographical notes have been brought up to date only in so far as seemed strictly necessary. In the interests of uniformity of style Mr. Grierson has omitted some of the annotation to his essay, and Mr. Richardson has omitted some material in an Appendix to his essay which is now readily available in a fuller form elsewhere. With these exceptions the essays are reprinted substantially in their original form. The Council of the Society gratefully acknowledges the kindness of the authors and (for the essay of Mr. McFarlane) of Dr. Helena Wright, in agreeing to the republication of their essays.

The last essay in the volume is by Mr. K. B. McFarlane, whose untimely death in 1966 deprived the Society of one of its most loyal and distinguished Fellows. Before his death he had agreed to edit this volume, and he had made a preliminary selection of essays, which did not include his own. His successor is conscious that this is perhaps the only improvement he has been able to make, and in concluding his work he wishes to express his own sense of the loss which the Society and all students of English history have suffered by Mr. MacFarlane's death.

R. W. S.

1 The Kiev State and its Relations with Western Europe

The early history of Russia is still in many respects an unexplored field, and the place which the first Russian political organisation occupied in Europe from the tenth to the twelfth century is not yet appreciated as it deserves to be, even by Russian scholars themselves. The research carried out in this field in Russia at the end of the nineteenth and in the early twentieth century[1] was cut short for almost three decades by political events. It is only recently that the history of Kievan Russia has aroused a keener interest among the historians of Soviet Russia, as witness the many studies published in *Vestnik Drevnei Istorii* and especially the work of B. D. Grekov.[2]

But again, the interest of modern Russian scholars centres rather on problems which do not appeal to western historians. As an instance of the slight progress made towards a final solution connected with the early history of Russia, it is enough to cite the origin of Kiev and of the Russian nation. The complexity of the questions relating to the pre-history and early history of Russia was revealed to western scholars by Professor G. Vernadsky,[3] but many of them still remain unsolved. It is therefore impossible in a short paper like this to do justice to all the topics raised and to treat in detail of the early formation of the State of Kiev.[4] All we can do is to outline its main problems and to stress some

[1] See a short review of the most important works dealing with the early history of Russia in G. Laehr, *Die Anfänge des Russischen Reiches: Polit. Geschichte von 9. u. 10. Jh.* (Histor. Studien, vol. 189. Berlin, 1930), p. 116.

[2] *Kievskaya Rus* (Academy of SSSR, Moscow, 1939, 2nd edn., 1945).

[3] *Ancient Russia* (New Haven, 1934).

[4] I have dealt more fully with these problems of early Russian history in my book *The Making of Central and Eastern Europe* (London, 1949), pp. 163–80, 236–61.

features that bear more directly on the relations between the State of Kiev and Western Europe.

To begin with, it appears that the State of Kiev had its own pre-history, scarcely known to a wide public, but significant enough to explain in a way why it was so easy for a foreign race to set up a mighty State among the Slavonic masses settled on the Rivers Bug, Styr, Dnieper and Dniester. Then, the Scandinavian Norsemen had their forerunners in their rule over the Slavonic tribes. These were the Antes,[1] most probably a Sarmatian tribe, which is believed to have been attacked by the Goths when they settled on the eastern frontiers of the Roman Empire. The Antes had their centre of power between the Dniester and the Dnieper, and must have set up their empire among the Slavs of that region at the end of the second century A.D. The Goths, and after them the Huns, who raised their empire on the ruins of the ephemeral Gothic kingdom, barred the way and hampered the drift of the Antes and their Slavs towards the south and the Black Sea; but after Attila's death in 453 the Antes resumed their eastward drive towards the Don and the south, where they came up against the eastern frontiers of the Roman Empire. They would probably have followed the track of the Huns and the Goths and forced their way into the eastern provinces, had they not been prevented by the Avars from doing so. These sixth-century Avars did their work well and made an end of this political unit of Eastern Slavs, the first ancestors of the Russian State.

The foundation of this first Slav Empire on Russian soil is still a subject of debate, and the very name of the Antes is one of the major puzzles which Slavonic archaeologists and philologists are trying to solve. The most likely hypothesis seems to be that the empire was set up by a tribe of the Sarmatians who invaded these countries in the second century A.D., and succeeded in imposing their rule on their nearest Slavonic neighbours. The Sarmatians, who formed the fighting and governing class, were then swallowed up by the prolific Slav element to which they left their political system and their name. We can therefore say that the formation of the first State among the eastern Slavs was similar to that of the Danubian Bulgaria by the Turkik

[1] On the Antes, cf. my work *Les Slaves, Byzance et Rome au IXe siècle* (Paris, 1926), pp. 22 ff., 55 ff.

Bulgars. In this case, however, it is possible that if the Avars had not put an end to the empire of the Antes, the Slavonic State, instead of being due to the Scandinavians of the north, would have started from the south, and the Slavonic State, instead of bearing the Scandinavian and Finnish name of Russia, would have borne a Sarmatian name from a tribe of Iranian stock.

This consideration may clear the way to the solution of another puzzle in Old Slavonic history, the origin of the Croats and the Serbs. There exist some vague accounts of the existence of an empire north of the Carpathians and on the Upper Vistula which flourished in the sixth and seventh centuries and was called the Empire of White Croatia. The reports are few and confused, but the existence of such an empire can hardly be denied. Some of the Sarmatian tribes were driven by the Huns as far as the region of the Upper Vistula, where they settled among the Slavs in occupation, united them, and founded a State which rose to prominence after the destruction of the empire of the Antes by the Avars. The existence of this empire called White Croatia was known to King Alfred[1] and to Constantine Porphyrogenitus, and also to such Arab writers as Kardisi, Ibn Rosteh and an anonymous Persian geographer of the same period. The fact that Slavs called Croats were to be found in countries that were later known as Russian, Polish and Czech authorises us to assume that the empire of White Croatia extended north of the Carpathians over modern Galicia, the Upper Vistula, the Upper Oder and perhaps even parts of Silesia and Eastern Bohemia. But it seems now established that the Iranians penetrated even further and imposed their leadership and their name on the Slavs who lived in modern Saxony, between the Rivers Saale, Elbe and Mulde and were called Sorbs, Serbs or Sorabs. Even among these Slavs, the Serbs of Iranian stock seem to have formed the preponderating and

---

[1] J. Bosworth, *King Alfred's Anglo-Saxon Version* (London, 1859), p. 18. See the study by K. Malone, 'King Alfred's North, A Study in Medieval Geography', *Speculum*, v (1930), 139–67. But Malone's correction of Alfred's geographical information is not warranted. Alfred is right in locating the Horoti to the east of the Dalamentsan, since he was thinking of the White Croats in modern Galicia, not south-east, where the existence of a White Croat tribe in Eastern Bohemia is established by other evidence.

military element, but to have assimilated the language of their subjects.

This should help us to understand what Constantine Porphyrogenitus says about the arrival of the Croats and the Serbs in the south, which he dates from the reign of the Emperor Heraclius.[1] He moreover credits the Croats and the Serbs with the destruction of the Avar overlordship among the Southern Slavs. His account, which Slavonic scholars have so far refused to accept, is true and deserves every credit. If we admit the existence of a White Croatia and a White Serbia, we shall find it proportionately more consistent to admit the expansion of the Moravian Empire starting in the ninth century from the valley of the Morava and reaching by the end of the same century the Upper Vistula, the Bug and the Styr. For Svatopluk of Moravia merely annexed to his realm the empires of White Croatia and White Serbia. These two countries were fully organised, but must have had their strength sapped by the emigration of a substantial portion of the Sarmatian military class to the south. These findings have their importance in early Russian history: the rivalry between Russia and Poland at that early period can be explained as a drive from either side for the spoils of the Moravian Empire, which had absorbed White Croatia when the Magyars overran Great Moravia.

The Sarmatians were succeeded in Kiev and in what is now Southern Russia by the Khazars,[2] who belonged to the Turko-Tartar branch of races that probably helped the Slavs of later Southern Russia to shake off the yoke of the Avars for good, and stepped straightway into the position which the Avars had vacated. Their empire, which had its centre on the Volga delta in Itil, was neighbour to the Bulgars in the Middle Volga. The Bulgar State, known to contemporaries as the Great Bulgaria, existed till the thirteenth century, when it was overthrown by the invading Mongols. There was then serious danger that the Eastern Slavs, the future Russians, would be permanently subjected to Asiatic

[1] See *Constantini Porphyrogeniti de Administrando Imperio*, chs. 29–76, eds. G. Moravesik and R. J. H. Jenkins, vol. 1 (Budapest, 1949), pp. 122 ff.; vol. 2, ed. R. J. H. Jenkins (London, 1962), pp. 93 ff.

[2] On the Khazars, see ch. v of my book *Les Légendes de Constantin et de Méthode vues de Byzance* (Prague, 1933), pp. 148–78.

influences and fall a prey to the powerful Asiatic hordes as they swept by on their way to attack what remained of the Roman Empire in the east.

It may sound strange, but it is nevertheless true to say that the eastern Slavs were saved from that fate by the Germanic Norsemen from Sweden. An Anglo-Saxon account handed down by King Alfred[1] tells us that in the second half of the ninth century the Vikings penetrated into Biarmaland, on the shores of the White Sea, where they opened commercial contact with the native Laplanders and kept up relations with the Baltic and Finnish populations on the shores of the Baltic that can be traced as far back as the eighth century. From there the Norsemen must have heard of the two flourishing empires established on the River Volga, the Khazars and the Bulgars.[2] The Khazars at that time carried on a brisk trade with the Arabs of Bagdad, for the Volga was an unique artery of communication.

But the Norsemen were also on the scent, and they soon discovered the great natural artery by which all these exchanges were going on, though probably not from the Gulf of Riga but from the Gulf of Finland and from Lake Ladoga. Ladoga offered easy access to the Volga by way of Beloozero, but there was a third route, via Lake Ilmen, which the Slavs had reached already before the ninth century. On both these routes two important Norse colonies, Beloozero and Novgorod, were founded, and the native population soon grew familiar with the regular expeditions of Norse warriors and traders.

Incidentally, it should be mentioned here that modern Russian scholars have not been successful in their latest attempt to deny the Germanic origin of the Russians, nor has Professor Vernadsky succeeded in proving that the Russian State started not in the north but in the south, in the Taman Peninsula of Kerch, and that the Russians were

[1] Bosworth, *op. cit.*, pp. 19 f. See also Alan S. C. Ross, *The Terfinnas and Beormas of Ohthere* (Leeds School of English Language, Texts and Monographs, no. vii. 1940), new edition with commentary on the passage and recent bibliography.

[2] See new materials on the commercial relations between the Bulgars on the Volga and the northern peoples in J. Marquart, 'Ein arabischer Bericht über die arktischen Länder aus dem 10. Jh.', *Ungarische Jahrbücher*, iv (1924), 322 ff.

rather a Sarmatic tribe of the Antes-As — the Ruks-As. All these theories are doing violence to known historical facts, and we must hold out for the theory that the Russians were Scandinavians, most probably from Sweden and that the Finns shared in the coining of the name of Russia. It may derive from the Swedish *rodd*, 'rowing'. Early documents frequently mention *Rods lagen*, the part of Sweden nearest to Finland and the first with which the Finns became acquainted. The Finns transferred the name to the whole Swedish land and to the nation, which they still call *Ruotsi*. The Finnish name for Russia is Venäjä.

Though the contact established by the Norsemen between the Khazars and the Arabs was of some importance, yet it did not produce in European history so profound a change as did the discovery by the Norsemen of a route from Novgorod via the Dnieper and the Black Sea to Constantinople. The Norsemen traded with Byzantium from the first half of the ninth century. A third important Nordic colony was established east of Smolensk, where the Volga and the Dnieper run in close proximity. On the way to Constantinople there existed no full-fledged State, only loosely knit Slavonic tribes such as the Krivitchi, the Radimitchi, the Severianes and the Polianes, so that the temptation for the Norsemen to make the best of their opportunity proved too strong.

The Russian Primary Chronicle picturesquely describes the settling of the Scandinavians among the Slavs.[1] The situation matured first in the north both among the Slavs and the Finns who lived there, and Novgorod began to take shape in the first half of the ninth century.

But as trade with the Byzantine Empire and its profitableness increased, the Norsemen considered it imperative to establish colonies farther south on the Dnieper, their main route to the Black Sea and Byzantium, and there was one place better than any, whose strategical importance and economic advantages were evident: Kiev, on the confluence of the River Desna with the Dnieper. It must have been an

[1] See the English translation with introduction by S. H. Cross, *The Russian Primary Chronicle* (Harvard Studies and Notes in Philology and Literature, xii. 1930), pp. 144 ff.; 2nd edn. by O. P. Sherbowitz-Wetzor (Cambridge, Mass., 1953), pp. 53 ff.

important commercial centre even before the arrival of the Norsemen,[1] as its value had not escaped the attention of the Khazars who owned it and from there ruled over the Slavonic tribes of the neighbourhood. But as the Khazars were not able to afford the necessary protection against the Magyars, who at that time lived in Southern Ukraine, and against other nomads, the local Slavs were only too glad to exchange Khazar rule for the overlordship of the Norsemen, whose immediate interest it was to protect their city and to keep the Dnieper route safe. This must have happened much earlier, as indicated by the Primary Chronicle, probably during the first half of the ninth century.

The tradition which attributes the occupation of Kiev to Askold and Dir rests on solid ground; but the Norsemen must have belonged to a clan other than those who settled in Novgorod,[2] and as all the clans were keen on imposing their leadership on as many Slavs as they could, the different clans must have been jealous of each other. This would explain the hostilities that later broke out between Novgorod and Kiev.

The growth of the new Kievan State can be summarised in a few words. In 860 the rulers of Kiev and of the Slavonic tribes between the Dniester and the Dnieper made in the best style of Scandinavian tradition an unsuccessful attempt to plunder the treasures of Constantinople. But pressed by the Byzantines and by the Khazars, Askold and Dir thought better of it and decided to keep on good terms with Byzantium. They officially became Christians and a bishopric of Kiev was created for the benefit of Norsemen and Slavs.[3]

The whole history of Russia would have shaped differently had Christianity at its first stage taken root in Kiev and spread thence to

[1] N. K. Chadwick, *The Beginnings of Russian History* (Cambridge, 1946), pp. 12 ff., rightly points out that the centres where the Norsemen settled must have been flourishing long before their arrival, the very reason why the colonists felt attracted. The land of the Polians played its part as early as the Sarmatian period of Kievan prehistory.

[2] This is also vouched for by the *Primary Chronicle* (ed. Cross, an. 6368–6370). It is not sure, though possible, that they were of Hálogaland origin, as suggested by N. K. Chadwick, *op. cit.*, p. 24.

[3] For particulars, see my books *Les Slaves, Byzance et Rome*, pp. 138, 146; *Les Légendes*, pp. 172 ff.

other lands occupied by the Slavs in east and west. Unfortunately, the first Christianisation of the Russians was of short duration. Kiev was captured by Prince Oleg of Novgorod (about 882), Askold and Dir were killed, and Kiev became pagan once more and had to wait for another century to become Christian again.

Oleg was the real founder of the Kievan State. He linked Kiev with Novgorod and applied his statesmanship to the fusion of the Varyag upper class and the Slavonic elements along friendly lines. His name deserves therefore a place beside the names of two other great Norse conquerors who altered the course of European history — William the Conqueror and Robert Guiscard. The commercial treaty with Byzantium concluded by Oleg in 911 and renewed by his son Igor in 944 enabled the Byzantines to penetrate into Kiev peacefully and paved the way for the policy of Igor's widow Olga, who went to Byzantium to receive baptism.[1]

At the same time as the Russians came under the cultural influence of Byzantium, we hear of their first attempt to come into closer contact with the West, when Olga sent an embassy to Otto I of Germany, the victor over the Magyars at the Lechfeld in 955, with the request to send a bishop to Kiev. This seemed so extraordinary to many Russian historians that they simply refused to admit the authenticity of the Annals which reported it. The report is however genuine; and Olga's move becomes understandable if we remember that the Scandinavian elements in Kiev were suspicious of Byzantium's political and religious influence, and that Olga tried to allay their apprehensions and intended to neutralise Byzantine interference by closer contact with the Roman Empire as renewed by the king of Germany, Otto I.

On the other hand, it had been Otto's one desire to extend his influence as far as possible over Slavonic lands, and at the time of Olga's embassy, the king was nursing ambitious plans of including the Slavonic East bodily in his new empire. This scheme was embodied in the foundation of the metropolis of Magdeburg, which in his dreams was destined to embrace all the Slavonic nations from the Elbe to the east as far as ambition could reach. Olga's embassy was therefore a

---

[1] For a detailed discussion of the sources and the bibliography on the baptism of Olga, see Laehr, *op. cit.*, pp. 103–6.

godsend, and gave him the feeling that his plans were nearer realisation than it had seemed possible to his sceptical counsellors.[1]

But Otto's schemes and Olga's plans came to grief at the very outset. Probably before Otto's envoy, the bishop Adalbert, had reached Kiev, Olga had been forced to hand over all effective authority to her son Svyatoslav, and the new master of Kiev had no time for either Byzantine or western Christianity. There was even a serious danger under Svyatoslav's reign that the fascinating civilisation of the Khalifs might outshine that of Christian Byzantium, and that instead of Christianity in either its western or eastern form it would be Islam that would cross the Dniester, the Dnieper, the Carpathians and obtain a footing perhaps even among the Magyars. Besides, when Svyatoslav defeated the Bulgars of the Middle Volga, who had become Musulmans, he was so charmed by the Arab culture that had found entry into Bolgar, the capital of the Bulgarians, that he made up his mind to transfer his capital to the Volga.[2]

The danger was averted by Byzantium. Svyatoslav yielded to the attraction of the Danube and instead of settling on the Volga, fought the Danubian Bulgars on Byzantine invitation and in these adventures met his death.

The fate of the Kievan State was finally decided by Vladimir, Svyatoslav's illegitimate son, of whose conversion the Russian Primary Chronicle gives us a graphic account.[3] According to this Russian source, Vladimir was baptised in Cherson by a Byzantine bishop. This report has been questioned on the ground that the hierarchy of Kiev had

---

[1] The religious policy of the Ottos deserves closer attention on the part of historians. A. Brackmann tried to break new ground in his interesting studies, especially in 'Die Ostpolitik Ottos des Grossen', *Hist. Zeitschrift*, cxxxiv (1926), 254 ff., but he underestimated the Slavonic element and the Polish reaction against Otto's designs. We have outlined Otto's plans in a short paper 'The First Wave of the Drang nach Osten', *Cambridge Historical Journal*, vii (1943), 129 ff., and more fully in my *Making of Central and Eastern Europe*, pp. 27 ff.

[2] See the recent study on the Volga Bulgars by A. P. Smirnov, 'Ocherki po Istorii drevnikh Bulgar' (*Trudy Gosud. Istor. Muzeya*, xi, Moscow, 1940), 55–136.

[3] *Ad a.* 6494–6497 (Cross, *op. cit.*, 183–207); also the complete list of sources bearing on Vladimir's conversion in H. Koch's study 'Byzanz, Ochrid und Kiev', *Kyrios*, iii (Berlin, 1938), 290–2.

been established by Rome and not by Byzantium. The main evidence for this argument is a statement in the Annals of Lampert to the effect that in 973 a Russian embassy attended the last diet held in Quedlinburg by Otto I. This would indicate that Vladimir's successor Yaropolk must have reopened negotiations with the emperor. There is also a statement in the Russian Chronicle of Nikon that Vladimir received an embassy from the pope in Kiev. The episode, if true, would be interesting, and the theory it supports has made an impression in some quarters.[1]

But when examined in detail, the theory does not hold water. The Roman embassy to Kiev at the time that Vladimir became a Christian is correct enough: only, it was not sent by the pope, but by the Empress Theophano, the widow of Otto II, who was at that time in Rome and who had special reasons for being interested in Vladimir's baptism, since his new wife was a Byzantine princess and Theophano's cousin. His marriage with a Byzantine princess had been Vladimir's *sine qua non* for his acceptance of Christianity.

The Byzantine princess did not fancy the union, but she had to make the best of it and find consolation in the knowledge that for her sake her husband had dismissed his five wives and 800 concubines, an extravagant number even for a Viking — a figure probably improved upon by the chronicler to demonstrate the baptismal transformation of a pagan soul. Theophano knew by experience what it meant to be married to a semi-barbarian and may have felt sympathy for her cousin. Hence she sent her some relics of saints with a few words of consolation. If the pope had anything to do with the embassy, it was only to send his blessing to the Russian duchess and her husband and to endorse the message of the Empress Theophano.

[1] The theory was developed by N. de Baumgarten, 'Vladimir et la Conversion de la Russie', *Orientalia Christiana*, xxvii (1932). We are told there that Scandinavian priests had acquainted Vladimir with the principles of Christianity and that Olaf Tryggvason finally prevailed on Vladimir to embrace the faith. Yet, it is well known that Christianity made very slow progress in Novgorod, where Scandinavian influence was most marked. This would make Scandinavian Christian influence in Russia very doubtful. The 'western theory' was lately developed by M. Jugie in his book, *Le Schisme byzantin* (Paris, 1940). pp. 177–86. See also my *Making of Central and Eastern Europe*, pp. 179 ff.

Though the Byzantine origin of Russian Christianity cannot be questioned, it would be going too far to see in this religious dependence of Kievan Russia on Byzantium any limitation of its political independence. This problem still preoccupies scholars, and many postulate a kind of vassalage of Russia under Byzantium.[1] But this is an exaggeration. The relationship that existed was based on Russia's free acceptance of Byzantine political philosophy. Like the Byzantines, they looked upon the Basileus as the representative of God on earth, and therefore as the supreme head of all Christians and sole legislator in matters concerning Christianity.[2]

With regard to the traces of western canon law found in the organisation of Kievan Christianity, as for instance the introduction of tithes, a Frankish custom unknown to Byzantium, there is no need to suppose that they were due to Rome or to the Scandinavian clergy who converted the Russians ahead of the Byzantines. There is an alternative and better explanation of how such western practices found their way into Kievan Russia, for Russian influence spread westward when Vladimir occupied the so-called Red Cities (Czervien) together with Przemysl. It was there he came upon the Poles who at that time were emerging into history under their first known duke, Mieszko I. He became a Christian in 966 with the assistance of the Czechs. Those regions had been part of White Croatia and their spoils had been a subject of dispute between the Russians, the Czechs and the Poles. After the defeat of the Magyars by Otto I, Boleslas I of Bohemia extended his dominion over Moravia, a great portion of Slovakia, and over Silesia and Cracow, territories which the Poles were soon to claim for themselves. Thus it came about that three Slavonic empires met on the Carpathians and that Vladimir's Russia came into contact with the western Roman Empire as renovated by the Germans, Bohemia being part of that empire. The gate to the west stood wide open to Vladimir and his Russians. It is this combination of circumstances which is so often overlooked by historians who happen to be interested in this period.

[1] See Vasiliev, 'Was Old Russia a Vassal State of Byzantium?' *Speculum*, vii (1932), 350 ff. Cf. N. K. Chadwick, *op. cit.*, pp. 71 ff.

[2] See further, F. Dvornik, *Early Christian and Byzantine Political Philosophy* (Washington, 1966), Dumbarton Oaks Studies no. 9, 2 vols.

It was through this gate that western literary documents in Old Slavonic translations reached the new Christian State and contributed to the growth of its Slavonic literature. It is true that the merit of passing on the Slavonic language really belongs to the Bulgarians,[1] though Bohemia also enriched it with Slavonic works. Recent discoveries have revealed what Slavonic literature meant to the life in Bohemia in the tenth and eleventh centuries. The disciples of St. Cyril and St. Methodius, the inventors of the Slavonic alphabet in Great Moravia, had found refuge in Bohemia, and some of them must have survived in what is Slovakia today and the region of Cracow, as these countries had not been destroyed but only subjected by the Magyars. The Legend of St. Methodius, written in Moravia before the catastrophe, thus found its way into Russian territory. The eight manuscripts that have survived are all of Russian origin, which is remarkable, since the Legend was unknown to the Serbs and the Croats; but then, the Magyars blocked the way. In the same manner, a fragment of the Old Slavonic missal was saved by Kiev. Great literary activity continued in the Przemyslid Empire throughout the tenth and eleventh centuries and endowed Kievan Russia with both translations and original works. Among them we find the oldest Life of St. Wenceslas, written in Slavonic soon after 929, and the Slavonic Life of his grandmother Ludmila, now lost, but which was known in Kievan Russia and embodied in the Lessons of the saint's feast by the Russian Church.[2]

Another Life of St. Wenceslas written in the tenth century in Latin by Gumpold of Mantua was translated in Bohemia, enlarged, and taken to Kiev. A Latin Life of St. Vitus, patron saint of Saxony and Bohemia, was also translated in the latter country and is found in a Russian collection dating from the twelfth century and called the *Uspenski Sbornik*. Again, the account of the martyrdom of St. Apollinaris of Ravenna, in Old Slavonic of Bohemian origin, is found in a Russian manuscript of the fourteenth century. The translation of the

---

[1] Their share is somewhat overdone by the partisans of the so-called Bulgarian theory first elaborated by M. D. Priselkov and later developed by H. Koch, *op. cit.*, pp. 254–92. There is no serious evidence for the Bulgarian origin of the Russian hierarchy.

[2] For more details on these recent discoveries, see the study by M. Weingart in *Svatováclavský Sborník* (Prague, 1936), pp. 863 ff.

Latin Life of St. Benedict of Nursia can be read in a manuscript of the same century and the martyrdom of Pope St. Stephen in another of the fifteenth. Other cases in point are a short homily on the feast of SS. Peter and Paul, a short sermon for Easter on the Baptism and Ascension of Jesus Christ, and another homily on St. John the Baptist and SS. Cosmas and Damian.[1]

Some of these texts may be credited to St. Methodius' favourite disciple St. Clement who fled to Bulgaria, as for instance the sermons on SS. Peter and Paul and on St. John the Baptist, and the Easter sermon. As regards the translation of Pope Stephen's martyrdom, the editor has discovered striking similarities of style between the translator and the author of the Life of St. Methodius. Another relic of Old Slavonic literature, a sermon by St. Gregory the Great, translated from the Latin and found in a Russian manuscript of the thirteenth century, offers many similarities to the style used in the so-called Glagolitic fragments of Kiev referred to above. What is more, a similar affinity of style is found to exist between the writers of those documents and the author of the Old Slavonic Life of St. Wenceslas. This would establish the Czech origin of the two documents.

More instances could be quoted to show that in spite of the official schism of 1054 between the Western and Eastern Churches, a lively intercourse in the religious field brought Kievan Russia and Western Europe together. And Bohemia was the principal liaison agent. That would explain how the cult of SS. Wenceslas and Ludmila, two Czech (but Latin) saints, came to be popular in Russia in the eleventh century. There are indications that without gaining the same popularity, the cult of St. Adalbert (Vojtěch), bishop of Prague, the great friend of Boleslas the Great of Poland, was known in Russia at the same period.

An interesting document in this connection is a prayer to the Blessed Trinity, of western origin and belonging to the eleventh century, which could only have found its way into Kievan Russia, where

---

[1] Most of the documents were published by A. I. Sobolevsky in *Izvestya Otdeleniya Russk. Yazyka i Slovesnosti Imp. Akad. Nauk*, viii (1903), x (1905), xi (1906), in the *Sbornik* of the same Institution (vol. lxxxviii), and in *Russkyi Filologicheskii Vestnik*, no. 1 (1900). See also F. Dvornik in *Église et les Églises* (Chevetogne, 1954), vol. 1, pp. 323–49.

it was popular in the eleventh and twelfth centuries, from the Przemyslid Empire. Here are the names of the western saints whose intercession is asked for in this prayer: SS. Magnus, Canute, Olaf, Alban, Botulf, Martin, Victor, the Popes Linus, Anacletus, Clement and Leo, the saintly brothers Cyril and Methodius, Wenceslas and Adalbert. The composition or the translation of this prayer probably belongs to the end of the eleventh century, since St. Canute and St. Olaf died in 1086 and 1072 respectively, and it has come to us in different versions found in Russian manuscripts dating from the fourteenth to the sixteenth century; but as A. I. Sobolevsky rightly points out, it has kept words that betray lineage from the Old Slavonic period.

This choice of saints is characteristic. St. Magnus, Abbot of Füss in Swabia, who died about the middle of the seventh century, was a disciple of SS. Columban and Gall and was held in great veneration in Germany at the time the prayer in question was composed. The legendary Life attributed to the hermit Theodore, a contemporary of Charlemagne's father Pipin, pretends that Magnus was of princely origin and belonged to the Scots royal family, but it is more likely that he was of German extraction. The Life was written in the tenth century, probably anonymously, by an author who used as his main source the Lives of SS. Columban and Gall. In the eleventh century, Othloh of St. Emmeram in Regensburg wrote another Life of the same saint.

The spread of the cult of Canute of Denmark and of the Norwegian king Olaf to Russia is not surprising, considering her many contacts with Scandinavia.[1] The spread of this cult to Germany would explain the juxtaposition of those two Christian heroes with another favourite German saint in a prayer composed at the end of the eleventh century. St. Alban, martyred in 406, was a patron saint of Mainz, and his Life was written in 1062 by Goswin, canon of the same city. Botulf was an Anglo-Saxon saint who died at the end of the seventh century

---

[1] On the church of St. Olaf in Novgorod which was set apart for the Scandinavian and German merchants, see W. Abraham, 'Powstanie Organiz. Kosciola Latinsk. na Rusi', *Rozsprawe* of the Polish Acad., Phil. Hist. Cl., 1904, pp. 47 ff.

as Abbot of Icanhoe, and his cult must have been revived in the tenth century when his relics were translated in the reign of King Edgar. St. Martin can be no other than the bishop of Tours, whose cultus is still popular throughout Central Europe. St. Victor[1] should probably be identified with the famous martyr of Solothurn in Switzerland, where he is venerated in association with St. Ursus and the soldiers of the legendary legion of Thebes, especially at St. Gallen.

Bearing in mind Bohemia's relations with Saxony, Mainz and Regensburg, we can imagine how the cult of those northern saints passed into that country. It was there, then, that the prayer was, if not written, certainly translated from Latin into Old Slavonic, since such a selection of Germanic and Slavonic saints could only have been made in eleventh-century Bohemia. There is no valid reason for assuming direct penetration into Russia from Scandinavia.

Another Old Slavonic prayer, for protection from the devil, has also a curious miscellany of western saints, some of them taken from the prayer to the Blessed Trinity, but with the addition of SS. Lucy, Cecilia and Walpurga. The Collection in which the prayer is found has other prayers which in the opinion of their editor A. I. Sobolevsky, may likewise be translations from a Latin original, especially the one attributed to St. Gregory the Great and addressed to St. Ambrose in the manner of the Latin *Confiteor*. As the manuscript belongs to the thirteenth century there should be no difficulty in dating it from the twelfth, when other prayers of western origin found their way into Russia.

The main link in this religious intercourse was the Abbey of Sázava near Prague, founded by St. Procopius, which kept its Slavonic character till 1096. Among its treasures was a relic of SS. Boris and Gleb, who were canonised by the Russian Church in 1071. But that was not the only centre. When the monks of Sazava were expelled for the first time in 1055, they took refuge in northern Hungary, evidence of the existence of another Slavonic institution in that country, which must have survived the suppression of Sázava.

[1] For the lives of these saints, see *Acta Sanctorum*: St. Magnus (6 Sept.), St. Canute (10 July), St. Olaf (29 July), St. Alban (21 June), St. Botulf (17 June), St. Victor (30 Sept.).

The Czechs were not the only go-betweens. The feast of the Translation of the relics of St. Nicholas from Myra in Asia Minor to Bari was probably not due to Bohemia. An office of the Translation was composed in Kiev in Old Slavonic soon after 1091;[1] and as the Byzantines looked upon the Translation as robbery, the introduction of the Latin feast into Russia has its significance. In 1066 the Byzantines settled some Russian mercenaries in Bari, and Praxedis, daughter of Vsevolod of Kiev and wife of the Emperor Henry IV, may have had something to do with the Latin feast. She was in touch with Matilda of Tuscany and Gregory VII and returned to Kiev in 1095.

Such religious contacts were possibly made via Germany and Regensburg, as attested by Scottish monks who lived in that city. We read in the Life of St. Marianus,[2] abbot of the Scottish foundation, of German traders travelling from Regensburg to Kiev, and we are told of a monk Mauricius who took advantage of these relations to go to Kiev and ask the king of the city (Vladimir Monomakh who died in 1125) for a contribution towards the completion of the abbey. The Scottish monks must have been popular in Kiev, for they built there a church and a monastery, probably towards the end of the twelfth century, to minister to the German colony and other foreign merchants who traded with Russia. Their foundation in Kiev was wrecked at the destruction of the city by the Mongols.[3]

We may in this connection mention another case of religious contact in the twelfth century. We read in the *Translation of the Relics of St. Godard*[4] that a number of pilgrims returning from Russia (*quidam peregrinantes de Ruzia*) were attacked by robbers and rescued by the intercession of St. Godard. The expedition was apparently a religious pilgrimage to the shrine of Kiev. As the *Translation* was written after 1132, the incident should be placed within the first decades of the twelfth century. At that time, the two Churches were held apart by an official schism.

To help one to grasp the position held by the Kievan State in con-

---

[1] For particulars, see B. Leib, *Rome, Kiev et Byzance* (Paris, 1924), pp. 65–74.

[2] 'Vita S. Mariani', *Acta Sanct.*, 9 Feb., ch. iv.

[3] For details, see W. Abraham, *Powstanie Organ. Kosc. Lac.*, 69 ff.

[4] *Mon. Germ. Hist.*, SS. xii. 647.

temporary Europe, it is well to remember that the ducal family of Kiev was matrimonially connected with every court of eleventh- and twelfth-century Europe. Vladimir married the sons and daughters of his last liaison to western princes and princesses — Svyatopolk to a daughter of Boleslas the Great of Poland, Premislava to Ladislas the Bald of Hungary, Yaroslav to Ingegerde of Sweden, Mary to Casimir I of Poland; and it is believed that in 1025 Boleslas the Great married Vladimir's daughter Predslava. Yaroslav followed his father's policy. His son Izyaslav married a sister of Casimir I of Poland; the daughters Elizabeth, Anne and Anastasia married Harold of Norway, Henry I of France and Andrew of Hungary respectively; and his sons Igor and Svyatoslav married Kunigunde of Germany, daughter of Otto, Margrave of Meissen, and the German Oda, whose mother may have been a daughter of Henry III's brother. Yaroslav's successor Vsevolod broke with the habit and turned east by marrying a daughter of the emperor Constantine Monomachus; but his daughter Praxedis (Eupraxia) went to Germany to become first the wife of Henry von Stade, Margrave of the Nordmark, and after the Margrave's death, wife of Henry IV, while his son and successor, the famous Vladimir Monomakh, found his wife in distant England, when he married Gytha, daughter of Harold, the last Saxon king, and niece of Sven, the king of Denmark. Two Polish princes, Boleslas II and Mieszko, married Russian princesses: the former, Vicheslava, daughter of Yaroslav's son Vladimir, and the latter, Eudoxia, daughter of Izyaslav. Boleslas III of Poland also married a princess of the Izyaslav line, Zbislava, daughter of Svyatopolk and sister of Predslava, who married a son of Coloman of Hungary. Vladimir Monomakh's children followed the tradition, Euphemia marrying the Hungarian king Coloman, and Mstislav, Christina of Sweden. Lastly, his daughter Malmfrid married Sigurd of Denmark and her sister Ingeburge married St. Canute of Denmark.[1]

---

[1] Details, sources and bibliography will be found in B. Leib, *op. cit.*, 143–78. Saxo Grammaticus' account (*a.* 1067, in *SS.* xxix. 67) of the unfortunate English princess's marriage to the Russian duke is pathetic enough. Cf. also S. H. Cross, 'Medieval Russian Contacts with the West', *Speculum*, x (1935), 137–44. N. de Baumgarten, *Généalogies et mariages occidentains des Rurikides Russes du Xe au XIIIe siècles*, Orientalia Christiana, nos. 35, 94 (Rome, 1927, 1934).

Kiev's contacts with the Scandinavian countries were of course true to tradition, but those with Poland and Hungary were a significant demonstration of friendship. Suggestive, too, were Kiev's relations with Germany and the deference paid in France and Saxon England to the prestige of the court of Kiev.

The part which Russia played in the commercial history of Europe also deserves consideration. The earliest document which points to brisk commercial exchanges between Kiev and the rest of Europe is that of Raffelstetten (903–906).[1] It regulated the duties to be paid by Russian and other traders on entering the Ostmark and crossing the Danube. The city of Enns was the first of the German towns to benefit by this trade, but Regensburg became its main centre,[2] which increased in importance when pilgrims and crusaders used it on their way to the Holy Land and to Constantinople as a stage for rest and supplies. From the eleventh century till the beginning of the thirteenth Regensburg enjoyed the same trading facilities with Russia as Novgorod enjoyed later. The complaints sent from Regensburg by Conrad III to John Comnenus of Constantinople about traders being waylaid and killed in Russia,[3] and the privileges granted to the Regensburgers by the Duke Leopold of Styria,[4] are evidence of a brisk intercourse. The Regensburg merchants must have had a clearing house in Kiev, since a German trader operating there settled a considerable sum of money, which a Regensburg trader owed him, on the convent of St. Emmeram.[5]

The famous Jewish merchant and traveller Petachias,[6] who described his travels through the lands of the Tartars, Turks, and Armenians to

[1] Published in *Mon. Germ. Hist., Capit. Reg. Franc.*, pp. 244 ff.

[2] Relative documents were published in V. Vasilevskii's study 'Drevnaya Toroga Kieva s Regensburgom', *Zhurnal* of the Ministry of Instruction, 1888, no. vii. 121 ff.

[3] See W. Bernhardi, *Jahrbücher der Deutschen Geschichte: Konrad III* (Leipzig, 1883), pp. 271 ff.

[4] A. V. Meiller, 'Öster. Stadtrechte u. Satzungen', *Archiv f. Kunde Öster. Geschichtquellen*, x (1853), 92–6.

[5] *Codex Traditionum S. Emmerammensium* in Pez, *Thesaurus Anecdotorum* (Augsburg, 1721–9, t. i, pars 3), p. 173.

[6] *R. Petachiae Itinerarium*, in B. Ugolinus, *Thesaurus Antiq. Sacr.* (Venice, 1767), vi. 1168 ff.

Babylon, Bagdad and Palestine, was a native of Regensburg. He started on his journey in 1182 from Bohemia, crossed Poland to Kiev, 'city of Sarmatia', and crossed the Dnieper 'into the lands of the Tartars'. Other documents speak of the transit through Hungary of Russian trade, while many ornaments of Byzantine origin or made in Kiev such as bracelets, rings and buttons, which are found in Czech graves of the period, tell their own tale.[1] Besides their own products such as furs, horses and beeswax, the Russians thus exported cloth and silks imported from Byzantium, where Russian traders had their own quarters.

The *Anonymous Gallus*[2] mentions an alternative route of Russian trading through Poland. The northern route via the Baltic was at the beginning in Russian hands and their merchant fleet sailed to Scandinavia, where the island of Gotland was used as a place of call, to Lübeck and Denmark.[3] A charter granted in 1188 by the Emperor Frederick I to Lübeck mentions the Russians first, and in the following year German merchants and Novgorod discussed the first draft of a commercial agreement.[4] But in the thirteenth century this trade fell into German hands and became the monopoly of the Hanseatic League. It had its own clearing house in Novgorod and special treaties regulated its operations.[5] The northern route interested Flemish traders, and in the twelfth century their cloth made of English wool found a good market in Novgorod.[6] Later, when English cloth came into its own, the English had a hard fight with the Hansa throughout the fifteenth century in the defence of their trading rights with Novgorod.[7] French

---

[1] J. Schránil, *Die Vorgeschichte Böhmens und Mährens* (Berlin, Leipzig, 1928), pp. 298 ff., tables 65–74.

[2] *SS.* ix. 425.

[3] Confirmation of Russian trade in the eleventh century is to be found in an English document, 'Ex Libris de S. Thoma Cantuarensi', *SS.* xxvii. 41.

[4] *Hansisches Urkundenbuch* (Halle, 1876–86), i. 41, no, 33; L. K. Goetz, *Deutsch-Russische Handelsverträge* (Hamburg, 1916), pp. 15–72.

[5] For details, see L. C. Goetz, *Deutsch-Russische Handelsgeschichte des Mittelalters* (Lübeck, 1922), pp. 31–46.

[6] Cf. H. Pirenne, 'Draps d'Ypres à Novgorod au commencement du XIIe siècle', *Revue Belge de Phil. et d'Histoire*, ix (1930), 563.

[7] L. C. Goetz, *Deutsch-Russ. Handelsgesch.*, pp. 152 ff., 160 ff., 289 ff.

enamels and articles of Latin devotion were also popular in Kievan Russia, to judge at least by archaeological finds.[1]

Frequent references to Russia in the *Chansons de Geste* and the French romantic poetry of the time show that the Kievan State was very much in Europe's thought, and a detailed analysis of the Russian allusions in French literature has been made by G. Lozinskij.[2] To French writers, Russia was a reality. In Ipomedon (s. xii), Octavian (s. xiii), Cléomadès (s. xiii) and Thèbes (s. xii) Russia is located beyond Germany as Poland's neighbour, and beyond the Danube as Hungary's neighbour. Merchants from 'Great Russia' bought Beuve de Hamtoun in Hungary as a slave and sold him in Armenia. The third French version of the poem is more explicit and specifies the maritime Varangian route to Russia and the Black Sea from England through the North Sea and the Baltic. It should, however, be observed that the Anglo-Norman romance of Sir Beues of Hamtoun displayed no more interest in Russia than did the other versions of the same romance.

In this class of literature, Russia was regarded as a very rich country and a home of valiant knights. Her main products, furs and horses, are often mentioned besides precious cloth, gold and silk, which were of Byzantine origin, but imported into the West by Russian traders.[3]

Western pilgrims and crusaders met Russians in Constantinople and in the Holy Land, but these were in the service of the Byzantine emperors and not always friendly to the crusaders. This would explain why French epic poets often depict Russia as a pagan country and use the name Rossia, derived from the Greek Rôs.

In English contemporary literature, information about Kievan Russia is scanty, but knowledge about that country must have been as widespread in England as in France and Germany owing to the proximity of Denmark and Scandinavia. Adam of Bremen was quite clear on the position of Russia and knew of the old Varangian route over the Baltic and Lake Ladoga to Novgorod (Ostrogard), and thence

---

[1] Cf. B. Leib, *op. cit.*, pp. 77, 96 ff.

[2] 'La Russie dans la littérature française du moyen age', *Revue des Études Slaves*, ix (1929), 71–88, 253–69.

[3] Lozinskij, *op. cit.*, pp. 262 ff.

over Lovat and the Dnieper to Kiev and the Black Sea.[1] Adam's description is hazy, but his general conception was correct. Gervase of Tilbury,[2] who left his home as a boy and lived on the Continent, had a good recollection of the travelling facilities from Britain to Russia by way of the Baltic. Henry of Mainz[3] showed similar competence with his map of the world (1110), which links the Baltic with the Black Sea by the River Tanais. Better still is the famous Hereford map of the world (1276/83) which connects the Baltic with the Black Sea by way of the 'fluvius Meotides et palludes'.[4] Russia is located north of the Danubian delta.[5]

These brief indications make it clear that the old Varangian tradition of Kievan Russia was still alive in the minds of western and northern Europe as late as the thirteenth century. It was killed by the crusaders' preference for the Mediterranean route. The Hansa only traded with Northern Russia,[6] and the Mongol invasion swept Russia off the stage of European politics and commerce. Echoes of the catastrophe are heard in English chroniclers[7] and in Chaucer's Canterbury Tales.[8] After that, confusion reigns in the minds of western writers whenever they refer to Russia.[9]

---

[1] *Gesta Hammaburg. eccl.*, ii. 19; iv. 1, 10–14 (*SS.* vii. 368, 372 ff.).

[2] *Otia Imperialia* (*SS.* xxvii. 371).

[3] K. Miller, *Mappaemundi* (Stuttgart, 1895), iii. 21 ff.

[4] *Ibid.*, iv. 16 ff.

[5] The Map of the Psalter of London (*ibid.*, iii. 37 ff.), dating from the second half of the thirteenth century, also places 'Ruscite' on the left bank of the Lower Danube.

[6] The Map of Ebstorf (about 1248; *ibid.*, v. 24 ff.) reflects the new knowledge of northern Russia.

[7] For instance, in the Continuation of Gervase of Canterbury's *Gesta Regum*, a. 1240 (*SS.* xxvii. 310); *Annals of Burton, ibid.*, 474; *Matthew of Paris, Chronica Maiora*, in *ibid.*, xxviii. 207 ff., 292.

[8] Complete Works (ed. W. W. Skeat) iv. 2 (Prologue, v. 54), 461 (The Squiere Tales, v. 10).

[9] This is what the monk of Malmesbury says of Russia in his *Eulogium*, ch. 121 (ed. F. S. Haydon, p. 944): 'Rucea sive Rucena provincia est in Minori Asia; habet ab Oriente Gothiam, a Septentrione Pannoniam, ab Occidente Graeciam. Cum Boemis et Sclavis concordat in idiomate. Haec in quadam sui parte Galatia est vocata, ad quam Paulus Apostolus Epistolas dirigebat.' Cf. also ch.

We may conclude from this rapid survey that Russia was never more conscious of her common interests with Western Europe than in the period between the eleventh and thirteenth centuries, and this at a time when Europe stood in the greatest need of a friendly intermediary between the Latin and the Greek worlds. Kievan Russia belonged to the Greek cultural sphere and had thoroughly assimilated the cultural treasures of Byzantium. These she had every opportunity to transmit to the Latin world. Greco-Slavonic traditions were still alive in the Przemyslid Empire in the eleventh century, and given the close relationship between Poland and Bohemia, a new Slavonic power was rising on Russia's western frontier that would have provided the ideal link between the Latin and Greek cultures. After the annexation of the Przemyslid Empire, Poland under Boleslas the Great had sufficient strength to build a 'Sclavonia' able to stem the Saxons' *Drang nach Osten* and provide a friendly meeting ground between East and West. Greco-Slavonic traditions were still alive in the region of Cracow which had treasured up so much of the Moravian Old Slavonic culture and new Greek influences were pouring into Poland from Russia; Mieszko II, Boleslas' successor, was even complimented by Matilda of Swabia for being able to praise the Lord in Slavonic, Latin and Greek.[1]

However, fate decided otherwise. Conrad II broke up this potential 'Sclavonia'. Kievan Russia, exhausted by internal divisions and subjugated by the Mongols, vanished from the scene, and the Latin and Greek worlds lost their last opportunity to reach a friendly understanding. The western crusades embittered the relations between East and

---

67 (p. 62) on the Slavs. The monk takes this information not from the *Geographia Universalis*, an anonymous work preserved in the fourteenth-century manuscript No. 123 of the Arundel Collection in the British Museum (fo. 17r, 18r, 19) — as F. S. Haydon believes — but from the fifteenth book of Bartholomaeus Anglicus' famous work *De Proprietatibus Rerum* (ch. 131, 140, ed. G. B. Pontanus a Braitenberg, Francfurt, 1601, p. 693, 697), written about 1250. As the study of the Arundel Manuscript has shown, this part of the anonymous Geography was simply copied from Bartholomaeus' work. It should be noticed that the English Franciscan is not as emphatic in placing Russia in Asia Minor as is the author of the *Eulogium*. Bartholomaeus places 'Ruthia' in Minoris Asiae confino' His information on the Baltic Slavs is surprisingly accurate.

[1] See her letter to Mieszko in *Mon. Poloniae Histor.*, i. 323.

West, and when in the fifteenth century Russia stepped out of the mist, she faced a Europe too proud of its superior culture to comprehend what its first ambassadors and travellers had reported from Muscovite Russia. There lie the roots of Europe's tragedy.

ADDITIONAL NOTE

The problems concerning the relations between the State of Kiev and Western Europe have been attracting, lately, the attention of Soviet literary historians. M. P. Alekseev in his study 'Anglo-Saksonskaya Parallel k Poucheniyu Vladimira Monomakha', *Institut Russkoy Literatury, Trudy Otdela Drevne-Russkoy Literatury*, ii (Moscow, 1935), 39–80, believed he had found in an Anglo-Saxon composition which, according to him, Gytha had read in the library of Leofric, bishop of Exeter (1050–72), the source of her husband Vladimir Monomakh's admonition to his sons. Alekseev's argument is not, however, conclusive. Such works were numerous in Byzantine literature, and it is more natural to suppose that Monomakh derived his inspiration from Byzantium. M. P. Alekseev gives in his study some interesting details, but no new substantiated facts, concerning this intercourse between Kiev and the West. The same applies to the study of D. V. Ainalov, 'K Istorii Drevne-Russkoy Literatury', *ibid.*, iii (1936), 5–10. For more details on this subject, cf. my study 'Byzantine Political Ideas in Kievan Russia', *Dumbarton Oaks Papers*, vols. 9, 10 (1956), pp. 73–121.

F. DVORNIK

2 The Byzantine Empire in the Eleventh Century : Some Different Interpretations

I was originally provoked into a consideration of this particular problem by reading Ostrogorsky's *Geschichte des byzantinischen Staates*.[1] A long-needed and courageous attempt to reconstruct the history of the empire and characterised by acute and penetrating analysis, this book is nevertheless marked by a certain unevenness of treatment. Side by side with brilliant sections on the achievements of the tenth century and the complications of the fourteenth (this latter perhaps the finest part of the book) must be set the brief and inadequate account of the years 1025–81. Ostrogorsky is not alone. Misstatements and omissions continue, and often in unexpected places.[2] Recent much used general histories, as for instance the third volume of the medieval section of the Glotz *Histoire générale*,[3] still repeat the old emphasis on 1081 as the dividing-line between a time of painful disaster and the new era of Comnenian glory. This paper is then a plea for the reassessment of the history of Byzantium in the eleventh century in the light of all available evidence.

My first point concerns the place of the years 1025–81 in the pattern of Byzantine history. The middle Byzantine period is usually described in some such way as this. — From 843 to 1025 the Empire extended

NOTE. This paper is reprinted as it was originally read, except that some references to later editions have been given and in one or two cases a note on recent work has been added.

[1] G. Ostrogorsky, *Geschichte des byzantinischen Staates* (*Byzantinisches Handbuch in Rahmen des Handbuchs der Altertumswissenschaft*, ed. by Walter Otto), Pt. i, vol. ii (Munich, 1940). 3rd edn., Munich, 1963; the English translation of the 2nd edn., Munich, 1952, was published by Blackwell, Oxford, 1956; an English translation of the 3rd edn. is in the press.

[2] See the reviews of *Byzantium*, ed. N. H. Baynes and H. St. L. B. Moss (1948), in *Journal of Theological Studies*, l (1949), and *Byzantinoslavica*, x (ii).

[3] C. Diehl and G. Marçais, *Le monde oriental de 395 à 1081* (Paris, 1944).

and consolidated its frontier particularly in the north and the east, its internal life was tolerably well ordered, and at the same time its artists and scholars were creating the masterpieces for which their generation was famous. This era of prosperity and achievement was succeeded by what is variously described as political and moral decadence and decline, accompanied by an intellectual flare-up in the mid-eleventh century stimulated by the activities of the brilliant and encyclopaedic, but corrupt, scholar, Michael Psellus. The incompetence which followed the death of Basil II in 1025 was only ended in 1081 with the accession to the imperial throne of the Emperor Alexius Comnenus, whose dynasty restored prosperity for the greater part of the twelfth century. This Comnenian prosperity was irretrievably undermined and the empire fatally disrupted by the events of the last quarter of the twelfth century, which led to the Fourth Crusade, the sack of Constantinople in 1204 and the establishment of the Latins in a substantial area of Byzantine territory. The pattern presented is one of high prestige — decline — recovery — collapse.

It is however nearer the truth to regard the years 1025–1204 as a single unit characterised by fundamental changes. I suspect that the racy gossip of Michael Psellus expatiating on the foibles of the Emperor Constantine IX, and the exceedingly partial pen of Anna Comnena magnifying the achievements of her father the Emperor Alexius, have influenced us more than we realise. The years 1081–1180 had only a veneer of prosperity, and it is a mistake to allow the contrast between the mid-eleventh-century rulers and the efficient Comneni to obscure the fact that certain significant developments which radically altered the history of Byzantium were common to both periods.

The internal life of the East Roman Empire in the eleventh century and after is marked by the growth of what Byzantinists often describe as 'feudalism'. The struggle of the state to protect the smallholder against the great landowner was relaxed;[1] the law making the rich responsible for the taxes of the poor was repealed; immunities and

---

[1] Ostrogorsky shows something of the difficulties involved and the subtlety of evasive methods, even in the tenth century, in 'The peasant's pre-emption right: an abortive reform of the Macedonian Emperors', *Journal of Roman Studies*, xxxvii (1947), 117–26.

privileges were granted with increasing frequency to the great lay and ecclesiastical landlords. Such changes affected imperial defence, for since the seventh century the state had to some extent relied for its soldiers and sailors on the small farmer holding his land under a hereditary obligation of military or naval service. And this system of defence was further undermined in the eleventh century by allowing men to redeem their obligation to military service by the payment of a lump sum. Diminution of imperial authority, such as is reflected in the failure of the state under Michael VII to maintain its corn monopoly against the privileged classes,[1] is most noticeable in increasing separatism: Lesser Armenia was established towards the end of the eleventh century;[2] Cyprus claimed independence under a member of the Comnenian house in 1185; and Trebizond broke away and formed a separate kingdom just before the Fourth Crusade.[3]

There were in addition economic difficulties in the last quarter of the eleventh century which threatened the stability of the Byzantine gold coin, the nomisma, on which Constantinople had built its position in international trade,[4] and further complications were introduced into both economic and political life by reason of the activities of the great trading cities of Italy, more particularly Venice, Pisa and Genoa.

Changes in the character of the Empire from the mid-eleventh century onwards were due also to certain external factors which introduced radical alterations on all three frontiers. And the effects were as disastrous in the twelfth as in the second half of the eleventh century.

In the Balkans there was growing insecurity both by reason of raids

[1] G. I. Bratianu, 'Une expérience d'économie dirigée: le monopole du blé, à Byzance au XIᵉ siècle', *Byzantion*, ix (1934), 643–62, and in *Études byzantines d'histoire économique et sociale* (Paris, 1938), pp. 141–57.

[2] See Sirapie Der Nersessian, *Armenia and the Byzantine Empire: a brief study of Armenian Art and Civilization* (Cambridge, Mass., 1945), pp. 11–12.

[3] See A. A. Vasiliev, 'The Foundation of the Empire of Trebizond (1204–1222)', *Speculum*, xi (1936), 3–37, and 'The Empire of Trebizond in History and Literature', *Byzantion*, xv (1941), 317–77.

[4] G. Ostrogorsky, *op. cit.*, pp. 260 ff., who cites W. Wroth, *Catalogue of the Imperial Byzantine coins in the British Museum*, i (London, 1908), 540 ff., pls. lxi and lxii, showing a normal nomisma and 6 variants. See now Ostrogorsky, *op. cit.*, 3rd edn., p. 274 and note 1.

from nomads living beyond the Danube and from the increasing independence of the Croats and the Zeta and from the conquered Bulgarians, whose resentment at unwise Byzantinisation was strong in
both the eleventh and twelfth centuries.[1] The eastern frontier was
subjected to the spasmodic but increasingly effective attack and infil-
tration of the Turks, themselves of course by no means a united body.
The Seljuks who defeated Romanus IV in 1071 failed to come to terms
with his successor in Constantinople and proceeded to establish themselves in the kingdom of Rum, while the Ghazi Danismends, their
rivals, settled further to the north.[2] From then onwards the old Asia
Minor, saved by the Isaurians, augmented and strengthened by tenth-
and eleventh-century acquisitions and long regarded as the essential
core of the Empire, a vital recruiting ground and source of revenue,
was lost to the Byzantines. Equally disquieting were developments in
the west, where the Byzantines were ousted by Norman adventurers,
who successfully established themselves in south Italy and Sicily and
then proceeded in the '80s of the eleventh century to inaugurate the
policy which was eventually — in other hands — to reshape the course
of Mediterranean and Byzantine history in the later Middle Ages.
Under Robert Guiscard they laid claim to the Byzantine Empire itself.

Norman and western ambition, only thinly disguised by taking the
name of 'crusade', and cleverly exploiting the enthusiasm of the reformed papacy, had as its object the conquest of Jerusalem and the
Holy Land and their retention in Latin hands. It is this embarrassing
corollary to the eleventh-century establishment of the Normans in Italy
and the Turks in Palestine and Asia Minor, that indissolubly links the
history of the two centuries. The Comneni could to some extent break
the shock of the crusading movement, but they could not retrieve the
imperial position or re-establish their claim to lost provinces now in
other hands. With the twelfth-century intrusion of the Turks and the

[1] D. Obolensky, *The Bogomils: a study in Balkan Neo-Manichaeism* (Cambridge, 1948), pp. 169 ff., shows the importance of the Bogomils and Paulicians
in organising resistance to Byzantinisation in both the eleventh and twelfth
centuries.

[2] On this whole question, see P. Wittek, 'Turkish Asia Minor up to the
Osmanlis', in *The Rise of the Ottoman Empire* (London, 1938).

Latins into neighbouring lands and the infiltratio of the latter into the Byzantine Empire itself, the political balance of the Near East was upset and the more important forces which were ultimately to lead to the destruction of the Empire were released. The Latin conquest of 1204 opened the door to the later Ottoman.

Developments which characterised the political and economic life of the Empire in the eleventh century are, then, aggravated in the twelfth century. When Diehl speaks of 'the new era' of the Comneni and the 'glorious' character of their achievement,[1] he is allowing (and he is not alone) capacity for statesmanship to obscure the extent to which the Comnenian rulers were faced with economic insecurity, increased dependence on mercenaries and allies with navies, the menace of separatism and forced reliance on an almost independent nobility. All this binds the twelfth to the eleventh century and sharply distinguishes the political life of both from the earlier period.

The same is true of the ecclesiastical relations between Rome and Constantinople. The violent quarrel of 1054 cannot be taken out of its context. But while all would agree that it can only be understood in the light of past history, few sufficiently emphasise that its full implications were drawn out by events in the succeeding 150 years. This schism of 1054 between the two churches was not in itself necessarily 'definitive' or 'final' as so many scholars still lead the uninitiated to believe.[2] It was not regarded in contemporary official circles as unhealable: the actual wording of the anathema, directed only against the Patriarch Michael Cerularius and his associates with its references to 'the orthodox city', indicate that at the time a door was left open.[3] In the years after

[1] Diehl, *op. cit.*, p. 565.

[2] E.g. Herbert Bloch, 'Monte Cassino, Byzantium, and the West in the earlier Middle Ages', *Dumbarton Oaks Papers*, Number 3 (Cambridge, Mass., 1946), p. 191, and even worse in *A History of Byzantine Music and Hymnography* (2nd edn., Oxford, 1961), p. 167, where Dr. Wellesz writes 'the liturgical controversy between Cerularius and Leo IX in 1054 was the final inducement to a permanent schism'.

[3] Cardinal Humbert, *Brevis et succincta commemoratio*, in J. P. Migne, *Patrologia Latina*, cxliii. 1001, and in C. Will, *Acta et scripta quae de controversiis ecclesiae graecae et latinae saecula xi composita extant* (Leipzig and Marburg, 1861), p. 153.

the Cardinal Humbert had shaken the dust of Hagia Sophia from his feet evidence of various kinds points to the possibility of an understanding. It is forty years ago since Holtzmann drew attention to a manuscript in the British Museum which contains, among other documents, an account of a synod held in September 1089 under the presidency of the Emperor Alexius Comnenus to consider Urban II's complaints that the pope's name had been wrongly (i.e. without judgement of a synod) struck off the diptychs. The synod could evidently find no written decision on this matter and the emperor insisted that, provided the customary systaticon or profession of faith reached Constantinople, the pope's name could be restored to the diptychs, and promised that this would be followed by consideration of disputed points by a synod at which the pope or his representative was present.[1] Further evidence of a less official nature, the experiences of travellers to the Holy Land for instance, is used by Bernard Leib and George Every to demonstrate that throughout the eleventh and for a good part of the twelfth century amicable relations between the various branches of the Church continued at any rate in practice.[2] Official schism between Constantinople and Rome did not necessarily affect relations between Rome and Jerusalem on the one hand, or Jerusalem and Constantinople on the other. The drama of the heated quarrel between the Patriarch Cerularius and Cardinal Humbert has tended to obscure other factors, such as the effect on the ecclesiastical situation of the slowly growing political and economic tension, aggravated by the crusading movement, which led to the Latin capture of Constantinople in 1204. It was not in 1054 but in the late twelfth and early thirteenth centuries that the minds of the orthodox were so hardened that all attempts at reunion in the later Middle Ages were foredoomed to failure.

To speak of political and economic and ecclesiastical difficulties and to stress *change* in an adverse sense would however be to give an unbalanced picture of the eleventh century. Growth and vitality having their roots in a living tradition were as evident then as at any time. And

---

[1] W. Holtzmann, 'Die Unionsverhandlungen zwischen Kaiser Alexios und Papst Urban II in Jahre 1089', *Byzantinische Zeitschrift*, xxviii (1928), 38–67.

[2] B. Leib, *Rome, Kiev et Byzance* (Paris, 1924); G. Every, *The Byzantine Patriarchate, 451–1204* (2nd edn., London, 1962).

there was too that underlying unity which was personified in the emperor, a unity which gave meaning to the Empire even when its final conquest by the Ottomans was a question not of years but of months. It is this unity and this living tradition which explain the contrast in the later Middle Ages between on the one hand the hopeless-ness of political and military inadequacy and on the other the main-tenance of full imperial claims and the late flowering of art and learning.

Some foreshadowing of this kind of situation is found in the eleventh century.

Take for instance the Byzantine conception of imperial authority. In the course of a thousand years or more this changed in details of emphasis and interpretation. Grabar's fine analysis of the conception of the imperial office as reflected in official art,[1] and Ensslin's brilliant essay on the emperor and imperial administration in *Byzantium*[2] are two convincing demonstrations of the error of overstressing a 'static' condition. But — behind such changes remained the common belief in the earthly empire as the *corpus politicum mysticum* and in the emperor as the representative of God. There were, however, clearly appointed limits in the ecclesiastical sphere beyond which the imperial authority could not run, and the working basis of the Byzantine polity was a close-knit interdependence of church and state. The term 'caesaropa-pism' is of course an anachronism after the days of the iconoclasts though there is still some reluctance to recognise this fact.[3] In essentials the relationship between emperor and patriarch, from the days of the iconoclasts onwards at least, remained unchanged, though not entirely unchallenged. The real high light of the Patriarch Michael Cerularius's career was not his attack on Roman authority and usage which pro-

[1] A. Grabar, *L'empereur dans l'art byzantin* (Paris, 1936).

[2] W. Ensslin, 'The emperor and imperial administration' in Baynes and Moss, *Byzantium*, pp. 268–307, though he does rather glide over the church and state controversy and follows von Sickel and Dölger (cf. p. 270).

[3] Cf. Baynes and Moss, *Byzantium*, p. 162: 'the tradition of Caesaropapism which dated back from the earliest days of Byzantium emerged from the Iconoclastic controversy unshaken' — a curious lapse on the part of Delehaye, but corrected by very different statements by N. H. Baynes in the Introduction (p. xxviii) and by W. Ensslin in his essay (p. 276).

voked the anathema of 1054, but his quarrel in 1058 with the Emperor Isaac I Comnenus and his conspicuous failure to gain his point; all he got was a good write-up in his obituary notice. He was a proud and overbearing man, and, failing to dominate the emperor whom he had helped to the throne, he attempted to make the Church supreme at the expense of the imperial office. The tension of the situation is reflected in Scylitzes' brief account of the imperial reaction to what are described as patriarchal 'snarlings',[1] and the drama of the quarrel lives in the elaborate and informative *Accusation*.[2] This last is an invaluable document which sets out the main charges of treason and heresy, and produces a wealth of detailed supporting evidence from the patriarch's public and private life, ranging from assumption of the insignia of imperial office to most injudicious dabbling in spiritualism.[3] The patriarch, arrested by order of the emperor, did not live to stand his trial; the *Accusation* was not needed after all, but was replaced by a diplomatic *Funeral Oration*.[4]

But the moral of Cerularius's defeat is its demonstration of the strength of the imperial tradition. Though it was a period of political uncertainty, the normal relation between church and state was still maintained.

Then there is a considerable body of evidence to show that the eleventh century was characterised by creative activity of the highest significance. It is here that the traditional account of this period most needs to be filled out and in some respects restated. It is here that one is most conscious of certain misrepresentations, not only in Ostrogorsky's *History* but also in other recent work. Apart from its imperial tradition,

---

[1] Scylitzes, ii. 643 (ed. I. Bekker, *Corpus script. hist. byzantinae*, Bonn, 1839, and in J. P. Migne, *Patrologia Graeca*, cxxii).

[2] Ed. L. Bréhier, *Revue des études grecques*, xvi (1903), 375–416, and xvii (1904), 35–76, and more recently by E. Kurtz and F. Drexl, *Michaeli Pselli Scripta Minora* (Milan, 1936), i. 232–328. This document might well be translated into English.

[3] For some interesting sidelights on medieval séances, see E. H. R. Dodds, 'Theurgy and its relationship to Neoplatonism', *Journal of Roman Studies*, xxxvii (1947), 55–69.

[4] Michael Psellus, *Funeral oration for the Patriarch Michael Cerularius* (ed. Sathas, *Bibliotheca graeca medii aevi*, iv (Paris, 1874), 303–87).

the peculiar strength and glory of Byzantine civilisation had always been the Christian life of the Empire and educational and literary achievement — on the one hand monasticism and the development of art and liturgy, on the other the activity of its university and scholars.

Of the quality of eleventh-century monastic life there is no need to speak here: it has long been recognised that there was in the eleventh century no break with tradition. The foundation of houses in Asia Minor, on Mount Athos, in Constantinople and elsewhere continued and we know something of the way in which monks lived and thought. Against some lack of effective central control or absence of staying power, particularly in small rural foundations, must be set the writings and ideals of such as Symeon the Young, Nicetas Stethatus or John of Euchaita.[1]

The lives not only of monks but of laity too, were further enriched by the liturgical artists and craftsmen of the period, and it is here especially that I would plead for more generous recognition of recent work. Distinguished contributions to our knowledge of such liturgical activity have been, and are being, made by such scholars as Dr. Tillyard and Dr. Wellesz[2] in the field of Byzantine music, by Dr. Otto Demus and others particularly on mosaic decoration as an important aspect of monumental art.[3] We can now decipher with tolerable certainty the music used in the church services; we are now beginning to appreciate the full significance of the design and execution of the eleventh-century mosaics and to apply to this study the canons of a far more exact criticism than ever before. And the place of hymnography in this liturgical activity can be further illustrated by the collection of eleventh-

[1] See J. M. Hussey, *Church and Learning in the Byzantine Empire 867–1185* (Oxford, 1937), pp. 158 ff. John Mauropous in his *Vita S. Dorothei* shows us something of what a small eleventh-century house meant to the villagers in a country district in Asia Minor in much the same way as the *Life of St. Theodore of Sykeon* does for the seventh century (see E. Dawes and N. H. Baynes, *Three Byzantine Saints*, Oxford, 1948).

[2] E. Wellesz, *A History of Byzantine Music and Hymnography*, contains a bibliography which lists the more important books and articles by Dr. Wellesz and Dr. H. J. W. Tillyard.

[3] O. Demus, *Byzantine Mosaic Decoration: Aspects of Monumental Art in Byzantium* (London, 1948). See also below, p. 34, n. 2.

century canons written by John Mauropous, for such collections were meant to be used in the Church services and were closely linked with the music to which they were composed.[1] There is now no excuse for the omission of some appreciation of these developments from any book claiming to describe the Byzantine world.

Music, canons and mosaics cannot be treated in isolation; they are indissolubly joined each to the other in a single liturgical framework. They conformed to certain well established rules and patterns and the accepted laws of composition must be understood before the full achievement of the artist can be rightly appreciated.

The iconography of the mosaic decoration of the middle Byzantine period aimed at promoting in its beholder a sense of participation. In Demus' view it was in the great monastic churches of the eleventh century, Hosios Loukas, Nea Moni of Chios, and Daphni, that this was most perfectly achieved. Their mosaics formed a considered scheme of decoration which was an integral part of a liturgical arrangement of the Church. This decoration was so planned as to bring out the teaching of Byzantine theology with its Christological emphasis, and more than that, for as he entered the narthex or stood in the nave the participant in the services did not simply learn something about the great truths of Christian teaching, but he could realise that he himself was actually present in both seen and unseen worlds. The very technique of the middle Byzantine mosaic painting produced images which were not 'framed' or artificially separated from the beholder; the beholder is himself — and here I quote Demus — 'enclosed in the grand icon of the church; he is surrounded by the congregation of the saints and taking part in the events he sees'.[2]

The same intention lies behind the hymns and music of the period. They knew no 'originality' in an individualistic sense of the word. Both were part of a tradition of hymnography whose roots were in Jewish and Syrian soil[3] and which had grown out of the *troparion* and

[1] J. M. Hussey, 'The Canons of John Mauropous', *Journal of Roman Studies*, xxxvii (1947), 70–3.

[2] O. Demus, *op. cit.*, p. 13. See also E. Diez and O. Demus, *Byzantine Mosaics in Greece: Hosios Lucas and Daphni* (Cambridge, Mass., 1931).

[3] See E. Wellesz, *Eastern Elements in Western Chant* (*Monumenta Musicae Byzantinae*, Subsidia, II, Amer. Ser., i, Oxford – Boston, Mass., 1947).

the *kontakion* into the more elaborate *canon* which developed from the eighth century onwards and which is admirably represented in its late form in the monumental collection of the eleventh-century John of Euchaita. After the end of the eleventh century, I do not know of any substantial addition to the corpus of canons, but the existing melodies continued to be increasingly elaborated and embellished and the accepted *Heirmologion* or book of tunes thus enlarged and enriched. These canons and their music show the variety possible within the appointed limits. The acceptance of a pattern presented no obstacle to a Byzantine and on its basis he was accustomed to create fresh poetic or musical variations without abandoning the essential link with the older works. This was not restrictive or mechanical and it had a purpose. Thus in the case of a canon each of its nine odes or hymns, whatever festival or occasion may have been in mind, was also associated with some special canticle of the Old or New Testament, and in this way singers and listeners, reminded of the *Benedictus* or *Magnificat*, or whatever might be the model, were carried in thought to the great hymns of divine inspiration and could in turn feel that they too in their humble way were linked with the ranks of the heavenly hierarchy.

As Dr. Wellesz has pointed out, much remains to be done in this field. But in his last work he has at any rate provided a first-class introduction to hymns and music and their place in the liturgy, in terms which can be understood by those who are not liturgiologists or musicians. And, which is equally important, both here and in earlier works such as the edition of the September *Stikerarion*, Dr. Wellesz' attitude to his subject marks an epoch.[1] I have taken only one or two outstanding instances of recent contributions in the fields of music and art. There is an interesting report by Dr. Weitzmann on Byzantine art and scholarship in America which shows the material which is rapidly being made available and reflects that change of attitude which is so marked a feature of present-day Byzantine studies.[2] Work such as this

[1] E. Wellesz, *A History of Byzantine Music*, and *Die Hymnen des Sticherarium für September* (*Monumenta Musicae Byzantinae*. Transcripta, i, Copenhagen, 1936).

[2] K. Weitzmann, 'Byzantine Art and Scholarship in America', *American Journal of Archaeology*, li (1947), 394–418. See also P. Lemerle's biblio-

makes it possible for the historian to reconstruct the liturgical approach and background which in a Christian empire was so important a part of the everyday existence of all, however humble and unlearned, monk, cleric and layman alike.

The intellectual world on the other hand was much more highly specialised and more limited in its sphere of influence. Here again it is a mistake to take Anna Comnena at her face value when she comments on the achievement of the period before her father's accession in 1081. She admits interest in learning in the mid-eleventh century and pays a tribute to Michael Psellus,[1] but she still thinks it necessary to point out that when Alexius became emperor, he found all education 'in a very poor way and the regular study of letters apparently banished afar'.[2] On raking over the ashes, so Anna goes on to tell us, he discovered only a few live sparks and these were concentrating on the preliminaries of Aristotelian philosophy. He at once, and very properly implies Anna, directed their attention from Greek literature to the divine books. (The emphasis was no doubt on the word 'divine', but one should remember that a study of the Bible and the Fathers can be a severe intellectual discipline.) The modified but still inadequate version of Anna which continues to haunt some general histories consists of a passing reference to a reconstituted university in the mid-eleventh century followed by a fairly full but somewhat biased account of the scholar Michael Psellus. Ostrogorsky, in many respects so acute and penetrating in his analysis, is a recent instance of a historian who appears to take this view,[3] influenced, I suspect, partly by Neumann.

---

graphy on all aspects of Byzantine art, 'Bulletin Archéologique 1940–1947', *Revue des études byzantines*, vi (1948), 199–240.

[1] Anna Comnena, *Alexiad*, v. 8 (ed. and trans. B. Leib, ii, Paris, 1943, 33–4). Cf. Sirapie Der Nersessian, *op. cit.*, pp. 26 ff., for the Armenian Gregory Magistros' somewhat different comment on intellectual life in Constantinople.

[2] Anna Comnena, *op. cit.*, v. 9, pp. 38–9, translated by E. A. S. Dawes (London, 1928), p. 136.

[3] Ostrogorsky's *History* does not of course profess to deal in detail with all aspects of Byzantine civilisation, and certain subjects are reserved for other volumes in the series. But he does nevertheless give some account of learning and of Psellus and in so doing lays himself open to criticism. See, however, his comment in the English edition (Blackwell, Oxford, 1956), p. 291, n. 1; this remains unchanged in the 3rd edn. (Munich, 1963), p. 271.

Now Neumann's *Die Weltstellung des byzantinischen Reiches*, written in 1894, remains one of the best introductory essays to the eleventh century.[1] Although like Diehl he tends to overstress orientalisation, his account of the political history of the period does in the main still stand. It is followed by a spirited chapter on Psellus, who is described as a solitary figure among the multitude of boring and arid minds which disfigure the pages of Byzantine literature.[2] Neumann then analyses Psellus' political career, laying bare his self-seeking and lack of sincerity but very fairly pointing out the difficulty of maintaining detachment and consistency at the court of a despotic ruler. What was originally a guarded statement is expanded in Zervos' book on Psellus,[3] and blunted in the course of repetition appears in Ostrogorsky in a somewhat different version. Both in cultural activities and in his moral corruption Psellus has now become 'the most representative figure of his age'.[4] It is clear that Psellus was an ambitious and unscrupulous man; he was too an ardent scholar with an encyclopaedic range of knowledge. He was passionately devoted to philosophy, particularly Platonic studies; like most of his contemporaries he was interested in the occult world; he wrote poetry, funeral orations, panegyrics, theological treatises and innumerable letters; he produced a first-rate history of his own times; and, whatever his shortcomings, he was a convinced Christian.

But in literary achievement, though exceptional in his range — and

[1] C. Neumann, *Die Weltstellung des byzantinischen Reiches vor den Kreuzzügen* (Leipzig, 1894; repr. Amsterdam, 1959). French translation by Renauld and Kozlowski in the *Revue de l'orient latin*, x (1905). My page references are to the French translation.

[2] Neumann, *op. cit.*, p. 140.

[3] C. Zervos, *Un philosophe néoplatonicien du XIᵉ siècle: Michel Psellos* (1920), *passim* (e.g., p. 59: 'parmi les savants de cette époque et tous ceux qui viendront après lui dans Byzance, il n'en est pas un qui ait été aussi complètement l'image de son temps que ce philosophe et homme d'État').

[4] Ostrogorsky, *op. cit.*, p. 230: 'In seinem überaus fruchtbaren Wirken auf kulturellem Felde wie auch in seiner unheilvollen politischen Tätigkeit und abgründigen moralischen Verdorbenheit ist Psellos die repräsentivste Gestalt dieser Zeit' (3rd edn. (Munich, 1963), p. 270, reads 'markanteste' for 'repräsentivste'). Ostrogorsky is of course aware of the work of Psellus' contemporaries, but he seems to me to give a misleading impression of their activities and their characters.

no one would wish to depreciate his achievement — Psellus does not stand alone, nor can his contemporaries in general be charged with precisely his own defects of character. The names of other scholars about whom we know a certain amount and may hope to know still more in the near future immediately come to mind: Xiphilinus, whose work has recently been examined by one of Professor Dölger's pupils in Munich;[1] Cecaumenus, the definitive edition of whose works, after crossing the Atlantic and back, is due to appear in Brussels;[2] Theophylact of Bulgaria, whose letters at least we may hope to see in a critical edition.[3] These and other of Psellus' contemporaries each have their own particular bias and interest, and none of them can be described as morally corrupt.

Further, the works both of Psellus and of the scholars and authors just mentioned only represent one side of the Byzantine literary tradition. The *written* tradition can be divided into at least two branches: one, to which Psellus and some of his friends belonged, looked back to classical models and consciously tried to use classical forms, syntax and metres, and often (as Professor Dawkins has so lucidly explained in a recent essay) showed by some mistake that many such forms had now dropped out of everyday use.[4] But there was another body of literature whose style was much nearer to the spoken language, lives of the saints for instance (sometimes for that very reason deliberately remodelled into a more 'correct' version by later purists),[5] or religious poetry covering a fairly wide range from canons and hymns in our sense of the word to mystical poems describing the Christian experience. The

---

[1] Κ. Γ. Μπώνης, ''Ιωάννης δ Ξιφιλῖνος', *Texte und Forsch. zur byz.-neugr. Philol.*, xxiv (Athens, 1938).

[2] The late Georgina Buckler's edition of Cecaumenus, delayed by the war, is announced as forthcoming in the *Corpus Bruxellense Historiae Byzantinae*. (This had reached the page-proof stage in 1949, but it still remains unpublished.)

[3] It is understood that this is being prepared by Dr. Alice Leroy-Molinghen.

[4] R. M. Dawkins, 'The Greek Language in the Byzantine Period', in Baynes and Moss, *Byzantium*, pp. 252–67.

[5] This happened for instance in the case of the ninth-century St. Theodora of Thessalonica, whose *Life* is discussed in a learned and perceptive review by Dr. Paul Maas in the *Byzantinische Zeitschrift*, xii (1903), 614 ff., where he compares the style of the three different versions which we have.

Hymns of the Divine Loves, written by Symeon the New Theologian, or Symeon the Young, one of the greatest spiritual leaders produced by Byzantium and published in about 1035 by his friend and pupil and biographer Nicetas Stethatus,[1] have been used by his fellow Christians either in Greek or a Russian translation from that day to this. The Latin translation in the *Patrologia Graeca*[2] which is all that is generally available in the west, conceals the significant fact that the metre used by Symeon is the popular verse, either 15, 12 or 8 syllabled, paroxytonic and ignoring quantity. This can be seen from the Greek original, still for the most part in manuscript, where the hymn looks like continuous prose but is separated by points into lines of equal syllabic length.[3] This was also pointed out by Dr. Maas, who edited four of the hymns in 1922 in a paper hidden away in the *Festgabe Albert Ehrhard*.[4] Maas once meant to produce a critical edition and did a good deal of preliminary work on the manuscripts, and it is Maas who emphasises in his brief but highly significant introduction that Symeon was the first notable writer to use these metrical forms and probably did much to popularise the so-called 'political verse'. The importance of the content of his 'hymns' as well as of his prose works has long been recognised,

---

[1] Nicetas Stethatus, *Vita Symeonis Junioris* (ed. I. Hausherr and G. Horn, *Orientalia Christiana*, xii, 1928), *cap.* 140, pp. 204–6, where Nicetas tells how he came to give Symeon's works to the public. Nicetas describes these writings as *kontakia* (*Vita, cap.* 131, p. 190). Perhaps they are more properly called *The Loves of the Divine Hymns*, cf. Monac. MS. gr. 177, f. 209.

[2] J. P. Migne, *Patrologia Graeca*, cxx. 507 ff. There is a German translation by K. Kirchhoff, *Symeon der neue Theologe: Licht vom Licht: Hymnen* (Hellerau, 1930). This is not generally accessible in England, and I hope to publish my own translation of both *orationes* and hymns which was completed before the war when I was working on the Greek text of Symeon's writings. The Greek text of some of the sermons (with a French translation) is now available in the *Sources chrétiennes* edited by B. Krivocheine, *Catéchèses*, i–iii. Paris, 1963–65, and the *capita* have been edited in the same series by J. Darrouzès, *Chapitres théologiques, gnostiques et pratiques*, Paris, 1957. See also J. Koder, 'Die Hymnen Symeons, des Neuen Theologen', *Jahrb. der österreichischen byzantinischen Gesellschaft*, xv (1966), 153–99.

[3] Cf. Monac. MS. gr. 177, f. 209 ff.

[4] P. Maas, 'Aus der Poesie des Mystikers Symeon', in *Beiträge zur Geschichte des christlichen Altertums und der Byzantinischen Literatur: Festgabe Albert Ehrhard*, ed. A. M. Koeniger (Bonn–Leipzig, 1922), pp. 328–41.

particularly in Holl's study.[1] For the monastic historian and more especially for the theologian and the student of orthodox spirituality these *orationes* and hymns and *capita* form one of the most important single contributions made in the medieval Greek-speaking world, and their influence on later generations is only now receiving impartial re-examination. This is particularly true in connection with the background of the hesychast movement in the fourteenth century and is still not sufficiently recognised.[2]

Symeon is of course an exceptionally important figure: a spiritual leader and a powerful influence in lay circles in Constantinople, a successful if somewhat intimidating monastic reformer and abbot, a landmark in the development of a popular, in contrast to what is sometimes described as the aristocratic, literary tradition. He belongs to a world for the most part outside the experience of Michael Psellus, though no less than Psellus he is a Byzantine of his day and generation.

The inadequacy of describing either intellectual and literary activity or indeed the temper of the age in terms of Michael Psellus may be demonstrated by one final reference to a scholar and author who was himself one of Psellus' greatest friends, but who can with more truth be singled out as representative of the interests and activities of an educated eleventh-century Byzantine.

John Mauropous (to use his nickname), sometimes called John of Euchaita (after his see in Asia Minor), is revealed in his own writings and in the impression he made on contemporaries as one of the most likeable of eleventh-century humanists.[3] His austerity and self-

---

[1] K. Holl, *Enthusiasmus und Bussgewalt beim griechischen Mönchtum. Eine Studie zu Symeon dem Neuen Theologen* (Leipzig, 1898). Cf. J. M. Hussey, *Church and Learning*, pp. 201 ff.

[2] See H. Delehaye, 'Byzantine Monasticism', in Baynes and Moss, *Byzantium*, p. 158, and H. Grégoire, 'The Byzantine Church', in *ibid.*, pp. 115–16, where the general reader may not realise how great an injustice is done both to Symeon and to hesychasm. For recent studies of hesychasm, see especially the work of J. Meyendorff and others cited by Ostrogorsky, *op. cit.*, 3rd edn., pp. 391, 422.

[3] On both John Mauropous and Symeon the New Theologian, see J. M. Hussey, *Church and Learning in the Byzantine Empire 867–1185*, pp. 39 ff. and 234 ff.; 'The Canons of John Mauropous', *op. cit.*; and *Ascetics and Humanists in eleventh-century Byzantium*, (Dr. Williams's Trust, London, 1960).

discipline were mellowed by a genius for friendship; he had the quiet satisfaction of a poet in the things around him; less passionate and less critical than Symeon the New Theologian, he learnt to walk a more even path on heights that Symeon only sometimes knew. Mauropous after his boyhood in Asia Minor started out as a private coach in Constantinople, giving his spare time at nights to his own research; then owing to the unwelcome good offices of his friend and pupil Psellus he became a personage in imperial circles and prominent in the reconstruction of the university in the mid-eleventh century, with a position as lecturer in the Faculty of Philosophy; he is known to have become a monk, for a time at any rate in a house in Constantinople, and he was a bishop in Asia Minor (much against his will, he says). We do not know the year of his death, only that it was on 5 October and in extreme old age.[1] There is no evidence known to me for the positive statement still handed down from book to book that it was in 1060;[2] it may very probably have been in the early years of Alexius Comnenus' reign some twenty years later. All his life he was distinguished not only for his tact and other gifts as an administrator and a teacher, but for his single-mindedness, his detachment and his integrity. When he died an Office was written in his honour by his nephew Theodore, but we do not know how long his cult lasted, and Mercati says that his name is not in any known calendar.[3] It does of course appear with a tribute to his saintliness in the account of the institution of the festival of the Three Fathers in the Office of Orthros in the *Menaion* for 30 January.

His own body of written work consists mainly of poetry, letters, sermons and the life of a contemporary saint. I doubt whether it gives him any claim to be called 'the last Father of the Church',[4] but it

[1] This is stated in his Office, recently published from Vaticanus MS. Pal. Gr. 138 by S. G. Mercati, 'Ufficio di Giovanni Mauropode de Euchaita composito dal nepote Teodoro', in *Mémorial Louis Petit* (*Archives de l'orient chrétien*, i, published by the Institut Français d'études byzantines, Bucharest and Paris, 1948), p. 350.

[2] A recent instance is E. Wellesz, *History of Byzantine Music*, p. 207. The date has been changed to '*c.* 1081' in the 2nd edn., Oxford, 1961, p. 237.

[3] S. G. Mercati, *op. cit.*, p. 348.

[4] E. Wellesz, *op. cit.*, 2nd edn., p. 237 (quoting J. M. Neale, *Hymns of the Eastern Church*, 2nd edn., London, 1863, p. 160).

certainly does bear out some of the points which I have tried to make. His poetry illustrates admirably the two-stream literary tradition, for some is in classical metre and some (the greater part and still nearly all unpublished) in the form of the canon. Throughout his writings, particularly in his letters and sermons, we have a moving commentary on the *insecurity* of the times in which he lived, but however conscious he was of what he calls 'the rough seas of the present day', and whatever the tension and conflict of his own personal life, there was no uncertainty in his mind as to the validity of the Byzantine conception of a Christian Roman Empire, and no hesitation as to the responsibilities of its citizens, whether lay or ecclesiastic. If we want to understand why the Byzantine Empire had so long a life, we should think in terms not of Michael Psellus but of John Mauropous. If we attempt to rewrite the history of the civilization of the Byzantine Empire in the eleventh century, or at any other time, then we must begin by recognising what has been described as 'the connection between tradition and perfection'.[1]

J. M. HUSSEY

[1] K. Weitzmann, 'Byzantine Art and Scholarship in America', *American Journal of Archaeology*, li (1947), 418.

3 Archbishop Wulfstan, Homilist and Statesman[1]

When Wulfstan II, archbishop of York from 1002 and bishop of Worcester from 1002 to 1016, alias *Lupus episcopus*, died at York on 28 May 1023, his body was taken for burial to the monastery of Ely, in accordance with his wishes. From the twelfth-century historian of this abbey we get the only medieval account of the prelate,[2] a brief, and in some respects unreliable, account. Among other things, it states that miracles were worked at his tomb, but there is no hint elsewhere that Wulfstan had any special claims to sanctity. There was certainly never any question of canonisation; hence there was little motive for the writing of his life by his contemporaries or successors. When we consider how little we should know of the activities of Dunstan or Oswold if we had been denied the contemporary lives of these saints, it is perhaps not remarkable that political historians of the period refer to Wulfstan, if at all, merely as the author of a sermon, the famous *Sermo Lupi ad Anglos*,[3] revealing contemporary conditions in England, or as the consecrator of Cnut's church at Ashingdon. Even in ecclesiastical histories Wulfstan is given no prominent place. Some mention his appointment to York, some his refoundation of St. Peter's at Gloucester and his consecration of Ashingdon, none, except recently Professor Darlington, who calls him an ardent reformer,[4] suggest that he had any influence on the Anglo-Saxon Church of his time or later.

Yet, leaving aside as biased by private considerations the claims of the Ely historian, we find scattered references to the archbishop in the records of the period that suggest that he was not without influence on

[1] I wish to thank Professor B. Dickins for reading and criticising this article.

[2] *Liber Eliensis*, ed. E. O. Blake (Camden Third Series XCII), ii, cap. 87, pp. 155–7.

[3] See my edition of this text in Methuen's Old English Library, 3rd edn., 1963, to which subsequent references refer, unless otherwise stated.

[4] *E.H.R.*, li. 392.

affairs. Legal historians have, of course, noted that he is mentioned in connection with Ethelred's code issued at Enham, though they are guarded as to the precise nature of this connection. In general, however, the fact that we can to some extent reconstruct his life is due to his being an author as well as a churchman. The identification of him with the author of the *sermones Lupi*, first made by Wanley in 1705,[1] and since proved beyond any reasonable doubt,[2] is the starting-point for any real knowledge of his work and its significance. It is for this reason that I place the homilist before the statesman in the title of this paper, in which I propose to summarise what can be learnt about this prelate and to consider his place in the history of his time. Enough progress has been made in the last twenty years for it to be worth while to take stock of the results. A final estimate can be given only when we have critical editions of all the genuine homilies and of the work known as the *Institutes of Polity*, both of which are in the hands of excellent scholars, Miss Dorothy Bethurum and Professor Karl Jost.[3] It might have been possible to take the subject a little farther today if conditions did not deny one access to several manuscripts of primary importance in this investigation.[4]

Wulfstan might long ago have been given his proper position if Napier had brought out the volume of notes and introductions to his edition of 1883,[5] which contained all the homilies claimed for Wulfstan by Wanley, and a few others. It is quite clear that several homilies in Wanley's list are not by Wulfstan, and Napier showed in 1882[6] that only the two homilies that immediately follow the rubric *Incipiunt sermones Lupi episcopi* in all the three manuscripts in which it occurs, together with two others with separate rubrics ascribing them to

[1] In G. Hickes, *Liguarum Veterum Septentrionalium Thesaurus*, ii. 140 f.

[2] Despite the *Dictionary of National Biography*, which considers the identification made without 'any convincing reason'.

[3] These works have now appeared: *The Homilies of Wulfstan*, ed. Dorothy Bethurum, Oxford, 1957; *Die 'Institutes of Polity, Civil and Ecclesiastical'*, ed. Karl Jost (Swiss Studies in English 47), Berne, 1959.

[4] See my *Sermo Lupi ad Anglos*, pp. 17–37; Bethurum, *op. cit.*, pp. 24–49, 69–101; and work cited p. 47, n. 5 below.

[5] *Wulfstan: Sammlung der ihm zugeschriebenen Homilien nebst Untersuchungen über ihre Echtheit*, quoted in this article by the number of the homily.

[6] *Über die Werke des altenglischen Erzbischofs Wulfstan*.

Lupus, can be proved genuine by the evidence of rubrics. There are, however, several texts[1] in a style so similar to that of the 'four genuine homilies' that no one would doubt Wulfstan's authorship but for a theory that there were 'Wulfstan imitators'.

The 'Wulfstan style' is very distinctive and has been frequently described.[2] It is a forcible, trenchant style, pre-eminently suited for preaching. It uses a few simple rhythmical patterns and it obtains a strong emphasis, chiefly by the frequent use of intensifying phrases such as *mid ealle* 'entirely', *georne* 'eagerly', *ealles to swiðe* 'all too greatly'. It possesses a characteristic vocabulary and syntactical peculiarities. Lists of words, often arranged in pairs, are a frequent feature, as, for example, in this passage from a homily based on a chapter of Leviticus: 'Then to your harm shall poverty and misery increase, strife and perse-cution, devastation and famine; and your hearts shall be greatly afraid and the might of your enemies shall grow grievously strong, and, driven asunder, terrified, you will often flee as cowards from a little band. And bad harvests shall oft come upon you through storms, and theft and pestilence shall bring you low, and you shall be given into the power of enemies, who will impoverish and greatly oppress you';[3] or in the descriptions of hell that are not rare in his work: 'There is everlasting fire cruelly stirred up, there is everlasting terror, there is everlasting pain, there is sorrowing and lamentation, and ever unceasing complaint, there is moaning and groaning, there is every misery and the throng of all devils.'[4] Some of these traits would be easy to imitate, and, if Wulfstan was the forceful person I believe him to have been, it would be strange if he exercised no influence on his followers. Every text with a sprinkling of the phrases mentioned above need not be his.[5] But when

[1] Including the so-called pastoral letter (Napier, xix–xxii), which begins in one version 'Wulfstan archebisceop'.

[2] See my edition of the *Sermo Lupi ad Anglos*, pp. 17 f., and the works cited, *ibid.*, p. 17, n. 3.   [3] Napier, xxviii (p. 133).

[4] *Ibid.*, xxii (p. 114). It is not possible in translating to give the effect obtained by rhyme and alliteration, e.g., *sorgung 7 sargung 7 á singal heof; wanung 7 granung*, etc.

[5] Even the Lord's Prayer is not proof against their insertion: one Old English version (Napier, xxvi) is equivalent to 'Lead us not into temptation all too greatly'.

we find works possessing not only the obvious characteristics of his style but also the minor syntactical mannerisms and the preferences in vocabulary, it is more probable that Wulfstan himself is the author. This can hardly be doubted when the work in question reveals an independence of mind incompatible with slavish imitation in style, or when its influence on later laws and canons is so strong as to suggest that it emanated from a person of high standing.[1] Wulfstan had a reputation as a stylist already by 1002, for an anonymous ecclesiastic, writing to him in Latin no later than this year,[2] speaks of 'the most sweet sagacity of your eloquence and the prolixity as well as the profundity of your elegantly arranged narrative'. As he uses Wulfstan's attainments as his excuse for declining to undertake some translation himself, he apparently did not think them easy to imitate.

An article by Professor Jost, published in 1932,[3] has greatly advanced Wulfstan studies. It not only establishes the authenticity of two important homilies, *De baptismate* and *De cristianitate*,[4] but it throws light on Wulfstan's scholarship and methods. For each of these homilies is based on a series of extracts[5] from Latin canonists, and, whereas it had hitherto been assumed that the collection was made by someone else for the homilist's use, Jost points out that the translator reveals familiarity with the original works, sometimes translating parts of the contexts of the selected passages. This suggests that he had made the compilation himself, and for these two homilies alone he read works of Theodulf of Orleans, Jesse of Amiens, Amalarius of Metz, Atto of Vercelli, St. Augustine, as well as Alcuin's *Liber de virtutibus et vitiis*, the Benedictine Rule and the *Poenitentiale Pseudo-Ecgberti*. In one place in the homily *De cristianitate*, instead of translating a simple passage of his original,[6] the author replaces it by a quotation from another work in the Wulfstan style, the unpublished *De regula canonicorum*, a translation of a chapter of

[1] See Jost, *Anglia*, lvi. 305.
[2] See my note in *E.H.R.*, lii. 460 ff.
[3] 'Einige Wulfstantexte und ihre Quellen', *Anglia*, lvi. 265 ff.
[4] Napier, v and x. Jost has found an earlier version of v in C.C.C.C. MS. 302, which is closer to the Latin original.
[5] Napier, iv and ix.
[6] I.e., *seniores honorate, iuniores diligite*. See Jost, *op. cit.*, p. 287.

Amalarius.[1] As the meaning is exactly the same, it is difficult to see why a different author should have troubled to do this; and this fact, taken together with strong stylistic evidence, makes it extremely probable that the *De regula canonicorum* is Wulfstan's work. Jost goes on to show that this text can hardly be divorced in authorship from the so-called 'Canons enacted under King Edgar'[2] which use the same source with the same omissions and the same explanatory addition. Though neither text is derived from the other, both have Wulfstan phrases. The canons survive in two manuscripts perhaps from Worcester, and only one describes them as *Eadgares gerædnes*. As Ælfric's pastoral letter for Wulfsige (993–1001) has been used, this rubric is an error.[3] We may notice that it is these canons that are the main reason for Stubbs's statement, 'The ecclesiastical laws of the period [i.e. Dunstan's time] are of the same constructive and progressive stamp.'[4] It seems that we must give the credit to Wulfstan, not, with Stubbs, to Dunstan.

This picture of Wulfstan as a man well versed in canonistic literature, excerpting carefully from Latin authors before writing his vernacular sermons, can be strengthened by noting the relationship between a series of Latin extracts from Isaiah and Jeremiah and his homily VI, between a similar series from Leviticus and homily XXVIII, between a collection of references to Antichrist[5] and homily XII.[6] Work on Wulfstan's sources is still in its infancy. To those mentioned by Jost can be added a sermon of Abbo of St. Germain[7] and the letters of Alcuin.[8]

---

[1] Now edited by Bethurum, *op. cit.*, pp. 192 f.

[2] Viz., the first of the five texts printed by Thorpe under this title and the only one with the slightest claim to it, i.e. the rubric in one manuscript.

[3] Wulfstan himself seems to have looked back on Edgar's reign as a golden age of law and order. See VIII Atr 37 and ASC 975D. Perhaps there was a tendency in later times to attribute undated codes to his reign.

[4] *Memorials of St. Dunstan* (R.S., 1874), p. cvi.

[5] Napier, xi.

[6] On pp. 13 f. of my first edition of the *Sermo Lupi ad Anglos*, I suggested that these homilies were authentic, judging by style alone. Since then, I have found their Latin sources in manuscripts otherwise connected with Wulfstan.

[7] Cf. *infra*, pp. 47 f., 50.   [8] Cf. *infra*, p. 59.

An examination of early manuscripts also adds to our knowledge of Wulfstan's learning and interests. As early as 1874 Stubbs[1] noted that Vespasian A. xiv contained a Latin poem of panegyric addressed to Wulfstan, under whose patronage the book had been written. No one troubled to follow up this information. It gives us definite proof of Wulfstan's interest in manuscript compilation, and the manuscript in question contains texts that tally with his interests as we know them from other sources, for example the canons of the Synod of *Celchyth* of 816,[2] of the Council of Hertford,[3] various papal letters, the Constitutions of Odo[4] and several letters of Alcuin, including one which Wulfstan uses in his *Sermo Lupi ad Anglos.*[5] A manuscript hitherto unknown to Wulfstan scholars[6] is the Copenhagen MS., Gl. kgl. S. 1595 (4to), of the early eleventh century. In addition to a group of penitential letters written by or addressed to Wulfstan, it contains the complete version of a homily of Abbo of St. Germain, of which Wulfstan used an extract for his homily XXXII;[7] the series of Latin excerpts above mentioned that are the sources of homilies V, VI and XII; the two pastoral letters written for Wulfstan by Ælfric; two copies of the chapter of Amalarius which is the source of Wulfstan's *De regula canonicorum*;[8] and several Latin texts that occur also in a Worcester manuscript (C.C.C.C. 265).[9] The only Old English in the manuscript is a short passage in the Wulfstan style,[10] and I have Mr. Ker's permission to mention his discovery

[1] *Op. cit.*, p. liv.

[2] A. W. Haddan and W. Stubbs, *Councils and Ecclesiastical Documents relating to Great Britain and Ireland*, iii. 579–84.   [3] *Ibid.*, iii. 118–21.

[4] D. Wilkins, *Concilia Magnae Britanniae et Hiberniae*, i. 212–14.

[5] See *infra*, p. 59. On this and other manuscripts connected with Wulfstan, see my article 'Wulfstan at York', *Franciplegius: Medieval and Linguistic Studies in Honor of F. P. Magoun, Jr.*, eds. J. B. Bessinger, Jr., and R. P. Creed (New York, 1965), pp. 214–31; also works cited, p. 43, n. 4 *supra*.

[6] I owe my knowledge of it to Mr. Neil Ker, who pointed out that it contained the penitential letters mentioned below.

[7] Cf. *infra*, p. 50.

[8] The extract is contained in C.C.C.C. 265.

[9] See next paragraph.

[10] Published, not quite accurately, by F. Holthausen in *Zeitschrift für deutsches Altertum*, xxxiv (Neue Folge, xxii), 228, repeated by Karl Jost, *Wulfstanstudien* (Swiss Studies in English 23, Berne, 1950), pp. 268 f.

that this is in the same hand as the poem in Vespasian A. xiv addressed to Wulfstan. There can be little doubt that the manuscript was compiled for Wulfstan's use or by his instructions. In addition to works already mentioned, it has several more homilies by Abbo of St. Germain, Amalarius's *Ecloge de officio misse*, another treatise on the mass and some homilies as yet unidentified, apparently mainly concerned with practical instruction rather than abstruse theology.

It has long been recognised that C.C.C.C. 265, called by Miss Bateson 'a kind of theological commonplace book specially intended for a bishop's use',[1] is a Worcester book. It shares a number of texts with the Copenhagen manuscript, sometimes in the same order.[2] Among them is the source of Wulfstan's *De regula canonicorum*, and the group of penitential letters. Mr. Ker assigns this manuscript to the mid-eleventh century, later therefore than Wulfstan's episcopate, but as, in addition to the texts mentioned above, it has the source of homily V and a continental canon which is probably the source of a chapter in the laws of Ethelred issued under Wulfstan's influence,[3] it appears to be at least partially made up of material collected at Worcester during his time.[4] Its other contents include letters of Alcuin, a large collection of canons and penitentials from various sources, and in particular the work known as the *Excerptiones Pseudo-Ecgberti*. One secular code written in Old English and Latin appears among these items of purely ecclesiastical interest. This is Edgar's fourth code, but its inclusion ceases to appear strange when we remember that it was issued on account of the plague of 962, this misfortune being attributed to the people's sins. It enforces a stricter payment of Church dues. As its tone closely resembles much of Wulfstan's writing, this code may well have had a special interest for him.[5]

[1] *E.H.R.*, x. 712. See D. Bethurum, 'Archbishop Wulfstan's Commonplace Book', *P.M.L.A.*, lvii (1942), 916–29.

[2] Like the Copenhagen manuscript, it has Ælfric's two Latin pastoral letters immediately followed by the source of Wulfstan's homily *De baptismate* and a treatise on the Mass. The two manuscripts share also Amalarius, *Ecloge de officio misse*.

[3] *Infra*, pp. 52 f.   [4] Or at York; see the article cited, p. 47, n. 5.

[5] It is perhaps the interest taken in this code by Wulfstan which has preserved it for us, for the only other manuscript is Nero E. i, probably from Worcester.

Several of the texts in this manuscript, including the *Excerptiones Pseudo-Ecgberti*, though in a different version, appear also in Nero A. i, a manuscript containing many Anglo-Saxon laws and some of Wulfstan's homilies. One of these is a version of the *Sermo Lupi ad Anglos*, annotated, according to Mr. Ker, by the hand he has detected in the Copenhagen manuscript and in Vespasian A. xiv, as we have already seen, and he would date this hand as early eleventh-century.[1] This supports Keller's opinion that the manuscript is from Worcester, the most likely scriptorium to have produced three manuscripts all with some connection with Wulfstan.[2]

Another manuscript that shares many texts with those under discussion is C.C.C.C. 190, given by Bishop Leofric to Exeter. Fehr considers it so closely connected with Ælfric that he would bring it from Eynsham.[3] His strongest reason is that it contains a Latin text in the abbreviated form in which Ælfric used it when writing his second pastoral letter for Wulfstan. But on the other hand, it has the shortened form of the Benedictine Office which is the immediate source of the Old English version in the Wulfstan style[4] and Fehr explains the presence of this in an Ælfric manuscript by suggesting that Ælfric had supplied Wulfstan with this curtailed version. Fehr seems not to have

---

[1] It used to be dated late eleventh-century.

[2] I now consider York equally possible; see p. 47, n. 5.

[3] *Englische Studien*, xlvi. 337 ff. His other arguments are not very cogent. The manuscript contains Ælfric's pastoral letter for Wulfsige as well as those for Wulfstan, but so does the undoubtedly Worcester manuscript Junius 121. It has a text made up of passages from Athelwold's *Regularis concordia* and Amalarius, the authorities combined by Ælfric when writing for monks at Eynsham. This is an argument for the authorship of the work, but not for the provenance of the manuscript, for the compilation for the Eynsham monks has been preserved only in a Worcester manuscript, C.C.C.C. 265, and if Ælfric sent a copy of the one work, he may easily have done the same with this one. Since writing this article Fehr has realised that the version of the *Excerptiones Pseudo-Ecgberti* in C.C.C.C. 190 is not the one used by Ælfric. See his *Die Hirtenbriefe Ælfrics in altenglischer und lateinischer Fassung*, p. cv. This greatly weakens his case for an Eynsham origin for this manuscript.

[4] See E. Feiler, *Das Benediktiner-Offizium. . . . Ein Beitrag zur Wulfstanfrage* (Anglistische Forschungen 4), Fehr, *Englische Studien*, xlvi. 337 ff., and *The Benedictine Office*, ed. J. M. Ure, Edinburgh, 1957.

noticed that the manuscript has also the single sentence from one of Alcuin's letters that Wulfstan translated in his *Sermo Lupi ad Anglos*,[1] followed by a passage *De tribulationibus*, a probable source of this homily, and also the extract from Abbo's sermon *De coena domini* translated by Wulfstan in homily XXXII,[2] the complete sermon being in the Copenhagen manuscript. If Fehr's theory is right, we can only assume that Ælfric made a practice of supplying Wulfstan with catenae ready for his use. But, taking into consideration what we now know of Wulfstan's activity in excerpting passages from Latin authors, and remembering that he had access to the complete works in question in Vespasian A. xiv and the Copenhagen manuscript, it is surely more probable that the manuscript under discussion is based on a collection made at Worcester, and that the shortened version of the source for Ælfric's pastoral letter was sent to him by Wulfstan when he commissioned the letter. Something similar may have happened with regard to the *Excerptiones Pseudo-Ecgberti*, as Fehr once believed,[3] but this cannot be determined until a detailed study has been made of this text. We have, however, evidence that Wulfstan did once send to another ecclesiastic some Latin passages for translation, for the letter quoted above[4] is a refusal to undertake such a task. Wulfstan may have repeated this action in his dealings with Ælfric. Intercourse between Ælfric and Wulfstan is shown also by their both using the decalogue in the form in which it occurs in the Boulogne-sur-Mer MS. 63, Wulfstan in his *De cristianitate*,[5] Ælfric in his second pastoral for Wulfstan.[6] This manuscript has the only surviving copy of Ælfric's letter[7] in reply to a lost letter of Wulfstan's, but of course either sender or recipient might have put this on record.[8] Other contents show some connection

---

[1] Cf. *infra*, p. 59.

[2] Wulfstan does not use the first paragraph (as printed in Migne, *Patrologia Latina*, cxxxii. 764 ff.), but begins with the section *Vere, fratres charissimi, hoc debetis scire unde fuit incoeptum hoc exemplum*, i.e. the passage in C.C.C.C. 190.

[3] *Englische Studien*, xlvi. 344. Cf. *infra*, p. 51.

[4] Cf. *supra*, p. 45.   [5] Jost, *Anglia*, lvi. 278 f.

[6] Fehr, *Die Hirtenbriefe Ælfrics . . .*, p. xi.

[7] *Ibid.*, pp. 222–7.

[8] On the relations of Wulfstan with Ælfric, see my *Sermo Lupi ad Anglos*, pp. 22 f.; P. Clemoes, 'The Old English Benedictine Office, Corpus Christi

with the Worcester group of manuscripts, but at this stage of the investigation it is impossible to decide which way round the influence was exerted. This examination of the manuscripts makes no claim to be exhaustive, but I think that enough has emerged to show great activity in the compiling of manuscripts at Worcester under Wulfstan's influence. To some extent an answer is provided to Miss Bateson's questions:[1] 'Who collected these manuscripts? Where were they collected?'

In view of all this, I cannot agree with Fehr's estimate of Wulfstan in the introduction to his edition of Ælfric's pastoral letters.[2] He feels that the answers given in the private letter, which Ælfric wrote in reply to one from Wulfstan, imply considerable ignorance on the part of the questioner, and he withdraws a previous suggestion that Ælfric owed his knowledge of the *Excerptiones Pseudo-Ecgberti* to Wulfstan with the statement: 'the monk or abbot could not learn much from the archbishop'. It must be remembered that Wulfstan's letter does not survive and we do not know for what purpose he wrote, whether asking for information on matters of which he was ignorant or for support against the views of opponents. Most of the answers relate to ecclesiastical practices current in England though forbidden by the canons and we need not assume abysmal ignorance on Wulfstan's part if he consulted Ælfric on the precise attitude of the canons. Not all the subjects are of an elementary nature;[3] to some queries Ælfric replies that he has never read anything relating to them; to one query, on the number of times a day a priest may celebrate mass, he can refer only to the usage of his teacher, Bishop Athelwold.

Although Wulfstan was evidently active in religious reform by his

---

College, Cambridge, MS. 190, and the relations between Ælfric and Wulfstan: A Reconsideration', *Anglia*, lxxviii (1966), 265–83. On Boulogne-sur-Mer MS. 63, see Enid Raynes in *Med. Aev.*, xxvi (1957), 65–73.

[1] *Op. cit.*, p. 713.   [2] P. cix.

[3] The letter deals with a range of subjects, the bars to entry into the priesthood, the limitation of the consecrating of the chrism to Holy Thursday, the abuse by which wine is mixed with water at baptism, the participation of the clergy in battle, etc. The passage in which Ælfric discusses the lawfulness of Caesarian section must have some connection with the Ely tradition that Wulfstan was born in this way.

own studies, by encouragement of manuscript compilation, by the
issue of a rule of life for canons and a code for the priesthood in
general, by the circulation of pastoral letters for the clergy of his
diocese and by the preaching of homilies to the laity, he had energy left
for other activities. His influence on secular legislation must now be
considered. Ethelred's code promulgated at Enham in 1008, which has
come down to us in two variant Old English versions[1] and in a Latin
paraphrase, is said in the last to have been issued at the instigation of the
archbishops Ælfheah and Wulfstan. Freeman, who had a high
opinion of this code, arbitrarily ignores Wulfstan's influence when he
says: 'The whole tone is at once pious and patriotic; the piety is of a
kind which, while it strictly enforces every ecclesiastical observance by
no means forgets the weightier matters of the law, judgment, mercy and
truth. In all this we can hardly fail to trace the hand of good Archbishop Ælfheah.'[2] The Latin paraphrase concludes with the statement:
'I, Wulfstan, archbishop by the grace of the disposing God, set down
in writing these same things,[3] for the memory of those who come
after and also for the benefit of those of the present day and those to
come, spurred on namely by the love of God and my neighbour.' It
has been suggested that this statement refers to the Latin version alone,
but this seems unnecessary caution when the vernacular codes are, like
all subsequent codes of Ethelred, undoubtedly in the Wulfstan style: a
style already fully developed in the original version of homily V and in
homily X, both of which are earlier than the code. Moreover, the
sources used include the so-called Canons of Edgar, probably, as we
have seen above,[4] a work of Wulfstan's, and the so-called Laws of
Edward and Guthrum, which I have suggested elsewhere to be another
of his works;[5] also the Capitula of Theodulf of Orleans, a text used by
Wulfstan on another occasion,[6] and probably a continental canon
against the too ready application of the death penalty which occurs

---

[1] Ethelred's Vth and VIth codes. On these and the Latin version, see K.
Sisam, *Studies in the History of Old English Literature*, pp. 278–87.

[2] *Norman Conquest*, i. 368.

[3] I.e. the edicts which all the *optimates* have sworn to keep.

[4] Cf. *supra*, p. 46.   [5] *E.H.R.*, lvi. 1 ff.

[6] See Jost, *Anglia*, lvi. 293 f.

only in the Worcester manuscript discussed above, C.C.C.C. 265.[1]
The great use made by Wulfstan of this code in his later work must also
be considered. His most famous homily, the *Sermo Lupi ad Anglos*, is
largely based on it.[2] Unless we allow that Wulfstan was the author of
the Old English code we are forced to assume that he set his name to
a Latin version of a vernacular code written by someone else in his
style, and later used his imitator's work for his own impressive homily.
This is not very probable and it seems therefore, that if, with Freeman,
we wish to attribute the 'weightier matters of the law' to Archbishop
Ælfheah, we must nevertheless allow Wulfstan credit for the language
in which it is couched and familiarity with the sources from which
it is drawn. A rather similar employment of Wulfstan to draw up a
legal document is on record in a charter[3] where, after a transaction
has taken place 'with King Ethelred's leave and the cognisance of
Archbishop Ælfheah and Archbishop Wulfstan and all the councillors who were alive at that time in England', it is stated that 'the
king commanded Archbishop Wulfstan to draw up a charter to this
effect'.

Though 1008 is the first year in which Wulfstan is mentioned by
name in connection with legislation, I believe, for reasons that I have

---

[1] The sentiment has not been expressed in general terms in previous legislation. The English code does not translate the Latin, but gives a summary in its
own words, and borrowing is therefore more difficult to prove. In my opinion
there is enough similarity to make it highly probable. The most relevant
passage reads: '*Castigandi sunt enim rei diris flagris vel vinculis et in carcerem
mittendi sunt et trabibus includendi et plumis piceque perfusi ad spectaculum publicum
in cippum mitti debent et diversis penis cruciandi sunt* ne anime pro quibus ipse
dominus passus est, in eterna pena dispereant.' The Old English statute (V
Atr 3, 3. 1) reads: '7 *ures hlafordes gerædnes 7 his witena is, þæt man Cristene men
for ealles to lytlum to deaðe ne fordeme; ac elles geræde man friðlice steora folce to
þearfe, 7 ne forspille for litlum Godes handgeweorc 7 his agenne ceap þe he
deore gebohte*', in which *friðlice steora* seems to summarise the various alterna-
tives of the Latin canon. Wulfstan has already given a closer rendering of the
last phrase of the Latin in the previous statute: *þæt man þa sawla ne forfare þe
Crist mid his agenum life gebohte.* For the complete canon, see M. Bateson, *op.
cit.*, pp. 726 f.

[2] See pp. 36 f. of my edition of this homily.

[3] KCD 898; A. J. Robertson, *Anglo-Saxon Charters*, lxxxiii.

stated in full elsewhere,¹ that he had already composed a code of regulations concerning ecclesiastical observance in the Danelaw, or in part of it. To this code he wrote a preamble explaining that the regulations had been in force since the earliest days of the Danish settlement, being agreed on first by Alfred and Guthrum, and afterwards by Edward and Guthrum. This is the document known as the 'Laws of Edward and Guthrum' and frequent use is made of it by the codes of Ethelred written in the Wulfstan style, and also by those of Cnut. Previous to 1008 no code betrays any knowledge of it. His work continued to influence legal writings in the reign of Cnut, whose codes share many passages with the Wulfstan homilies.²

Wulfstan's authorship has been claimed by Jost³ for the 'poems' in the Anglo-Saxon Chronicle 959 D E and 975 D (where E has substituted a prose summary). There are the familiar Wulfstan phrases, e.g. in 959, *hit godode georne*, 'things improved greatly', *swa him þearf wæs* 'as was needful for him', *Godes lage lufode* 'he loved God's law'; while in 975 there is a Wulfstan ring about *Godes wiþærsacan Godes lage bræcon* 'God's adversaries broke God's laws'. This is, however, clearest in the passage: *7 wydewan bestryptan oft and gelome, 7 fela unrihta 7 yfelra unlaga arysan up siððan, 7 áá æfter þam hit yfelode swiðe*, 'and they plundered widows oft and again, and many wrongs and evil injustices rose up afterwards, and it grew greatly worse ever after'.⁴ The similarity recognised by Earle⁵ between the 959 passage and Ælfric's Book of Judges is almost certainly borrowing on the part of the Chronicle, not vice versa. Whether these passages, summaries of the reigns of Edgar and Edward the Martyr respectively, are due to an imitator or to our

¹ *E.H.R.*, lvi. 1 ff.

² In two articles, *E.H.R.*, lxiii (1948), 433–52, and lxix (1955), 72–85, I have demonstrated that Wulfstan drafted Cnut's laws.

³ *Anglia*, xlvii. 105 f.

⁴ I print as prose, since phrases of an approximately equal length, with almost a verse rhythm, are a feature of Wulfstan's style. See A. McIntosh, 'Wulfstan's Prose', *Proc. Brit. Acad.*, xxxv (1949), 109–42. Jost prints *Institutes of Polity* in verse lines. Einenkel, in *Anglia*, vii. Anzeiger (1884), pp. 200 ff., suggested that the *Sermo Lupi ad Anglos* is a poem.

⁵ C. Plummer and J. Earle, *Two of the Saxon Chronicles Parallel*, ii. 152 (hereafter cited as Plummer).

author himself, they cannot be earlier than the extreme end of the tenth century. If Plummer's suggestion that the original of D and E was by this time in the Worcester diocese be accepted, this addition was more likely to be made at Worcester itself than at Evesham;[1] but in view of the close connection between Worcester and York, it is not necessary, in order to account for matters of Worcester interest, to assume that this version had left the north. If still in the north, this Wulfstan insertion speaks for York in preference to Ripon.[2]

Having considered the evidence for Wulfstan's varied activities, we are in a better position to reconstruct his career. Of his early training nothing is known. William of Malmesbury's opinion that he was not a monk[3] is offset by the Ely historian's statement that he was,[4] and Florence of Worcester[5] gives him the title of abbot in 1002, and this, though incorrect at this date, may have been true at an earlier period. In later life Wulfstan showed great interest in the Fenland abbeys and perhaps this implies some early connection with the region. Our first clear evidence about him is his consecration to the see of London in 996.[6] As bishop of London he issued penitential letters, which he later included in a small collection of such letters intended to be used as formulae.[7] It is at this time that he received the letter from an anonymous ecclesiastic refusing to translate some *archana* into Old English at the bishop's request, being debarred by the thought of Wulfstan's eloquence.[8] I have suggested elsewhere[9] that some of the eschatological homilies, regarding the end of the world as imminent, may be what

[1] See also the strong case for a Worcester rather than an Evesham origin of the later part of D made by Sir Ivor Atkins, *E.H.R.*, lv. 8 ff. His case against a York origin is less cogent.

[2] See *The Peterborough Chronicle*, ed. D. Whitelock (Early English Manuscripts in Facsimile, iv, Copenhagen 1954), 29 f.; *The Anglo-Saxon Chronicle: A Revised Translation*, ed. D. Whitelock, with D. C. Douglas and S. I. Tucker (London, 1961), pp. xiv–xvi.

[3] *Gesta pontificum* (R.S. 1870), p. 250.

[4] *Historia Eliensis, loc. cit.*   [5] Ed. B. Thorpe, i. 156.

[6] ASC 996 F. On the identity of this bishop of London with the homilist and later archbishop, see my article in *E.H.R.*, lii. 460 ff.

[7] See *supra*, pp. 47 f. The group occurs also in the Bodleian MS Barlow 37, fo. 12.

[8] See *supra*, pp. 45, 50.   [9] *Sermo Lupi ad Anglos*, 1st edn., pp. 12 f.

obtained him this reputation; as, for example, homily XII: 'for the greatest evil shall come upon mankind, when Antichrist himself shall come, that ever has been in the world; and it seems to us that it is very close to that time, for this world from day to day grows ever worse and worse. Now is there a great need for all God's messengers that they often warn God's people against that terror which is about to come on mankind, lest they be taken unawares and then too quickly ensnared by the devil.'[1]

In the penitential letters, Wulfstan calls himself *Lupus*, translating the first element of his name, and this name is used in the rubrics to some of his homilies. As he is never given it elsewhere, and as he always signs charters as *Wulfstan(us)*, I am inclined to think that it is a nom de plume rather than a nickname, and I suspect him, in using a literary *alias* at all, to be copying the Carolingian group of scholars, for he certainly was familiar with Alcuin's letters. I have sometimes wondered whether he could have had any thought of Lupus of Ferrières in his mind, but he is unlikely to have known enough about this author to have noticed the similarity of their interests.[2]

It is after his translation in 1002 to the combined sees of Worcester and York that we have evidence of great reforming zeal on Wulfstan's part, zeal no doubt occasioned by his realisation of the laxity of his northern province. He corresponded with Ælfric on canonistic matters and commissioned him to write two pastoral letters for him and to translate them into Old English. One of them he rewrote in his more emphatic style. He translated Amalarius *De regula canonicorum* and for the secular clergy he issued the so-called 'Canons of Edgar'. He addressed a general exhortation to the 'thanes, ecclesiastical and lay, entrusted to his direction in spiritual concerns', a document often called his pastoral letter.[3] His 'Laws of Edward and Guthrum' are concerned with breaches of church regulations primarily in a Danish area; and probably some homilies of clear exposition of the essentials of the

[1] Napier, p. 79.

[2] Even if he knew of the manuscript of German customary law which Lupus wrote for Count Eberhard of Friuli, or of his composition of synodal acts, we have no evidence for Wulfstan's own legal activities as early as his use of the name Lupus.

[3] Napier, xix–xxii.

Christian faith,[1] with tirades against heathenism, belong to this period. It would be in line with his other activities if the Law of the Northumbrian Priests had been drawn up at his instigation.[2] In 1008 he drew up the statutes issued by the king and witan and his influence lies behind all the later codes of this reign. Among them is an ordinance[3] enjoining a three-day fast on the nation, which is closely connected with a homily surviving in two versions.[4] This, which amplifies the code and illustrates divine retribution from the Old Testament, reads like a sermon preached about the time of the promulgation of the ordinance. A similar attitude is shown in homilies based on the denunciatory passages in the prophets and Leviticus, and the culmination is the *Sermo Lupi ad Anglos*, preached after Ethelred's exile, and probably in 1014, as is shown by the passage: 'and a very great treachery it is also in the world that a man should betray his lord to death or drive him, living, from the land; and both have happened in this land: Edward was betrayed and then slain and afterwards burned, and Ethelred was driven out of his land'.[5] Wulfstan's disapproval of the acceptance of Swegn is clear, and it would be interesting to know what action he took during the few months while Swegn was king in Northumbria. All that can be ascertained is that he was in York within a fortnight of Swegn's death, for he consecrated Ælfwig bishop of London there on 16 February.[6]

From time to time, we get glimpses of Wulfstan's participation in public affairs.[7] Like other bishops of Worcester, he issues leases of the estates of the see, one even after Leofsige had been appointed to succeed him in 1016. He appears as legatee in two wills and as executor in one of them. In 1012 the monks at Sherborne asked him to be their advocate before the king when the ætheling Edmund wished to obtain one of

---

[1] E.g. Napier, ii and iii.

[2] See D. Whitelock, *English Historical Documents* c. *500–1042*, pp. 434 f. and the article cited on p. 47, n. 5.

[3] Ethelred's VIIth code.   [4] Napier, xxxv and xxxvi.

[5] Ll. 75–80. See also note to ll, 79 ff.

[6] ASC 1014 D. Homily xxxvii, a sermon preached at the consecration of a bishop, may belong to this occasion or to his consecration of Æthelnoth as archbishop of Canterbury in 1020 or of Edmund as bishop of Durham about the same year.

[7] See *Sermo Lupi ad Anglos*, pp. 8–14.

their estates, a fact which supports other evidence for his influence with the king. He consecrated Cnut's church at Ashingdon in 1020 and consecrated Æthelnoth as archbishop of Canterbury, writing to Cnut to inform him that he had done so. He placed monks in the monastery of St. Peter at Gloucester, according to the cartulary of the abbey, in 1022.

Enough remains on record of this prelate for us to see him as a man of fiery zeal who, convinced that the misfortunes of his country were a retribution for sin, strove by all means to bring about reform, not confining himself to impassioned denunciation, though of this he was a master. He toiled to improve the standard of learning and morality of the clergy and to bring all classes to an understanding of the Christian faith and a due observance of the laws of the Church, and to put an end to the abuses of contemporary life.

It was a misfortune that Ethelred's reign produced no secular leader of Wulfstan's calibre who could have followed up this religious and moral reform with strong measures for repelling the invader and keeping internal order. The principles stated in the codes composed by Wulfstan are excellent, and agree too closely to the sentiments of his homilies for us to accept Freeman's assumption that Ælfheah is alone responsible.[1] If at times they read more like a treatise on legal principles than a code of statutes, as, for example, 'but every deed shall be carefully distinguished and judgment meted out in proportion to the offence, as shall be justifiable in the sight of God and acceptable in the eyes of men',[2] or if there is sometimes a note of rather vague appeal, as when, after listing crimes including 'shameful frauds and foul adulteries, and horrible perjuries and devilish deeds such as murders and homicides, thefts and robberies, covetousness and greed, etc.'[3] it continues lamely, 'and lo, let it be clearly understood that all such things are to be censured and not approved',[4] it is only fair to note also that the code can be explicit enough about the penalties where new law is

---

[1] For example, I take it that in referring to the mercy shown in this code Freeman is thinking chiefly of the attempt to stop the slave trade (V Atr 2, VI. 9) and to limit the application of the death penalty (*supra*, pp. 52 f). The first subject occurs in the *Sermo Lupi ad Anglos*, the second comes from a continental canon preserved at Worcester in a manuscript with other Wulfstan sources.

[2] VI Atr. 10. 2.   [3] *Ibid.*, 28. 2 f.   [4] *Ibid.*, 29.

being created, as in the statute on desertion from the army,[1] or on plotting against the king's life.[2]

In holding that the Viking raids were a divine retribution, Wulfstan is taking the same stand as Alcuin had done. In one passage on this theme he is actually translating from a letter of Alcuin's: 'There was a historian in the time of the Britons, called Gildas, who wrote about their misdeeds, how by their sins they so excessively angered God that finally he allowed the army of the English to conquer their land and entirely destroy the flower of the Britons. And that came about, as he said, through robbery by the powerful and through greed for wrongful gains, through the lawlessness of the people and through false judgments, through the slackness and base cowardice of God's messengers, who kept silent about the truth all too often, and mumbled with their jaws where they should have cried aloud. Also through the foul wantonness of the people and through gluttony and manifold sins they destroyed their country and themselves they perished.'[3] In other places also there are signs of Alcuin's influence.[4] If Wulfstan took up a purely ecclesiastical attitude to the problems of his time, this would have been in accord with a body of contemporary opinion; but the terms in which Ælfric's letter to him deprecates any interference by a bishop in secular affairs imply that Wulfstan held a different point of view. Ælfric says: 'take heed, lest perchance it is said to you by Christ: who constituted you judge of thieves or robbers?'[5] And a little later: 'and Paul said: no soldier of God is to involve himself in secular concerns'. We cannot now know whether Wulfstan paid heed to this and kept himself aloof from secular administration, or whether he strove for reform in this also, but, faced with the inertia and corruption of the lay magnates, worked without any noticeable result during Ethelred's reign.

---

[1] V Atr. 28. [2] *Ibid.*, 30.

[3] *Sermo Lupi ad Anglos*, ll. 184 ff. Cf. Alcuin to Archbishop Æthelheard, M.G.H., Abt. iv, *Epistolae Karolini Ævi*, ii. 47. The letter is contained in full in C.C.C.C. MSS. 190, 265, and in Vespasian A. xiv, and the sentence in question is entered separately on fo. 139 of C.C.C.C. MS. 190; see *supra*, p. 50.

[4] For example, he frequently stresses the cowardice of bishops who do not preach to the people of their sins, using the texts quoted by Alcuin again and again when writing to contemporary bishops: *clama et ne cesses; exalta quasi tuba vocem tuam; canes muti non valentes latrare.*   [5] Fehr, *op. cit.*, p. 226.

In conclusion, we may turn to the estimate of later generations. In the west midlands, he left no good reputation. Worcester cartularies call him *impius, reprobus,* and one accuses him of having robbed the monks.[1] William of Malmesbury speaks rather slightingly of him. The monks of Worcester may have thought that he subordinated their interests to those of his northern see. There is at any rate no record of any personal aggrandisement at their expense. One of his charters, it is true, leases a Worcester estate to his brother, but Oswold had settled a whole series of relations on the lands of the see without any aspersions being cast on his sanctity. We ought, however, to notice that Ælfric's letter to Wulfstan mentioned above[2] concludes rather curiously after the valediction, begging him remember the words of the prophet Micah on justice,[3] and regretting the absence from England of justice free from bribery: 'we are all blinded by gifts and pervert judgments as gifts instruct us, *non habentes retributionem uere iusticiae a deo*'.[4] The position of this warning, away from its natural context where the corruption of bishops has been mentioned in general terms, seems a little pointed, as if Ælfric, if not actually aware of a streak of cupidity in Wulfstan's nature, at least thought him exposed to particular temptation.

There is no suggestion of any flaw in his character in the Ely account.[5] He is 'an excellent man', 'strong in good qualities', 'all his qualities and deeds served religion'. As he had been a benefactor of the abbey and it possessed (and still possesses) his body, exaggeration of his importance and his virtues is to be expected. Yet I think we may claim that the following passage, in spite of its extravagant expression, is not entirely without foundation: 'by them (the kings, Ethelred, Edmund and Cnut), he was loved as a brother and honoured as a father, and frequently summoned to the highest affairs of the realm, as being the most learned of counsellors, in whom spoke the very wisdom of God, as if in some spiritual temple'.

DOROTHY WHITELOCK

---

[1] *Sermo Lupi ad Anglos*, pp. 8 f. Atkins, *op. cit.*, p. 19, calls attention to the scarcity of information about him in Worcester documents.

[2] *Supra*, pp. 50 f.   [3] Micah vi. 8.

[4] Fehr, *op. cit.*, p. 227.   [5] *Historia Eliensis, loc. cit.*

4 The Relations between England and Flanders before the Norman Conquest

The subject of the following paper is one which many scholars are likely to regard as being of only secondary interest.[1] During the later centuries of the Middle Ages, the relations between England and Flanders occupied a position of capital importance in the history of both countries. During the centuries that preceded the Norman Conquest, these relations were much less close than they were later to become, and correspondingly little is known about their character. But they are by no means devoid of interest, even if considered only as an introduction to the more important subject of the later relations between the two countries, and a study of their history is therefore not without justification. In the main, the period covered in this paper will be the two centuries before 1066. During almost the whole of this time, the counts of Flanders were masters of the region bounded by the Scheldt, the Canche, and the sea, and I shall use the word 'Flanders' as the equivalent of the county of Flanders at this date. This means that I shall include in my discussion the vassal counties of Boulogne, Saint-Pol

---

[1] The only detailed study of Anglo-Flemish relations in the period covered by this paper is that of J. M. Toll, *Englands Beziehungen zu den Niederlanden bis 1154* (Historische Studien, Heft 145; Berlin, 1921). It forms a very useful collection of material, but is based rather too exclusively on the literary sources and is somewhat uncritical in their use. The early section (pp. 36–48) of E. Varenbergh's *Histoire des relations diplomatiques entre le comté de Flandre et l'Angleterre au moyen âge* (Brussels, 1874) is quite obsolete, but there are some useful details and observations in W. Kienast, *Die deutschen Fürsten im Dienste der Westmächte*, i (Utrecht, 1924), pp. 42–5, and G. G. Dept, *Les influences anglaise et française dans le comté de Flandre au début du XIIIᵉ siècle* (Ghent, 1928), pp. 13–16. There is naturally much valuable material in the works of Freeman and other writers dealing with the late Anglo-Saxon period.

and Guines, as well as the regions of Artois and Saint-Omer which were separated from the county of Flanders by Philip Augustus.

The relations between England and Flanders were governed by the fact that Flanders, in this wide use of the word, was that part of the Continent which was closest to Britain. But the routes that were in use in the early Middle Ages differed considerably from those that are used today. Of the four chief harbours of this region, only one — Boulogne — goes back to Roman times, and up to the tenth century the Boulonnais and Ponthieu attracted nearly all the cross-channel traffic with Britain. The reason for this was that the dunes started at Calais and ran north-eastwards, and that the Plain of Flanders behind them was a country of forests and undrained fens and marshes. Even in Roman times it had been one of the least developed parts of Gaul, and much of it had been invaded by the sea in the course of the fourth and fifth centuries A.D.[1] It offered in itself little or no attraction to travellers, and its communications with the interior were almost non-existent. It was crossed by only one Roman road of any importance, that connecting Oudenbourg, near the modern Ostend, with Tournai on the Scheldt.[2] Oudenbourg was ruined during the period of the barbarian invasions, and the main line of harbours on the dunes — Calais, Dunkerque, Nieuport, Ostend — do not appear before the twelfth century. Almost our sole record of a landing on this coast during the intervening period is the statement of Theofrid of Echternach that St. Willibrord, in the seventh century, put in at Gravelines.[3] This is a manifest anachronism,

[1] The standard authority on the historical geography of this region is R. Blanchard, *La Flandre* (Lille, 1906), who places (pp. 143–6) the inundation of the Plain of Flanders in the late fourth or the early fifth century. Blanchard (pp. 151–90) also gives a detailed and most valuable account, which must now be supplemented by the more recent work of A. Briquet, *Le littoral du nord de la France et son évolution morphologique* (Paris, 1930), of the evolution of the Flemish coastline from Roman times to the present day.

[2] Cf. V. Guichez, 'Topographie des voies romaines de la Gaule belgique', in *Ann. de l'Acad. roy. d'arch. de Belgique*, xxxviii (1882), 281–3. Traces also exist of a minor road connecting Oudenbourg with Antwerp, and there were minor roads connecting Cassel with various fishing villages on the coast; cf. the map in Briquet, *op. cit.*, p. 361.

[3] Theofrid of Echternach, *Vita S. Willibrordi*, c. 5 (in *Acta SS.*, 7 Nov. iii. 463–4; cf. p. 424).

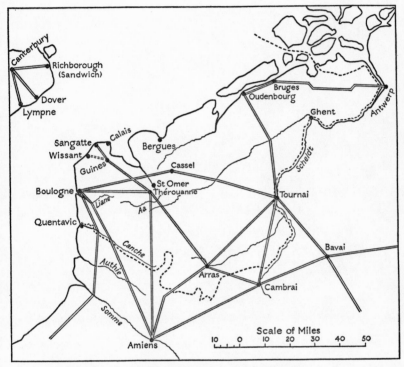

SKETCH-MAP OF THE COUNTY OF FLANDERS AT THE CLOSE OF THE TENTH
CENTURY.

The coastline at this date is largely conjectural. The position of the main Roman roads
is shown.

based on the fact that it was Willibrord who was the patron of the church at this village. It is not till the tenth and eleventh centuries that the rise of Bruges, which was connected with the sea on the north by the broad channel of the Zwin, brought to an end the virtual isolation of the Plain of Flanders.[1]

The main routes to Britain in the early period ran across the Boulon-nais, where the country presented no serious obstacles to hamper communications with the interior. Boulogne was in Roman times the chief port of embarkation, and was the focal point of a number of important roads. One of these ran north-eastwards to Cassel, whence one could go eastwards by way of Wervicq, Tournai, and Escaupont to Bavai in Hainault, where one reached the main roads connecting Tongres and Cologne with the south. Another road ran almost due eastwards to Thérouanne, the capital of the Morini. From Thérouanne there were main roads running southwards to Amiens and south-eastwards to Arras and Cambrai, while a minor road, known in later times as the *voie de Leulène*, connected it with Sangatte on the coast by way of Guines.[2] The other two main roads that converged on Boulogne connected the city with the south. The chief route was that which ran to Amiens and thence to Rheims, where it linked up with the road system of eastern Gaul, but there was also a less important route that followed the coast and ended up at Lillebonne, near the mouth of the Seine.[3]

This nexus of roads explains why the Boulonnais attracted nearly all the through traffic between Britain and the Continent. But the port of embarkation that was most in favour altered with the centuries. In Roman times Boulogne, at the mouth of the Liane, then a wide estuary extending as far inland as the modern village of Pont-de-Bricques, enjoyed a practical monopoly of communications with Britain. There was a certain amount of trade running directly from

[1] Bruges seems to have been connected with the sea by a southern channel as well. The 'statio haud longe a castello Brugensi distans' where Emma landed in 1037 (see below, p. 79) was perhaps Oudenbourg.

[2] See D. Haigneré, *Étude sur le Portus Itius de Jules César* (Paris, 1862), pp. 100–3. The Roman village lay somewhat to the west of the modern Sangatte and farther out to sea (Briquet, *op. cit.*, pp. 283–5).

[3] Cf. E. Desjardins, *Géographie de la Gaule d'après la Table de Peutinger* (Paris, 1869).

London and Colchester to the mouths of the Rhine and Maas,[1] and the lead route from the Mendips and the Midlands ran direct from Bitterne (near Southampton) to the mouth of the Somme and to Lillebonne at the mouth of the Seine, but otherwise, apart from fishing villages, there were no harbours save Boulogne on this part of the coast of Gaul. The monopoly enjoyed by the port is strikingly shown by the fact that when in May 360 Julian was anxious to prevent the news of his proclamation as emperor from reaching Lupicinus in Britain, he simply sent an agent to Boulogne with orders to prevent anyone from crossing the Channel without his permission.[1]

The prosperity of Roman Boulogne, seriously injured already by the disasters and the economic retrogression of earlier centuries, came to an end in the fifth century. There is no evidence that it succumbed to any direct barbarian attack; its walls no doubt saved it during the great invasion of 407, when the territory of the Morini was raided by the Germans,[2] and the story of its destruction by Attila[3] is nothing but a legend. But with the abandonment of Britain by the Roman legions it lost the greater part of its military and administrative importance. Its doom was sealed by the Anglo-Saxon conquest of south-eastern Britain, which cut the essential trade routes on which it relied, and the Frankish conquest of northern Gaul, which cut it off from the continental hinterland. What had formerly been the second port of Gaul sank to the level of a mere fishing village, from which it was not to emerge till quite modern times. The estuary of the Liane, despite the mud-flats and sand-banks which were allowed to accumulate in its channels, remained possible as an anchorage; it was there that Charlemagne stationed his fleet in 811,[4] and it was from Boulogne that a Viking fleet of 250 ships sailed against England in 892.[5] During the Merovingian and Carolingian periods it was no doubt occasionally used by travellers.

[1] Ammianus Marcellinus, *Gesta*, xx. 9 (ed. C. U. Clark, Berlin, 1910, i. 206).

[2] Jerome, *Epistola cxxiii (xci) ad Geruchiam*, § 15 (ed. I. Hilberg [*Corpus script. eccles. lat.*, t. lvi], Vienna, 1918), p. 92. On the walls of Boulogne, see A. Blanchet, *Les enceintes romaines de la Gaule* (Paris, 1907), pp. 123–4.

[3] *Chronicon Vedastinum* (*Mon. Germ. Hist., Script.*, xiii. 679).

[4] *Annales regni Francorum*, a. 811; ed. F. Kurze, Hanover, 1895, p. 135.

[5] *Anglo-Saxon Chronicle*, a. 893 [= 892] (ed. C. Plummer, i. 84).

The fact that King Caedwalla of Wessex, on his journey to Rome in 688, made a gift of 30 solidi to St. Wulmer for his abbey of Samer, close to the main Roman road some eleven miles south-east of Boulogne, suggests that it was at Boulogne that he landed in Gaul.[1] But this example is an isolated one, and by the end of the sixth century it may be assumed that the bulk of what little cross-channel traffic that there was went by way of Quentovic, though the old route from the Solent to the mouth of the Seine must still have been the most convenient for travellers from the west of England. It was by this route that St. Willibald travelled when setting out on his pilgrimage to Jerusalem in 720.[2]

During the Merovingian and Carolingian periods, Quentovic[3] near the mouth of the Canche enjoyed the same position of almost unchallenged supremacy as Boulogne had had in Roman times, though Duurstede in Frisia was a more formidable rival than any port in this region had been to Boulogne, and a certain amount of trade no doubt still went by the Seine route.[4] But the bulk of the trade went by way of Quentovic, and the port enjoyed a practical monopoly of the passenger traffic; the route from Britain by Quentovic is described as the *via rectissima* to Rome in Eddi's *Vita S. Wilfridi*,[5] which was written in

---

[1] *Vita S. Vulmari*, c. 10 (Mabillon, *Acta SS. ord. S. Bened.*, III. i (Paris, 1672), 236–7). The *Vita* dates from the ninth century (cf. L. Van der Essen, *Étude critique et littéraire sur les Vitae des saints mérovingiens de l'ancienne Belgique*, Louvain, 1907, pp. 413–14), and the tradition on this point may well be genuine, though it is usually regarded with suspicion.

[2] *Vita S. Willibaldi*, c. 3 (*Mon. Germ. Hist., Script.*, xv. i. 91). He started from the mouth of the Hamble, in Hampshire.

[3] On Quentovic, see J. Dhondt, 'Les problèmes de Quentovic', in *Studi in onore di Amintore Fanfani*, i (Milan, 1962), 183–248, which supersedes earlier studies.

[4] Rouen was apparently also a commercial site of some importance during Merovingian and Carolingian times; cf. E. de Fréville, *Mémoire sur le commerce maritime de Rouen*, i (Rouen–Paris, 1857), 25 *sq.* But the evidence on the matter is very meagre.

[5] *Vita S. Wilfridi*, c. 25 (ed. B. Colgrave, Cambridge, 1927, p. 50). The Quentovic route was that followed by Theodore of Tarsus in 669 (Bede, *Hist. eccles.*, iv. 1; ed. Plummer, i. 203) and St. Boniface in 718 (Willibald, *Vita S. Bonifatii*, c. 5; ed. W. Levison, Hanover-Leipzig, 1905, p. 20).

c. 710, and the neighbouring abbey of Saint-Josse was recognised as a regular halting-place for pilgrims.[1] It was not till the ninth century that disaster overtook it. A large part of the town was burnt by the Vikings in 842,[2] and after 864[3] it disappears from the literary sources, though money continued to be coined there by sovereigns up to the reign of Charles the Simple. The causes and date of its final disappearance are obscure. The *Annales Vedastini,*[4] which were composed at Arras and give full accounts of the movements of the Vikings, do not mention any attack on the town during the period which they cover (873–July 900), and their silence may be taken as decisive evidence of its immunity in these years. But in January 901 the monks of Saint-Josse arrived with their relics at Winchester in full flight from a Viking attack,[5] and although we have no French sources that are relevant we must assume a second destruction of Quentovic in the autumn or winter of 900. In 938 an attempt to restore the port was made by Louis IV,[6] in whose policy the maintenance of close relations with England formed an important element; but it was unsuccessful, and the disappearance of Quentovic was made absolute by the same cause that had destroyed the prosperity of Boulogne: the silting up of the estuary on which the port was situated.[7] The old site was gradually engulfed in sand, and now lies

[1] Lupus of Ferrières remarks that the *cella* of St. Josse was given by Charlemagne to Alcuin 'ad elemosinam exhibendam peregrinis' (L. Levillain, *Correspondance de Loup de Ferrières*, i (Paris, 1927), no. 19, p. 104).

[2] *Annales Bertiniani*, a. 842 (ed. G. Waitz, Hanover, 1883, p. 28); Nithard, *Historiae*, iv. 3 (ed. P. Lauer, Paris, 1924, p. 124).

[3] Quentovic and Rouen appear in the Edict of Pitres (*cap. xii*) of 25 June 864 among the nine towns of Gaul which were to retain their mints (A. Boretius and V. Krause, *Capitularia regum Francorum*, ii (Hanover, 1897), 315).

[4] Ed. B. de Simson, Hanover, 1909.

[5] For the date 901 (and not 903), see my article 'Grimbald of St. Bertin's', *EHR*, lv (1940), 556–7.

[6] Flodoard, *Annales*, a. 938 (ed. P. Lauer, Paris, 1905, p. 69): 'Ludowicus rex maritima loca petens, castrum quoddam portumque supra mare, quem dicunt Guisum, restaurare nisus est.' The identity of *Guisum* has been much discussed. Wissant, Guines, and Quentovic (*Wicus*) have all been suggested, but the arguments of Levillain (in *Bibl. de l'École des Chartes* XCI, 1930, p. 27, n. 2) in favour of Quentovic appear to me to be decisive.

[7] Cf. Levillain, *ibid.*, p. 25, n. 3. On the estuary of the Canche, see Briquet, *op. cit.*, pp. 177 *sq.*

several miles from the actual course of the Canche. In the tenth century the line of cross-channel traffic had thus to leave Quentovic, and move northwards to Wissant.

The harbour of Wissant[1] lay almost midway between Cap Gris-Nez and Cap Blanc-Nez, at the point where the English and French coastlines are closest (eighteen and a half miles) to one another. It was apparently formed by a breach made by the sea in the dunes that protected the coast. The small region thus submerged provided a safe anchorage from the storms of the Channel, and at the spot where the Rieu de Herlen reached the sea the port of Wissant grew up. One can date its appearance with fair accuracy as the middle of the tenth century, for Wissant was situated in the parish of Sombres,[2] and in the Itinerary of Archbishop Sigeric (990) the landing-place was still known by the name of the parent village (*Sumeran*) and not by that of the recently formed harbour.[3] Wissant itself does not appear by name in a contemporary document till the second half of the eleventh century.[4] Its proximity to the Kentish coast gave it the same advantage that is enjoyed today by Calais, and its position was enhanced in the eleventh and twelfth centuries by the rising commercial importance of Saint-Omer and Arras. While Bruges was the main harbour in the north of Flanders, Wissant occupied the same position in the south, though unlike Bruges it never developed any real industrial or commercial life

---

[1] Wissant = Wit-sand, *white sand*; cf. the eleventh-century *Vita S. Vulganii*, which declares that the saint 'appulit ad portum Witsant appellatum: qui videlicet locus ex albentis sabuli interpretatione tale sortitur vocabulum' (cap. 15; *Acta SS.*, 2 Nov. i. 572).

[2] Haigneré, *Étude sur le Portus Itius*, pp. 29–30.

[3] The Itinerary is printed by W. Stubbs, *Memorials of St. Dunstan* (Rolls Series), pp. 392–5; the stopping-places in the county of Flanders are given as Sombres (*Sumeran*), Guines (*Gisne*), Thérouanne (*Teranburh*), Bruay (*Bruwaei*) and Arras (*Atherats*).

[4] Hariulf in his *Chronique de l'abbaye de Saint-Riquier* (lib. iv, cap. xxiii; ed. F. Lot, Paris, 1894, p. 241), which was written *c.* 1088, describes how in 1068 Abbot Gervinus, intending to cross to England, 'ad maris ingressum properavit, quem nominant plebeiales Guizant'. Wissant is mentioned by English and Norman writers of the twelfth century when referring to events of 933, 1036 and 1051 (cf. below, pp. 72, 79, 82), but in each of these cases Wissant is probably no more than a guess on the part of the historian.

of its own. It was connected with the interior by a route which joined the Roman road from Thérouanne to Sangatte near Guines. It remained the chief port in this region till the rise of Calais towards the end of the twelfth century, and, as in the case of Quentovic, it ultimately became unusable owing to the sand storms that destroyed its harbour.

The greater part of Flanders, therefore, lay even at the best of times off the main routes of cross-channel traffic, and its isolation was accentuated during the Merovingian period by the diversion of this traffic to Quentovic in Ponthieu. During these centuries the relations between England and Flanders were probably of the slightest. Flanders was converted to Christianity almost exclusively by Frankish missionaries, and Englishmen seem to have played no part in the work. The activity of St. Willibrord was confined to Frisia, and his alleged visits to Flanders, if they ever took place, were of the most transitory description.[1] It is not till we reach the Carolingian period that we find traces of English activity in the country, and even then it is mainly of an ecclesiastical character, though presumably the correspondence between Offa and Charles the Great[2] refers to Flemish as well as other Frankish merchants. Two abbots of St. Bavo's of Ghent in the eighth century have English names, and were possibly Englishmen, but nothing is known of their lives.[3] Alcuin was a close friend of Abbot Rado of St. Vaast's of Arras, and rewrote at his request the biography of the patron saint of the abbey.[4] An Englishman named Fridegis, chancellor of Louis the Pious and abbot of St. Martin's of Tours, was abbot of St. Bertin's at Saint-Omer from 820 to 834. His reorganisation there of monastic life, which involved a reduction of the number of monks from 83 to 60 and the substitution of canons for monks at St. Omer's,

[1] See G. H. Verbist, *Saint Willibrord* (Louvain, 1939), pp. 207–9.

[2] See the *Gesta sanctorum patrum Fontanellensis coenobii*, xii. 2 (ed. F. Lohier and J. Laporte, Rouen–Paris, 1936, pp. 86–7), and *Epistola c* of Alcuin (in *Mon, Germ. Hist., Epist. Karol. Aevi*, ii. 144–5). Cf. now J. M. Wallace-Hadrill, 'Charlemagne and England', in *Karl der Grosse: Lebenswerk und Nachleben*, ed. W. Braunfels, i (Düsseldorf, 1965), 683–98.

[3] See my article, 'The Early Abbots of St. Bavo's of Ghent', *Revue Bénédictine*, xlix (1937), 40–1, 42–3, 61.

[4] See *Epp. lxxiv* and *ccxcvi* of Alcuin (*Epist. Karol. Aevi*, ii. 115–17, 454–5), and the verses in *Poetae aevi Carolini*, i. 308–13.

earned him the malediction of later chroniclers of the abbey.[1] Some of
the monasteries of southern Flanders, notably St. Bertin's and St.
Vaast's, were important centres of the so-called 'Franco-Saxon' style
of illumination and ornament,[2] but this is to be explained by their
association with English or English-trained scholars of the school of
Alcuin and not by any direct contact with England.

It is in fact only in the last two decades of the ninth century, during
the reign of Count Baldwin II (879–918) of Flanders, that the history
of Anglo-Flemish relations really begins. The way for the developments of this period was no doubt prepared by the historical accident
that Judith, the daughter of Charles the Bald, who had been wife in
succession to two English kings, Ethelwulf (died 858) and Ethelbald
(died 860), was married in 863 to Baldwin I of Flanders.[3] Although we
know that before she returned to the Continent she sold her possessions
in England,[4] the fact that she was step-mother to King Alfred may have
played a part in bringing him into communication with her own son
Baldwin II.

A similar function was probably performed by Grimbald of St.
Bertin's.[5] Grimbald had been a monk in the time of Abbot Hugh (834–
44), and during the middle decades of the century had apparently
acquired some reputation as a competent administrator and a scholar,
for in 886 he was brought from St. Bertin's to Rheims by Archbishop
Fulk, who had formerly been abbot of his Flemish monastery. His stay
at Rheims was a brief one, for in 886 or 887 he was invited to England
by King Alfred, and in 889 he was actually offered the see of Canterbury
on the death of Archbishop Ethelred. He assisted the king in his

[1] Folcuin, *Gesta abbatum S. Bertini Sithiensis*, c. 47 (B. Guérard, *Cartulaire de
l'abbaye de Saint-Bertin*, Paris, 1840, pp. 74–5; better edn. in *Script.*, xiii. 614–15).

[2] See E. Lesne, *Histoire de la propriété ecclésiastique en France*, IV. *Les livres.
'scriptoria' et bibliothèques* (Lille, 1938), pp. 394–8, and the works there cited.

[3] On Judith, see particularly Toll, *op. cit.*, pp. 2–12, and H. Sproemberg,
'Judith, Königin von England, Gräfin von Flandern', *Revue belge de philologie et
d'histoire*, xv (1936), 397–428, 915–50. Her career is important in the history
of Anglo-Frankish relations, but not, so far as we know, in that of those
between England and Flanders.

[4] *Annales Bertiniani*, a. 862 (ed. Waitz, p. 56).

[5] On Grimbald, see my article cited above (p. 66, n. 5), pp. 529–61.

translation of Gregory's *Pastoral Care*, and no doubt helped him in his other works of scholarship. Shortly before Grimbald's death (8 July 901) he co-operated with Alfred's successor Edward in the foundation of New Minster at Winchester, and though he died before the foundation was completed it was there that he was buried and his reputation for sanctity was preserved. It has been suggested that it was he who brought the manuscript known as the Utrecht Psalter to England. There is no very good evidence for this, but there is something to be said for connecting him with a ninth-century manuscript of Prudentius now in the library of Corpus Christi College, Cambridge (MS. 223). The manuscript contains some notes relating to St. Bertin's which prove it to have been written at that abbey, as well as some scribbled dates referring to events that must all have happened there during Grimbald's lifetime, while the names of two kings in an Anglo-Saxon hand of the tenth century — the insertion can perhaps be dated 918–22 — prove that it was in England soon after Grimbald's death. But the supposition that he brought the manuscript to this country is only a plausible conjecture; no doubt other Flemings besides Grimbald formed a part of the foreign element which Alfred encouraged and patronised at his court.[1]

More important than Grimbald's migration to England was the marriage between Alfred's youngest daughter Elftrudis (Ælfthryth) and Baldwin II. The marriage took place at some date between 893, when Asser describes Elftrudis as still living at her father's court and praises her learning,[2] and 899, the date of Alfred's death.[3] She was a beneficiary under her father's will, receiving the estates of Wellow (Isle of Wight), Steeple Ashton (Wilts.) and Chippenham (Wilts.),[4] but she probably disposed of these at some time to her brother, as they were not inherited by her children. Wellow and Chippenham were still royal

---

[1] Asser, *Vita*, c. 76 (ed. Stevenson, p. 60).

[2] *Ibid.*, c. 75 (pp. 57–9).

[3] That the marriage took place before Alfred's death we know from Æthelweard, *Chronicon* (ed. A. Campbell, Edinburgh, 1962, p. 2).

[4] W. de Gray Birch, *Cartularium Saxonicum*, ii (London, 1887), 178; better edn. by Miss F. E. Harmer, *Select English historical documents of the ninth and tenth centuries* (Cambridge, 1914), pp. 17–18. The will does not mention Elftrudis by name, but we know from Asser that it was she who was the youngest of Alfred's three daughters.

manors at the date of the Domesday survey, while Ashton passed into the possession of the abbey of Romsey, probably by grant of King Edgar.[1] Two of her four children and one of her grandchildren were named after her side of the family; her second son Adelulf was called after her grandfather Ethelwulf and her elder daughter Ealhswith after her mother, the wife of King Alfred, while Egbert, the second son of Arnulf, was named after his more distant ancestor, King Egbert of Wessex (died 839).[2] When Baldwin II died on 10 September 918, his servants proposed to bury him with his father at St. Bertin's. But Elftrudis wished to be interred in the same grave as her husband, and he was therefore buried instead at St. Peter's of Ghent, since St. Bertin's was closed to women.[3] She is said to have died in 929, but the authority for the date is unsatisfactory.[4] According to a forged charter, dated the day after her husband's death, to St. Peter's of Ghent, she granted to this abbey her estates at Lewisham, Greenwich, and Woolwich.[5] This donation appears to be a fiction of the eleventh century; there is no evidence that she ever possessed the estates in question, and the original grant of Lewisham and the other manors in England to St. Peter's appears to have been made by King Edgar in 964.[6]

[1] For Wellow, see the *Victoria County History, Hampshire*, i. 517; v. 274; for Steeple Ashton and Chippenham, see W. H. Jones, *Domesday for Wiltshire* (Bath, 1865), pp. 53, 9.

[2] The names of her four children are given by Æthelweard, *loc. cit.* Arnulf was presumably named after St. Arnulf of Metz, the ancestor of the Carolingian house, and Ermentrude after Baldwin II's grandmother, the wife of Charles the Bald. Egbert, the younger of Arnulf I's two sons, is mentioned in a charter of 10 July 853 (A. Van Lokeren, *Chartes et documents de l'abbaye de Saint-Pierre au Mont-Blandin* (Gand, 1868), no. 22, pp. 28-9).

[3] Folcuin, *Gesta S. Bertini*, c. 103 (ed. Guérard, p. 140; better in *Scriptores*, xiii. 627).

[4] *Annales Blandinienses*, a. 929 (ed. P. Grierson, *Les Annales de Saint-Pierre de Gand et de Saint-Amand*, Brussels, 1937, p. 17).

[5] The edition of this charter by Van Lokeren, *Chartes de Saint-Pierre*, i, no. 14, pp. 20-1, has been superseded by that of C. Vanden Haute, 'Notes sur quelques chartes de l'abbaye de Saint-Pierre de Gand', in the *Bull. de la Comm. roy. d'hist. de Belgique*, lxxi (1902), 411-14. There is an excellent discussion by J. Dhondt, 'La donation d'Elftrude à Saint-Pierre de Gand', *ibid.*, cv (1940), 117-64.

[6] See below, p. 74.

The marriage of Elftrudis with Baldwin II, which was the first of a long series of alliances between English princesses and continental rulers,[1] had no doubt a special political significance in view of the common sufferings of England and Flanders at the hands of the Vikings. But our total ignorance of the history of Flanders during the last eighteen years of Baldwin's reign makes it impossible to say whether there was any formal alliance between the two countries. Baldwin died in 918, and his dominions were divided between his two sons. Adelulf, the younger, inherited the Boulonnais and Ternois and the abbey of St. Bertin's, while Arnulf, the elder, inherited the remainder of the marquisate. Both of them remained in close contact with their cousin Athelstan (925–39). At some date between 925 and 933 Adeulf headed an embassy from Hugh the Great to the English king asking for his sister Eadhild in marriage, and bringing wonderful spices and jewels and such treasures as the sword of Constantine and the spear of Charles the Great as presents to the king.[2] In 933 Athelstan's brother Edwin was drowned in mysterious circumstances in the Channel; his body was washed up on the Flemish coast, and it was his cousin Adelulf who arranged for his burial with fitting honours at St. Bertin's.[3]

With the accession of Louis IV in 936 the relations between England and Flanders were merged in those between England and the West Frankish kingdom. Louis, the son of the luckless Charles the Simple, had been brought up in exile at Athelstan's court, and looked to Athelstan for support against his ambitious magnates. Since the maintenance of good relations with Arnulf was an essential element in the

[1] Five of the daughters of Elftrudis' brother, Edward the Elder, were married to foreign princes, Eadgifu I to Charles the Simple, Eadhild to Hugh the Great, Eadgyth to Otto the Great, Eadgifu to Louis, *princeps* of Aquitaine, and Aelfgifu to Conrad the Pacific of Burgundy.

[2] William of Malmesbury, *Gesta regum*, ii, 135 (Rolls Series, i. 149–51). William's source was a lost poem on the reign of Athelstan. The mission must have taken place between 22 March 925, the date of the death of Hugh's first wife, daughter of Rotilda of Chelles, and 13 November 933, that of Adeulf's death.

[3] Folcuin, *Gesta*, c. 107 (ed. Guérard, p. 145; *Script.* xiii, 629); *A.-S. Chronicle*, a. 933 (ed. Plummer, i. 107). Folcuin, who gives Edwin the royal title, implies that Edwin was in flight from England, but that his death was accidental. The story was embroidered by later legend.

continuance of free communication with England, the Count of Flanders was thus thrown into close contact with the French Crown.[1] When Louis landed at Boulogne early in 936, Arnulf was one of those who were there to welcome him,[2] and Louis' presence at Saint-Omer in August 937 is probably to be connected with his English policy.[3] The following year Arnulf co-operated with him in his attempt at the restoration of Quentovic.[4] In 939, when the count of Flanders captured Montreuil, he sent the wife and sons of Count Herluin of Ponthieu, who had been made prisoners, for safe-keeping to Athelstan.[5] But later came the strange incident of the English fleet, sent to help Louis against the rebel magnates, ravaging the Flemish coast.[6] The cause of this has never been satisfactorily explained. Freeman suggested that Athelstan foresaw Arnulf's coalition with the rebels later in the year and hoped to prevent it,[7] while the theory of the Danish scholar Steenstrup was that the initiative was taken by the English sailors and that the attack was made on the Danes settled along part of the Flemish seaboard.[8] But, although it seems clear that the attack was unauthorised,[9] it led to an abrupt change in Flemish policy. Arnulf joined the rebels against Louis IV,[10] and during the rest of his reign, though we have plenty of evidence for continued relations between England and Flanders, we

[1] Louis and Arnulf were cousins through their common descent from both Charles the Bald and King Alfred.

[2] Folcuin, *Gesta*, c. 102 (ed. Guérard, p. 138; *Script.* xiii. 626). P. Lauer (*Le règne de Louis IV* (Paris, 1900), p. 12, n. 7) disputes the value of this testimony on the ground that Adelulf (and not Arnulf) is described as being present, while he died in 933, but that *Adalolfus* is only a slip for *Arnulfus* is proved by the description of him as *markisus*, and the evidence is perfectly valid.

[3] This is the suggestion of Lauer, *op. cit.*, p. 27.

[4] Flodoard, *Annales*, a. 938 (ed. Lauer, p. 69); Richer, *Historia*, ii. 8 (ed. R. Latouche (Paris, 1930), i. 140).

[5] Flodoard, *Annales*, a. 939 (p. 72); Richer, *Historia*, ii. 12 (p. 146).

[6] Flodoard, *Annales*, a. 939 (p. 73). Cf. Richer, *Historia*, ii. 16 (p. 152).

[7] E. A. Freeman, *History of the Norman Conquest*, i (3rd edn.), 203, n. 3.

[8] J. Steenstrup, *Normandiets Historie* (Copenhagen, 1925), p. 101.

[9] It is suggested by Flodoard's phrase, 'nulloque negotio propter quod venerant peracto'.

[10] Arnulf's adhesion to the rebel cause is related by Flodoard immediately after his account of the attack on Flanders.

have no more evidence of friendly connections between the English and Flemish courts. The reception of St. Dunstan in Flanders argues, in fact, the existence of hostile relations.

Intercourse between the religious establishments of the two countries was at this period fairly frequent. St. Bertin's, because of its geographical proximity to the coast, appears to have taken the lead; so much so that in 944 the majority of the monks of the abbey, objecting to the reforms of St. Gerard of Brogne, fled to King Edmund, who settled them at St. Peter's of Bath.[1] Sixteen years later, in 961-2, Adelulf, the abbot-elect of St. Bertin's, was sent by Arnulf on a prolonged mission to England.[2] But the exile of St. Dunstan to Flanders in 956 brought into prominence the abbey of St. Peter's of Ghent, where the future archbishop stayed for nearly two years;[3] the grant of Lewisham, Greenwich and Woolwich by King Edgar to St. Peter's in 964 was made at his request.[4] It was through Dunstan that the monastic reform movement of Lotharingia and Flanders, inaugurated by St. Gerard of Brogne, came to exercise an important influence on the similar movement in England. It is true that it did not originate it, for Dunstan had reformed Glastonbury before he was driven into exile, but St. Peter's of Ghent had been one of the first houses reformed by St. Gerard in Flanders, and Dunstan's residence there for the best part of two years must have profoundly influenced both his outlook and his methods. In both Flanders and England the reform proceeded on closely parallel lines: the expulsion of canons in favour of monks, the maintenance of episcopal and to some extent of lay control, and the enforcement of the Rule of St. Benedict as modified to meet the circumstances of the time.

---

[1] Folcuin, *Gesta*, c. 107 (ed. Guérard, pp. 144-5; *Script*. xiii. 628-9), 'Athelstan' being a mistake for 'Edmund',

[2] Folcuin, *Gesta*, c. 110 (ed. Guérard, pp. 153-4; *Script*. xiii. 631-2).

[3] No details have survived concerning the exile of Dunstan in Flanders; see the brief statements in Stubbs, *Memorials of Saint Dunstan*, pp. 34, 59-60, 101, 193. The charter of Edgar (see next note) suggests that Dunstan practically ruled St. Peter's of Ghent as abbot, but this is no doubt an exaggeration.

[4] Van Lokeren, *Chartes de Saint-Pierre*, no. 38, pp. 40-2. It has been seriously interpolated and tampered with; see Oppermann, *Die älteren Urkunden des Klosters Blandinium*, pp. 101-4, and the article of Dhondt cited above (p. 71, n. 5).

When English monastic customs were codified, apparently by Bishop Ethelwold of Winchester, in the *Regularis concordia*, monks from Ghent were called upon to assist in the work.[1] It is even possible that Abbot Womar, who had received Dunstan at St. Peter's, may have helped in person; we know at least that he asked for the prayers of the monks of New Minster, and apparently visited England,[2] and that the date of his death (980) was entered in the Abingdon Chronicle,[3] which was particularly connected with St. Ethelwold.

After Dunstan's appointment as archbishop we still find him in relations with Ghent, and a letter to him from Abbot Wido of St. Peter's (980–6) has survived.[4] Count Arnulf II of Flanders (died 988) looked to him to keep Flemish interests in view at the English court,[5] and the archbishop is said to have visited St. Bertin's on his journey to Rome for the pallium in 960.[6] He is also known to have been friendly with Abbot Fulrad of St. Vaast's.[7] This last relationship is an interesting one, for St. Vaast's played a not unimportant part in the formation of the coronation *ordines* of France and England.[8] The manuscript known as

[1] See the preface to the *Regularis concordia* (ed. T. Symons, Edinburgh, 1953, p. 3).

[2] W. de Gray Birch, *Liber Vitae: Register and martyrology of New Minister and Hyde Abbey* (Hampshire Record Society, 1892), p. 24. Plummer (*Two Saxon Chronicles*, ii. 169) concluded from this that Womar resigned his abbey at Ghent and retired to Winchester, an idea which is quite without foundation (Toll, *op. cit.*, pp. 23–5).

[3] *A.-S. Chronicle*, a. 981 [= 980] (ed. Plummer, i. 124).

[4] Stubbs, *Memorials*, pp. 380–1; the dates are those of Wido's abbacy.

[5] See his letter in *ibid.*, pp. 359–61. Stubbs (p. 359, n. 2) ascribes the letter to Arnulf I, and connects it with the mission of Adelulf to England in 961, but since all the other letters regarding Dunstan in the same manuscript (Cotton Tiberius A. xv) belong to the decade 980–90, Arnulf II is more probable.

[6] John of Ypres, *Gesta abbatum S. Bertini*, xxix. 1 (*Scriptores*, xxv. 777); but since he wrote in the fourteenth century and there is no mention of the matter in Folcuin it is perhaps doubtful.

[7] Fulrad mentions the fact in his letter to Æthelgar (see below, p. 77).

[8] See J. A. Robinson, 'The Coronation Order in the tenth century', in *Journal of Theological Studies*, xix (1917), 56–72; a long series of works by P. E. Schramm, the chief of which are two articles, 'Die Krönung bei den West-franken und Angelsachsen von 878 bis um 1000', *Zeitschrift der Savigny-Stiftung*, liv (1934), Kan. Abt., xxiii. 117–242, and 'Ordines Studien II, III', *Archiv für*

the 'Leofric Missal', so called because it belonged in the eleventh
century to Bishop Leofric of Exeter (died 1072), was written at St.
Vaast's towards the close of the ninth or the beginning of the tenth
century, and there seems good reason to believe that it was brought to
England by Dunstan. At the same time, the so-called Sacramentary of
Fulrad (Rathold), which was written at St. Vaast's before 986, contains
one of the best copies of the *ordo* used in the coronation of King Edgar
in 973, which became in the twelfth century the basis of the coronation
ritual of France. The Edgar *ordo*, the compilation of which is generally
ascribed to Dunstan, is based on a number of coronation *ordines*, some
of them taken from the Leofric Missal or a common source, which
were used in the West Frankish kingdom in the ninth century. The
inter-relationship of these various *ordines* is still not entirely clear, but it is
difficult to believe that the necessary material for the compilation of the
Edgar *ordo* would have been available in England, while it might quite
well have been available at St. Vaast's, an abbey which had had particularly close relations with Charles the Bald and been the recipient of
a gift of a number of liturgical manuscripts from Queen Ermentrude.[1]
It has always been assumed, though without any real proof, that the
Edgar *ordo* was specifically produced for the coronation of 973. But
there is no evidence that it was not used for earlier coronations, and it
is not impossible that Dunstan may have composed it during the
enforced leisure of his Flemish exile in 956-7.

Throughout the second half of the tenth century our evidence of
Anglo-Flemish intercourse is reasonably abundant. In a manuscript in
the Cottonian collection a copy has been preserved of a whole mass of
correspondence between English and Flemish prelates that can be dated
between about 980 and 990. Besides the two letters of Arnulf II and
Wido of Ghent to St. Dunstan that have already been mentioned, the

---

Urkundenforschung, xv (1938), 3-55, 305-91, and his *History of the English
Coronation* (tr. L. G. Wickham Legg; Oxford, 1937); and P. L. Ward, 'The
Coronation Ceremony in Mediaeval England', in *Speculum*, xiv (1939), 160-78.
This last article modifies in certain important particulars the views of Schramm
on the date and provenance of some of the texts.

[1] E. Van Drival, *Cartulaire de l'abbaye de Saint-Vaast rédigé au xiie siècle par
le moine Guiman*, Arras, 1875, p. 111.

collection contains a letter from an unnamed English ecclesiastic to Arnulf II, asking the count to return an evangeliary which he had recently purchased but which had been stolen in England,[1] a letter from Abbot Fulrad of St. Vaast's to Dunstan's successor Æthelgar, and letters from Abbot Odbert of St. Bertin's to Æthelgar and to his successor Sigeric.[2] These letters mention casually the names of many minor ecclesiastics who seem to have been quite accustomed to travelling backwards and forwards between the two countries,[3] and allude to the gifts made by Dunstan and his successors to Flemish monasteries. Flanders was often visited by Englishmen, and England by Flemings. As early as *c.* 940 an Englishman is said to have come to help in the reconstruction of the abbey of St. Bavo's at Ghent as a result of a vision seen in his own country.[4] At about the same date we hear of an Englishman named Electus stealing the relics of St. Bertulf, which had been brought for safety to Boulogne during the Viking invasions with the intention of selling them to Athelstan, who had a great reputation as a collector of such objects.[5] In 982 or 985 an English nun named Teta induced the abbot of San Pancrazio at Rome to send to the abbey of St. Bavo's some relics of St. Pancras; she also presented it with a number of other relics on her own account.[6] English pilgrims passed

[1] Stubbs, *Memorials*, pp. 361–2. Stubbs regards Arnulf I as the recipient of the letter, but on the general consideration of the date of the other letters in the collection (see above, p. 75, n. 5) Arnulf II seems more likely.

[2] *Ibid.*, pp. 383–5, 388–9.

[3] Odbert's letters mention two clerks named Richar and Sigebert, and a monk of St. Bertin's named Grimwald, who is being sent to England, and Wido's mentions a monk of St. Peter's of Ghent with the very English name of Leofsin, who has been sent on a mission to Dunstan. There was a monk at St. Bertin's between 944 and 961 with the English-sounding name of Adalsige (Folcuin, *Gesta*, c. 111; *Script.*, xiii. 633).

[4] *Miracula S. Bavonis*, i. 9 (*Script.*, xv. 594). The *Miracula* date from *c.* 1000, but their information is usually trustworthy.

[5] *Vita S. Bertulfi*, c. 24–7 (*Script.*, xv. 635–6); *Sermo in translatione SS. Gudwali et Bertulfi* (in *Acta SS.*, 6 June, i. 742–3). Both these works date from the second half of the eleventh century, and are most untrustworthy; cf. Oppermann, *op. cit.*, pp. 200–9.

[6] *Neues Archiv*, viii (1883), 376. The indications of the date do not agree. The *Annales S. Bavonis* (in *Script.*, ii. 188) place the event in 985.

regularly through Saint-Omer.[1] We hear also of Flemings at the court of King Edgar (died 975),[2] and in the reign of Ethelred II, in regulations dealing with the market dues of London, Flemings are mentioned in company with Normans and Frenchmen and men of Ponthieu as frequenting the port, and provision is made for them to exhibit their wares and pay toll on them.[3]

During the early part of the eleventh century we lose track of Anglo-Flemish intercourse. Possibly it was somewhat diminished as a result of the disorders of the reign of Ethelred II and the creation of the Anglo-Danish Empire, which brought England into closer relations with Scandinavia. But we still hear of casual visits of English magnates to Flanders. In 1016 the youthful Edward the Confessor, then living in exile in Normandy, spent Christmas at Ghent, and promised to restore the English possessions of St. Peter's if and when he should become king.[4] In 1026 Cnut visited St. Bertin's on his famous pilgrimage to Rome, and made rich presents to the abbey.[5] But after Cnut's death in 1035 the situation underwent a sudden change, and the relations between Flanders and England suddenly and for the first time became a matter of almost primary importance to both countries. In the three-cornered struggle between the Danes, the Normans, and the house of Godwine for the English crown that was to occupy the foreground of English history during the next thirty years, Flanders was to be the

[1] We have already seen the cases of Archbishops Dunstan, Æthelgar and Sigeric. The *Miracula S. Bertini*, c. 4 (*Script.*, xv. 511), which date from about the year 1000, allude to a monk setting out for Rome who 'iunxit se Saxonibus ultramarinis Romam pergentibus', and evidently passing through the town. At Langres the party joined up with a caravan of merchants from Verdun on the way to Spain.

[2] William of Malmesbury, *Gesta regum*, ii. 148 (Rolls series, i. 165).

[3] F. Liebermann, *Gesetze der Angelsachsen* (Halle, 1903), i. 232 (*a.d.* 991-1002).

[4] Van Lokeren, *Chartes de Saint-Pierre*, no. 96, pp. 72-3; the act is dated 25 December 1016, and there is no reason to doubt its authenticity. Its existence settles decisively the much disputed question of the relative ages of Edward and his brother Alfred; if the latter was, as some authorities declare, the elder of the two, it is inconceivable that Edward would have granted a charter which anticipates his own accession to the throne.

[5] *Encomium Emmae reginae*, ii. 20, 21 (ed. A. Campbell, London, 1949, p. 36).

regular resort of political refugees whom the fortunes of the struggle had driven into exile, and was to form the normal base from which they were to intrigue for their return to England. Count Baldwin V of Flanders, allied by marriage ties and bonds of friendship with Emma, with the house of Godwine and with William of Normandy, was necessarily implicated in the struggle.

Baldwin V's first contact with English affairs came through the unlucky Alfred, the second son of Emma by her first husband Ethelred. In 1036 he passed through Flanders on his way from Normandy to England, and Baldwin offered him the loan of some troops to act as his bodyguard against possible enemies. But the atheling declined the kindly suggestion, and took with him only a few men from the Boulonnais on the disastrous expedition that was to end in his own blinding and death.[1] In the winter of 1037 King Harold drove his stepmother Emma into exile. She took refuge in Flanders, at the court of Baldwin V, where she was magnificently received by the count[2] and his countess Adela and given a splendid dwelling-place at Bruges.[3] There she sent for her son Edward, who dutifully came to visit her, but he naturally showed no relish for an expedition to England that could only be in the interests of his half-brother, and he soon afterwards returned to Normandy.[4] In the autumn of 1038 Harthacnut, having made terms with Magnus of Norway, was free to come to his mother's aid and settle accounts with Harold over the succession in England. He spent the winter of 1039–40 with his mother at Bruges, collecting ships for the projected invasion. By the spring of 1040 sixty ships had been got

[1] *Encomium Emmae*, iii. 4 (p. 42). The Norman sources of the twelfth century give Wissant as the starting-place of the expedition (cf. Freeman, *Norm. Conq.*, i (3rd edn.), 490, n. 2), but the references in the *Encomium* to the *fines Flandriae* and the men of Boulogne suggests that it may rather have been Boulogne.

[2] Her niece Judith, daughter of Richard II of Normandy, was his stepmother. The countess Adela had also married, as her first husband, Richard III of Normandy.

[3] *A.-S. Chronicle* (C and E), a. 1037 (ed. Plummer, i. 160, 161); *Encomium Emmae*, iii. 7 (p. 46). The account of Bruges given by the Encomiast is practically our earliest evidence of the importance of the place. The *statio haud longe a castello Brugensi* where she landed was perhaps Oudenbourg. This is the first time we hear of any port in the region of Flanders proper.

[4] *Encomium Emmae*, iii. 8 (p. 48).

together and all was ready, but before they sailed came the news of Harold's death (17 March) and the arrival at Bruges of an embassy, led by Ælfweard, bishop of London, to offer the crown to Harthacnut. He and his mother set sail from Flanders in the month of June; they landed on the 17th at Sandwich, and Harthacnut was duly crowned by the archbishop of Canterbury.[1] But he only lived for two years, and on his death (8 June 1042) he was succeeded by Edward the Confessor.

During almost the whole of the following decade the relations between the English and Flemish courts were most unfriendly. Emma and Harthacnut had no doubt done much during their residence at Bruges to prejudice Baldwin against Edward, and the count was in consequence prepared to welcome political exiles of any description who had been driven out of England. When Gunhild, the niece of Cnut, was banished with her two sons Hemming and Thurkil in 1045, she remained for some time at Bruges before going on to Denmark,[2] and the constable Osgod Clapa, the head of the Danish faction, probably followed the same course the next year.[3] Swegen, son of Earl Godwine, likewise spent the winter of 1046–47 at Bruges while on his way to Denmark after his banishment for having seduced the abbess of Leominster.[4] Baldwin even went so far as to throw open his harbours to pirates. In 1048 two Viking chiefs, Lothen and Yrling, made a sudden raid on the English coast, and landed and plundered in Kent and Essex and the Isle of Wight. Before the king and Godwine could collect ships enough to pursue them they had taken refuge in the harbours of Flanders, where they disposed of their spoil before sailing back to the north.[5]

---

[1] *Encomium Emmae*, iii. 8–13 (pp. 48–52); *A.-S. Chronicle* (C, E), a. 1039, 1040 (ed. Plummer, i. 160, 161). Cf. also Adam of Bremen, *Gesta episcoporum Hammaburgensium*, ii. 72 (*Script.*, vii. 332), and the *Chronicon abbatiae Rameseiensis*, c. 85 (Rolls Series, pp. 149–50).

[2] *A.S. Chron.*, (D) a. 1045 (p. 165); Florence of Worcester, *Chronicon*, a. 1044 (ed. Thorpe, i. 199).

[3] *A.-S. Chron.*, (C) 1046, (E) 1044, (D) 1047 (pp. 164, 165). Freeman refers to Osgod Clapa's visit to Flanders as if it were a fact, when really it is only a plausible conjecture.

[4] *Ibid.*, (C) 1046, (E) 1045 (pp. 164, 165–6).

[5] *Ibid.*, (C) 1048, (E) 1046 (pp. 166–7).

Edward was not slow to retaliate for these injuries. In 1049 the war between Henry III and the Count of Flanders, who was the chief ally of the rebel Duke Godfrey of Upper Lorraine, was reaching its crisis, and the Emperor, whose first wife Gunhild (died 1038) had been Edward's half-sister, appealed for help to the English king. According to the English account, Edward was asked to collect his fleet and watch the Channel in case Baldwin should attempt to escape by sea from the chastisement of the imperial arms. It is scarcely conceivable that under any circumstances Baldwin would have fled from Flanders, and it is more likely that the massing of ships in the Channel and the menace of an attack on the Flemish seaboard were designed to divert his energies and prevent him from concentrating his troops for the war in Lotharingia. In any case, Edward collected a fleet and kept watch at Sandwich while Henry delivered his attack on Baldwin by land; only when Henry had been victorious and Baldwin had come to terms did he venture to disband his ships.[1] But Baldwin himself had fallen back for allies on the Danish exiles, and Edward had scarcely dismissed his Mercian contingents before he heard that Osgod Clapa was lying with twenty-nine ships off Wulpen, not far from Bruges. The king hastily recalled as many ships as he could, but in the event they proved unnecessary. The greater part of the invading fleet was destroyed in a storm after a diversion against Essex, and Osgod had nothing to do but to send for his wife from Bruges, where he had left her before sailing, and return to Denmark.[2]

It was at about this time that Baldwin began to come into close contact with the house of Godwine. Swegen had already spent the winter of 1046–7 at Bruges, and in 1049 he was back again, banished for the murder of his brother Beorn.[3] Once again he wintered in Flanders under

---

[1] *A.-S. Chron.*, (C) 1049, (D) 1050 (pp. 166, 167). Cf. also Florence of Worcester, *Chron.*, a. 1049 (p. 201). Baldwin submitted to Henry in September at Aachen.

[2] *A.-S. Chron.*, (C) 1049, (D) 1050 (pp. 168, 169); Florence, *Chron.*, a. 1049 (p. 202). These various accounts are difficult to follow and not wholly compatible with one another. I have made the best I can of the story. Cf. Plummer, *op. cit.*, ii. 230.

[3] *A.-S. Chron.*, (C) 1049, (D) 1050, (E) 1046 (pp. 168–70); Florence, *Chron.*, a. 1049 (pp. 202–3). On the whole story, see Freeman, *op. cit.*, ii (3rd edn.), 100–10, and Plummer, *op. cit.*, ii. 229–31.

Baldwin's protection, till in March 1050 his outlawry was reversed and Bishop Ealdred of Worcester crossed to Bruges and brought about his reconciliation with the king.[1] Soon afterwards, in 1050 or 1051, Judith, daughter of Baldwin IV by his second marriage to a daughter of Duke Richard II of Normandy and so half-sister to Baldwin V, became the bride of Tostig, the third son of Godwine,[2] and when in September 1051 the great earl and his whole house were banished, Flanders was their natural place of refuge. Godwine, his wife, and his two sons Swegen and Tostig all fled to Bruges, where, like previous exiles, they wintered at Baldwin's court.[3] Baldwin is alleged to have written to Edward on the earl's behalf,[4] and no doubt assisted Godwine in collecting a fleet in the Yser with which to invade England. On 22 June the earl set sail, hoping to land in Kent, but Edward on his side had gathered ships to oppose him, and although the forces were separated by a storm Godwine judged it unsafe to risk a landing and put back to Flanders.[5] His second attempt was more successful, and on 15 September a meeting of the Witan at London reversed the outlawry passed on Godwine and his household a year before. Only one member of the family had no share in the restoration. Swegen, instead of joining his father's expedition, had set out from Bruges on a pilgrimage to Jerusalem, and died at Constantinople on the way home.[6]

After Godwine's restoration in 1052 we hear nothing more of hostilities between England and Flanders for thirteen years. Harold,

[1] *A.-S. Chron.*, (E) 1046, (p. 171); Florence, *Chron.*, a. 1049 (p. 203).

[2] Judith's parentage, a matter on which the sources are in extreme confusion, was elucidated by Freeman, *op. cit.*, iii (2nd edn.), 663–5; cf. pp. 656–8. Our only evidence for the date of the marriage is given by the rather untrustworthy *Vita Aedwardi regis* (ed. F. Barlow, Edinburgh, 1962, pp. 24–5), which declares that it took place about the time of Godwine's exile. It was certainly previous to this event, since the *A.-S. Chron.*, (D) 1052 (p. 175), refers to Tostig's wife as going into exile with the rest of the family.

[3] *A.-S. Chron.*, (C) 1051, (D) 1052, (E) 1048 (pp. 172, 175–6, 176); Florence, *Chron.*, a. 1051 (pp. 206–7).

[4] *Vita Aedwardi* (p. 26).

[5] *A.-S. Chron.*, (E) 1052, (F) 1051, (C) 1052 (pp. 177–8); Florence, *Chron.*, a. 1052 (p. 208); *Vita Aedwardi*, p. 26.

[6] *A.-S. Chron.*, (C) 1052 (p. 182); Florence, *Chron.*, a. 1052 (pp. 209–10). Cf. Freeman, *op. cit.*, ii (3rd edn.), 650–2.

who succeeded his father as virtual ruler of England in 1053, maintained friendly relations with Baldwin; in November 1056 he was actually at Saint-Omer, where he witnessed a charter of the count to St. Peter's of Ghent.[1] The relations of the great Flemish abbeys with England had continued in full operation even during the period of hostilities. In 1038 a certain Balger had procured some relics of St. Oswald of Northumbria and St. Edberga for the abbey of St. Winnoc of Bergues.[2] In 1044 Edward had fulfilled his promise to restore the English possessions of St. Peter's of Ghent, and had added to them some property in London.[3] Bishop Hermann of Ramsbury, who is variously described in our sources as a Fleming or a Lotharingian,[4] retired in 1055 to St. Bertin's, where he became a monk out of disappointment at having failed to annex the abbey of Malmesbury. He emerged from retirement in 1058 to take up the staves of both Ramsbury and Sherborne,[5] and brought back with him to England a monk of St. Bertin's named Goscelin, who had accompanied him on the journey he had made to Rome at Edward's orders in 1050, and who was to become one of the most prolific hagiographers of the century.[6] English visitors to Flanders

[1] Van Lokeren, *Chartes de Saint-Pierre*, no. 133, pp. 95–6. The diploma is dated 13 November 1056. In 'A visit of Earl Harold to Flanders in 1056', *Eng. Hist. Rev.*, li (1936), 90–7, I suggested that Harold may have been on his way to Hungary to induce the atheling Edward to return to England.

[2] A. Pruvost, *Chronique et cartulaire de l'abbaye de Bergues-Saint-Winnoc*, i (Bruges, 1875), 39–40. The account is apparently based on a lost *Translatio* written by Drogo of Saint-Winnoc and addressed to Abbot Rumold. Cf. *Acta Sanct. Bolland*, 5 August ii. 88, and 20 June iv. 29–30. Drogo also wrote a life of St. Oswald (*ibid.*, 5 August ii. 94–103).

[3] Van Lokeren, *Chartes*, no. 124, pp. 88–90. Cf. Oppermann, *op. cit.*, pp. 282–7, and the article of Dhondt cited above (p. 71, n. 5). The charter is largely interpolated.

[4] William of Malmesbury, *Gesta pontificum*, ii. 83 (Rolls Series, p. 182), describes him as 'natione Flandrensi', while Florence of Worcester, *Chronicon*, a. 1045 (ed. Thorpe, i. 199), describes him as 'de Lotharingia oriundus'.

[5] Florence, *Chronicon*, a. 1055, 1058 (pp. 214, 217); William of Malmesbury, *Gesta pontif.*, ii. 83 (pp. 182–3).

[6] Goscelin, *Historia translationis S. Augustini*, ii. 3 (in Migne, *Patrol. lat.*, clv. 32) mentions his journey to Rome in Hermann's company. There is an excellent study of Goscelin's life and writings by Barlow in his edition of the *Vita Aedwardi*, pp. 91–111.

in the years immediately preceding the Conquest were Bishop William of London, who was at Bergues St. Winnoc on 15 May 1060 in company with the count and countess of Flanders,[1] and the exiled Hereward. The details of the latter's visit — the shipwreck near Saint-Omer, his welcome by Count Manasses, his war with the count of Guines and his capture of the count's nephew Hoibrict, his wooing and his marriage with Torfrida, and his two expeditions with Duke Robert to *Scaldemariland*[2] — are in the main legendary, but the visit itself seems to have been a reality. The expedition of the future Count Robert I against Zeeland is known to us from another source, and probably took place in 1067,[3] and the romance has preserved the name of Manasses, who appears to have been Count of Saint-Pol at about this time. But if there were Englishmen in Flanders, there was at least one Flemish magnate in England. Count Eustace II of Boulogne is known to have been among the number of Edward's 'foreign favourites'; at some date after 1035 he had married Edward's half-sister Godgifu (Goda), widow of Count Drogo of Vexin,[4] and it was his skirmish with the men of Dover while on a visit to England in 1051 that had precipitated the crisis which resulted in Godwine's exile.[5] But Eustace probably did not return to England after the restoration to power of Godwine's family, and apart from him we hear of no Flemish magnates in England before the Conquest.[6]

[1] *Miracula S. Ursmari in itinere per Flandriam facta*, c. 9 (*Mon. Germ. Hist., Script.*, xv, pars 2, p. 839). I am indebted for this reference to the late Prof. J. F. Niermeyer.

[2] *Gesta Herwardi*, printed as an appendix to Gaimar's *Lestorie des Engles* (Rolls Series), i. 353–64.

[3] See J. Huizinga, 'Scaldemariland', in *Mededeelingen der Koninkl. Akad. van Wetensch., afd. Letterkunde*: deel 84, ser. B, no. 2 (1927), pp. 2–11 (86–95).

[4] The data relative to Godgifu's first marriage, confused by Freeman, are made clear by J. H. Round, *Studies in peerage and family history* (London, 1901), pp. 148–50. Drogo died in 1035.

[5] *A.-S. Chron.*, (D) 1052, (E) 1048 (pp. 172–5); Florence, *Chron.*, a. 1051 (pp. 204–5).

[6] Arnold I of Ardres may possibly have come to England before the Conquest and been one of the foreign favourites of Edward; cf. Lambert of Ardres, *Historia comitum Ghisnensium*, c. 111, 114 (*Script.* xxiv. 614, 615). On the lords of Ardres in England, see Freeman, *op. cit.*, iii (2nd edn.), 314, 725–6, and 'The

Since there exists an admirable article by an American scholar dealing with the part played by Flemings in the Norman conquest of England,[1] I do not feel that anything would be gained by my attempting to say anything on this topic here. Baldwin V held himself entirely aloof from the enterprise. Its success could in no way be contrary to his own interests. The fact that his daughter Matilda was married to Duke William must have tended to make him favour the invaders, for his only tie with Godwine's family was through Tostig, and Tostig had been banished in November 1065 and at the moment of Edward's death (5 January 1066) was living in exile at Saint-Omer.[2] The count's neutrality did not prevent him from giving shelter to Harold's family after the conquest had been achieved.[3] But neither did it hinder Tostig and William collecting recruits in Flanders, and among the followers of the Norman duke were Eustace of Boulogne and a great number of lesser Flemish magnates. Eustace and his followers played an important part in the Battle of Hastings and the subsequent military expeditions of William to the North and West, and were recompensed on an enormous scale; the Flemish element was second only in importance to the Norman when the land of England came to be distributed among the invaders. It is from this land settlement, and from the arrival of trading elements in the reign of Henry I, that one must really date the beginning of the period of close Anglo-Flemish relations that was to outlast the Middle Ages.

I have so far confined myself almost exclusively to the political and ecclesiastical connections between England and Flanders. The political connections, in the period I have been speaking about, were really of only secondary importance; the religious connection is of significance

---

Lords of Ardres', *Historical Essays*, 4th series (London, 1892), pp. 159–98; and J. H. Round, 'The Lords of Ardres', *Feudal England* (London, 1895), pp. 462–4.

[1] R. H. George, 'The Contribution of Flanders to the Conquest of England', in the *Revue belge de philologie et d'histoire*, v (1926), 81–97. There is much of value in Toll, *op. cit.*, pp. 38 ff., and Freeman's *Norm. Conq.*, *passim*.

[2] *A.-S. Chron.*, (C) 1065 (p. 192). Cf. the other versions of the Chronicle, and Florence, *Chron.*, a. 1065 (pp. 223–4).

[3] See Freeman, *Norm. Conq.*, iii (2nd edn.), 157–9, 752–5.

only in so far as it influenced the movement of monastic reform in England that is associated with the name of Dunstan. But I should like before I close to say a few words on the economic and cultural ties between the two countries.

So far as economic affairs are concerned, there is very little that one can say, for virtually no information on the subject has survived. We have seen already[1] that the list of tolls of 991–1002 mentions the presence of Flemish traders in London at this date, and this is almost the only piece of solid evidence that we possess.[2] The grant in 1044 of Warmansacre in London to St. Peter's of Ghent suggests trading connections between London and Ghent, for Warmansacre was on the waterfront and its wharves are mentioned in Edward's charter.[3] The fact that in 1050 some English sailors engaged in the Baltic trade called in their difficulties on St. Trond has been used as an argument to show that English merchants were familiar with Flanders and Brabant.[4] Certainly Bruges was already a port of some standing, and in southern Flanders Arras and Saint-Omer were growing commercial centres. But the probability is that at this epoch both England and Flanders traded more with Scandinavia than they did with each other. This at least is suggested by the mixed hoards of Anglo-Saxon and Flemish coins which are found in the Baltic countries and Russia, and by the fact that Flemish coins are not found in England or English coins in Flanders. The Flemish trade with England was presumably in cloth, the traditional export of Flanders since Roman times, and the Flemings no doubt received in return articles of luxury and hides and metals, as

[1] See above, p. 78.

[2] The scanty information that exists is given by G. G. Dept, 'Les marchands flamands et le roi d'Angleterre', *Revue du Nord*, xii (1926), 303, and *Les influences anglaise et française dans le comté de Flandre au début du xiiie siècle*, p. 15.

[3] The phrase used is 'infra Londonem partem terre de terra illa videlicet que Warmanakre anglice nuncupatur cum warvo eidem terre pertinente et cum omnibus rectitudinibus et consuetudinibus, que ad illam pertinent' (Van Lokeren, *Chartes*, p. 88). On Warmansacre, see W. Page, *London, its origin and early development* (London, 1923), p. 132–7, though his account of its history must be treated with some reserve.

[4] Stepelinus, *Miracula S. Trudonis*, ii. 74 (*Scriptores*, xv. 827–8), cited by Dept, *Les marchands flamands*, p. 303.

well as other commodities in which Flanders was deficient. An incident recorded in the *Miracula S. Winnoci* shows that there was also a certain trade in slaves.[1] According to the accepted belief the export of wool from England to Flanders, an export that was to make the fortunes of both countries, did not begin till the twelfth century, but although there is no evidence on the point it is not impossible that it may go back to earlier times.

During the second half of the eleventh century Goscelin and Fulcard, two monks of St. Bertin's who settled in England, made remarkable contributions to English hagiography,[2] but Flemish scholars who visited the country earlier than this have left little trace of their work behind them. We have seen already that Grimbald had helped King Alfred in the translation of the *Pastoral Care*, and that monks from St. Peter's of Ghent had assisted in the composition of the *Regularis concordia*, but otherwise there is nothing to record. Two monks who remained in Flanders, however, made important contributions to English historical literature. At some date between 1006 and 1011 a monk named Adelard of St. Peter's of Ghent composed at the request of Archbishop Elfege of Canterbury the series of lections on the life of Dunstan which ranks as the *Vita secunda* of the saint.[3] The *Vita* was certainly written at Ghent, and not, as one might suppose, on a visit of Adelard to England, for it contains a verbal quotation from the *Annales Blandinienses*.[4] The writer probably had the *Vita prima* — no

[1] *Miracula S. Winnoci*, c. 10 (*Mon. Germ. Hist., Script. rer. Merov.*, v. 784); a certain Merolfus, a native of the Boulonnais, is accustomed to sell slaves overseas. The incident described occurred in the tenth century. The *mercatores ultramarini* referred to no doubt included Irish as well as English traders; we know of the efforts made by St. Wulfstan in the eleventh century to put down the traffic in slaves between Bristol and Ireland.

[2] On Fulcard and his work, see Barlow, *op. cit.*, lii–lix.

[3] Stubbs, *Memorials*, pp. 53–68; on the author, date and manuscripts, see Stubbs' Introduction, pp. xxx–xxxi, xli–xlii.

[4] In referring to Arnulf I, Adelard writes (pp. 59–60): 'Hic tempore eodem nobile quoddam coenobium nomine Blandinium, a sancto quondam Amando structum, in majori elegantia renovavit, ibique magnum Dei sacerdotem Wandregisilum cum sociis archipraesulibus nutu Dei transtulit.' This echoes the *Annales Blandinienses*, which have under the year 960 the notice 'Hoc anno ab Arnulfo marchiso hoc Blandiniense coenobium in maiori elegantia est con-

doubt sent to him by Elfege — before him, but he was in any case very well-informed on English affairs. It is not clear whether he knew Dunstan personally, but he may well have done so, for he is almost certainly identical with the *Adelardus* who drafted three charters of St. Peter's of Ghent in 972, 974 and 984.[1] It is disappointing that he gives us no details about Dunstan's stay in Flanders, a subject on which some traditions might well have been preserved in his own abbey. The other work by a Flemish writer dealing with English history is that which is variously called the *Gesta Cnutonis regis* or the *Encomium Emmae*.[2] Its author — there is no reason to believe that he was an Englishman — was apparently a monk at St. Bertin's, where he saw Cnut on his journey to Rome in 1026. He made the acquaintance of Emma during the three years (1037–40) which she spent in exile at Bruges, and in 1041 he composed the *Gesta*, which is largely a panegyric on his patroness. It is a work of considerable interest and value, but the author was not above tampering with the truth in order to please the queen, and since she must have been the chief source of his information no impartiality can be looked for in his statements.

There is not much evidence available which would enable us to estimate the extent to which Flemish manuscripts came to England during this period. We have seen already that a manuscript of Prudentius from St. Bertin's and the manuscript known as Leofric's Missal from St. Vaast's of Arras were brought to this country in or about the tenth century, and further research in English libraries might reveal a number of other volumes of which the same is true. The abbey of St. Peter's of Bath, which was colonised in 944 by monks from St. Bertin's, provides us with a certain amount of interesting material. Its abbot Seiwold (Saeweald) fled to Flanders after the Conquest, and eventually presented a number of books to St. Vaast's of Arras. These volumes — a list of thirty-three of them is preserved on the last page of

---

structum' (P. Grierson, *Les Annales de Saint-Pierre de Gand et de Saint-Amand*, Brussels, 1937, p. 19).

[1] Van Lokeren, *Chartes*, nos. 45 (31 January 972), 48 (2 October 974), 61 (12 January 984).

[2] Ed. and transl. A. Campbell (Camden Third Series, lxxii. London, 1949), with very full introduction and appendices.

a manuscript at Arras — almost certainly formed part of the library at Bath, and ten of them, together with what appears to be a leaf of an eleventh, are still in existence. Of these eleven volumes one manuscript and the archetype of another must have been brought from St. Bertin's, and only three are either written in distinctively Anglo-Saxon hands or contain Anglo-Saxon glosses or notes. Some of these glosses, as well as the remaining manuscripts that have survived, are in continental hands, though the presumption is that they were written at St. Peter's. We may conclude from this that the monks from St. Bertin's succeeded in imposing their own style of writing at Bath, and that their influence did not die out till the middle of the eleventh century.[1]

There is little evidence for the presence of English manuscripts in Flanders at this time. We have seen already how Arnulf II acquired a valuable manuscript from some English monastic or cathedral library,[2] and a copy of Nennius, which was in the abbey of Marchiennes in the twelfth century,[3] must have been there already two centuries earlier, since it was used by the author of the *Chronicon Vedastinum*.[4] It has since disappeared, but it can be shown that two Nennius manuscripts of the twelfth century in English libraries are derived from it.[5] The library of St. Bertin's possessed an early eleventh-century manuscript containing

[1] Cf. my article, 'Les livres de l'abbé Seiwold de Bath', *Revue Bénédictine*, lii (1940), 96–116.

[2] See above, p. 77.

[3] The manuscript is mentioned in the twelfth-century catalogue of the library of Marchiennes under the title 'Historia Britannorum' (*Catalogue général des mss. des bibliothèques des départements*, sér. in 4°, t. vi (Paris, 1878), 767).

[4] *Script.*, xiii. 678; cf. p. 675, and *Mon. Germ. Hist.*, *Auctores antiquissimi*, xiii. 133. This Flemish copy of Nennius was also used by Lambert of Saint-Omer in the *Liber Floridus* (cf. L. Delisle, 'Notice sur les manuscrits du Liber Floridus', in *Notices et extraits des mss. de la Bibl. nationale*, xxxviii (1906), no. 78, p. 640) in the early twelfth century.

[5] Part of Cambridge University Library, Mm. v. 29, and part of Bodley 163 (2016). Both contain the pseudo-Hieronymian *Vita S. Methodii* under the curious title *Libellus Bemetoli* (mistake for *Beati Methodii* ?), and both contain a *Series comitum Flandrensium* (*Scriptores*, ix. 336) which is found in manuscripts in Flanders.

a number of Ælfric's works,[1] but it is impossible to say whether it acquired it before or after the Conquest, for Seiwold's books were not the only ones to come to Flanders after 1066. Gunhild, Harold's sister, who died at Bruges in 1087, bequeathed to the chapter of St. Donatian's a psalter with Anglo-Saxon glosses,[2] and the copy of Ælfric was perhaps a legacy from Harold's mother Gytha, who appears to have settled at Saint-Omer.[3] The history of Judith, Tostig's widow, is interesting in this connection. We know very little about her life in England.[4] She presented her husband with two sons, Scule and Ketel, who took part in the Battle of Stamford Bridge (26 September 1066) and later settled down and founded families in Norway. Bishop Ægelwin of Durham gave her in 1065 some of the hair of St. Oswin, and she also acquired some relics of St. Oswald. She accompanied her husband on his journey to Rome in 1061, and when he was banished in November 1065 she went with him to Saint-Omer, and after his death she settled down in Flanders. A few years later, through the agency of Archbishop Odo of Trier, she married Welf IV, later Duke of Bavaria, and she appears to have lived in southern Germany till her death in or soon after 1095.[5] Among the relics which she presented to the abbey of Weingarten were the bones of St. Oswald and some relics of the Holy

---

[1] This manuscript is now Boulogne 16; cf. B. Fehr, *Die Hirtenbriefe Aelfrics* (Bibl. der Angelsächischen Prosa, ix. Hamburg, 1914), pp. x–xiv. A mark of ownership on folio 2r° proves that it was in the possession of St. Bertin's by the thirteenth century at least.

[2] J. Meyerus, *Commentarii sive Annales rerum Flandricarum*, Antwerp, 1561, a. 1389, folio 209v. The manuscript has since disappeared. Meyerus confused the sister of Harold with Gunhild, daughter of King Cnut and wife of the Emperor Henry III, and wrongly attributed the legacy to the latter.

[3] *A.-S. Chron.*, (D) 1067 (ed. Plummer, i. 202).

[4] There is a useful if somewhat romantic account of Judith by M. Harrsen, 'The Countess Judith of Flanders and the library of Weingarten Abbey', *Papers of the Bibliographical Society of America*, xxiv (1930), 1–13.

[5] Her *obit* is given by the Weingarten necrology as 5 March (G. Hess, *Monumentorum Guelficorum pars historica* [1784], p. 136), and she was still alive when the list of her gifts and those of her husband to Weingarten (*ibid.*, pp. 153–4) was drawn up on 12 March 1094. She must therefore have died in 1095 or later. I do not understand why Hess (p. 154) makes her die on 13 March 1094.

Blood which she had received from her father,[1] and a leaf of a manuscript from Weingarten contains a list, drawn up on 12 March 1094, of various other gifts she had made to the abbey.[2] Although it is nowhere very clearly stated,[3] it may be presumed that five magnificently illuminated evangeliaries of the eleventh century of Flemish or English origin that were later in the possession of Weingarten formed part of her benefaction.[4] Of the two manuscripts executed in England, one (Pierpont Morgan Library, MS. 709) is in the New Minster style and can probably be dated 1020–30;[5] it has been suggested that Judith may have obtained it through her husband's uncle Ælfwig, who was abbot of New Minster from 1063 to 1066.[6] The other (Pierpont Morgan Library, MS. 708) is also in the New Minster style, but shows a certain Flemish influence; it may have been executed at Thorney.[7] Of the

[1] *De inventione* (in *Script.*, xv. 922–3).

[2] The list is given in Fulda, Aa. 21, folio 89v. It is printed in Hess, *op. cit.*, pp. 153–4.

[3] The list of her donations includes 'duo preciosissima scrinia in auro et artificio, tria plenaria — cum uno textu evangelii', which may refer to Pierpont Morgan MSS. 708 and 709 and Fulda Aa. 21 (Harrsen, *op. cit.*, pp. 6–7). There is no mention of the other two manuscripts. Two of the manuscripts (Pierpont Morgan 708 and Fulda Aa. 21) contain entries relating to Judith, but no assertion that the volumes were given by her. On the Fulda manuscripts one can consult the note of A. Haseloff, 'Aus der Weingartner Klosterbibliothek', in the *Deutsche Literaturzeitung*, 1905, col. 1998–9, and on the two manuscripts now in America see L. Dorez, *Les Manuscrits à peintures de la bibliothèque de Lord Leicester à Holkham Hall* (Paris, 1908), pp. 9–11 and Planche iii.

[4] Miss Harrsen suggests (p. 9) that Monte Cassino B.B. 437, an eleventh-century evangeliary executed in England, may have passed through her hands.

[5] See O. Homburger, *Die Anfänge der Malschule von Winchester im x Jahrhundert* (Studien über christliche Denkmäler; N.F., xiii, Leipzig, 1912), pp. 66–7.   [6] Harrsen, *op. cit.*, p. 3.

[7] This is the view of Miss Harrsen (p. 4), who gives a list of other manuscripts that on artistic grounds can be assigned to the same scriptorium; one of these, though decidedly earlier, was certainly executed at Thorney. I am rather less confident about the later ones, for there is no evidence that Fulcard of St. Bertin's was at Thorney before the Conquest, though of course there may have been Flemish influence at Thorney independently of him. It may perhaps be noted that Godwine apparently had interests at Thorney; according to one manuscript of the Chronicle, his family took refuge there before their flight to Flanders in 1051 (*A.-S. Chron.*, (D) 1052; p. 175).

three Flemish manuscripts, the provenance of two (Fulda, Ständische Bibliothek, Aa. 44 and Stuttgart, Hofbibliothek, II. 46) cannot be definitely determined,[1] but the third (Fulda, Aa. 21) is from St. Bertin's; the illuminations have clearly been executed by the same artist who was responsible for those in a sacramentary of St. Bertin's at Paris (Bibl. nat., MS. lat. 819).[2] These five manuscripts, and more especially the two executed in England, exercised an important influence on the school of Weingarten in the twelfth and thirteenth centuries.[3]

Illuminated manuscripts of the period with which I have been concerned in this paper are very rare, and it is not often that one can hope to establish such a series of connections as is possible in the case of the manuscripts of Judith of Flanders. But the investigation of this and similar questions seems to me to be one of the most promising lines of research in the future. It is not likely that further study of chronicles and charters will greatly add to our knowledge, and save for the earliest period the amount of archaeological material is not very great. But there are few lines of research more valuable than that of tracing the inter-relationship of manuscripts, of showing how they were loaned from one abbey to another and trying to fill in the gaps in their genealogy. Provided good editions of the texts concerned are available, this can be done just as well for the ordinary contents of monastic libraries as for the more precious volumes that were kept in sacristies. It would I think be true to say that only when a systematic study of the textual relationships of early English manuscripts with those in continental libraries has been undertaken, will we be able to form any accurate and precise idea of the relations of England with Flanders, as well as with other parts of the Continent, during the early middle Ages.

PHILIP GRIERSON

[1] Harrsen, p. 7.

[2] Harrsen, p. 6. For an account of the Paris MS., see V. Leroquais, *Les sacramentaires et les missels manuscrits des bibliothèques publiques de France*, i (Paris, 1924), no. 43, pp. 105-7.

[3] Harrsen, pp. 9-11.

5 English Families and the Norman Conquest

There can be no question that the redistribution of land after the Norman Conquest amounted to a tenurial revolution of the most far-reaching kind. It affected the lower classes of society less than their superiors. The Normans possessed no clear-cut system of manorial economy which could be applied as a whole to a conquered country. The later history of England proves that no attempt was ever made to apply a uniform method of estate-management to the various forms assumed by English rural life. The social differences between Anglo-Danish and Anglo-Saxon England were as strongly marked in 1150 as in 1066. But it is equally clear that the Conquest had come to the higher orders of English society as a catastrophe from which they never fully recovered. It was completed within twenty years from the landing of Duke William, and Domesday Book, which is its record, gives conclusive evidence of its intensity and range. In 1086, although many Englishmen were still in possession of considerable estates, it was the rarest of exceptions for an Englishman to hold a position which entitled him to political influence or gave him military power. Two Englishmen only, Thurkill of Arden and Colswein of Lincoln, held tenancies of the first order under the king himself. The English lords of 1086 are clearly survivals from a society which had been shattered by foreign conquest and their place in the new order which had superseded it was obviously insecure.

There is remarkably little information, even of a fictitious kind, to illustrate the personal history of the last pre-Conquest thegns. On any estimate, the laymen who possessed at King Edward's death estates which the Domesday clerks returned as manors must be reckoned in thousands rather than in hundreds. The number of those who as individuals are now more than names cannot easily be brought above a score. The legendary history of the resistance to the Conqueror, in which innumerable thegns are known to have taken part, is centred almost entirely on the single name of Hereward, the hero of the defence of Ely. Here and there, Domesday Book itself hints at a story. It mentions Englishmen who fell in the warfare of the year 1066, who went into exile, or came to terms with the new government. But the fate of most pre-Conquest landowners of thegnly rank can only be conjectured, and in approaching this question the enquirer in the last resort is thrown back upon generalities. There is no question of equal importance in English history for which the evidence is so fragmentary or so deficient in personal detail.

It is probable that many English families had become extinct even before Duke William's coronation through the death of heirs in battle. The year 1066 was marked by three general engagements, in two of which an English army was destroyed. A high proportion of the English force is known to have perished in the battle of Hastings, a long drawn-out defensive engagement ending in defeat. The English losses were remembered for generations. A chronicler writing at Abingdon after the middle of the twelfth century refers as a matter of common knowledge to the former tenants of his house called thegns, who fell in the battle of Hastings.[1] The losses at Stamfordbridge were less heavy, but a Norwegian king at the head of a great army, even if taken by surprise, cannot have been defeated easily. The strain of the fighting at Stamfordbridge and Hastings fell most heavily on the retainers of Harold and his brothers and, beyond their immediate circle, on the thegns of Wessex and eastern England. It is clear that the thegns of Northumbria and Mercia were not engaged in force in either of these battles. But in the first general action of this year, the battle of Fulford, fought by Edwin and Morcar for the defence of York against Harold Hardrada, they formed the mass of an English army which was annihilated. The battle of Fulford has received less attention than it deserves from modern historians, but it was remembered both in England and Norway as a murderous and protracted struggle in which the English force was only broken after a desperate resistance. It was, in fact, an engagement of the kind which, under the conditions of early warfare, brought the heaviest loss to the defeated side. The slaughter at

[1] *Chronicon Monasterii de Abingdon* (Rolls Series), ii. 3.

Fulford made it impossible for Edwin and Morcar to take any effective part in the campaign of Hastings and must have destroyed the younger members of many prominent families in northern England and the western midlands.

Allowance should also be made for the English losses in the sporadic revolts of the years between 1068 and 1071. There is no definite record of any general engagement in these years, though a battle on a considerable scale may well be represented by the statement of Ordericus Vitalis that King William annihilated a great force of rebels by an easy victory at Stafford in 1069.[1] But the impression given by the meagre record of this period is of constant hostility between Normans and Englishmen, flaring up here and there into risings which were generally suppressed quickly, but always with heavy loss to the defeated side. The numbers of those who fell in this dim struggle cannot even be conjectured, but in the aggregate they were probably greater than the English losses in the battle of Hastings itself. The greater part of the fighting took place in regions from which few men had gone out to the great battles of 1066, and in some degree it explains the disappearance of the Old English families once settled in the Severn Valley and the south-western shires.

The numbers of the Old English aristocracy were reduced by emigration as well as by death in battle. There is evidence from many quarters of a widespread movement of Englishmen into other countries. But it is not easy to obtain definite information about particular cases, or to determine in what countries refuge was principally sought. In view of the communication which is known to have been maintained between English rebels and the Danish court, it is natural to suppose that many Englishmen may have found a home in Denmark. If so, they have made no definite impression on Danish history. It is significant that the English personal names which are known to have been current in medieval Denmark are few, and for the most part seem to represent an intercourse between the countries which was earlier than the Norman Conquest.[2] There are no bearers of English names among the

---

[1] *Historia ecclesiastica*, ed. A. le Prevost, ii. 194.

[2] The name-group *Bōt*, for example, was introduced from England into Scandinavia about the middle of the eleventh century according to the evidence

seventeen retainers of King Cnut II who fell with him at Odense in 1086.[1] The recorded connection between England and Denmark in the Norman period of English history was mainly of an ecclesiastical or economic nature. There is no sign that it was affected by the presence in Denmark of families descended from English exiles of the Conqueror's reign.

There is direct evidence of a movement of Englishmen into Scotland in this period. The *Chronicle* states that many good men accompanied Edgar the Ætheling and his sister Margaret when they took refuge with Malcolm king of Scots in 1068. At least one prominent Englishman, Cospatric Earl of Northumbria, is known to have transferred his allegiance to King Malcolm and to have received from him the lands which afterwards supported the earldom of Dunbar. The charters of King Malcolm's sons show many Englishmen in their company, and the *Life of St. Margaret* by Turgot shows that before 1093 the Scottish court had been remodelled on English lines. There are many English place-names in southern Scotland. Some of them are of a great age and clearly descend from the time when the Northumbrian kingdom extended to the Firth of Forth. But others are much later. Many of them contain Scandinavian words and personal names which can hardly have been acclimatised in that country before the cession of Lothian to Scotland by King Edgar. For most of the century between the reign of Edgar and the Norman Conquest the relations between Northumbria and the Scottish kingdom had been hostile. It is probable that in part at least the Anglo-Scandinavian element in the place-names of Lothian represents a settlement of Anglo-Scandinavian families which had emigrated from northern England in the years immediately after 1066.

The most remarkable of all these movements is also the best recorded. It is clear from contemporary evidence that Englishmen in large numbers had entered the service of the Eastern emperor before the end of the eleventh century. The famous imperial guard of Varangians, mainly

---

collected by O. von Friesen in *A philological miscellany presented to Eilert Ekwall* (Uppsala, 1942), pp. 357–65.

[1] Ailnoth of Canterbury, *Historia Sancti Canuti Regis*, in Langebek, *Scriptores rerum Danicarum*, iii. 373.

recruited, as their name implies, from the Scandinavian north,[1] had been established before the date of the Norman Conquest. In his early life, Harold Hardrada, afterwards king of Norway, is known to have served the emperor in the east. There is no reason to think that the emperor ever ceased to draw recruits from Scandinavia. But there was no essential difference in equipment or tactics between English and Scandinavian armies of this period, and it is unlikely that any material distinction between the races was felt at the emperor's court. Nevertheless, it is clear that English adventurers formed an important part of the army which the Emperor Alexius used for the defence of the Balkans against Robert Wiscard in 1081. At the turn of the century, a south-Italian writer, recording the defeat of the Imperial Guard in the battle of Durazzo, describes it as a force of Englishmen.[2] A generation later, Ordericus Vitalis refers to the Englishmen to whom the emperor had entrusted the imperial palace and treasury. He also states that the emperor had intended to place an English force in charge of a fortress which he was building near Nicaea for the defence of his Asiatic coastlands against the Turks — a plan which a Turkish advance had made impracticable.[3] The evidence is fragmentary, but it is precise enough to show that before the end of the Conqueror's reign there had taken place a large-scale emigration of young English thegns from their own country to permanent service in the near east.

It is by no means easy to form more than a general conception of the state of the Englishmen who had come to terms with the Conqueror and remained at home. It was governed by accidents of personal circumstance which varied almost indefinitely between one case and another. The one certain factor in the situation is the Conqueror's determination to minimise so far as possible the difference between the condition of England under his rule and that which had prevailed in the days of King Edward. He wished to reign in England as King Edward's heir. He respected, and insisted that others should respect, the system of private relationships in which the landowners of the time

[1] The word is used in ancient Russian sources as a general description of all the Scandinavian peoples known in the East.

[2] Geoffrey Malaterra, *Historia Sicula*, iii. 27, Muratori, *SS. rer. Ital.*, v. 584–5).

[3] *Historia ecclesiastica*, ed. A. le Prevost, ii. 172–3; iii. 169.

before the Conquest had been involved. It was a cardinal principle of his government that a Frenchman to whom he had given land should hold it with all the rights and subject to all the encumbrances which the land had carried before he came to England. He also respected the integrity of the greater Old English estates, and it was not merely for administrative convenience that the property which an English thegn had held in 1066 was commonly transferred as a whole to the same new lord. There are a number of cases, few but significant, in which there is reason to think that one of the Conqueror's barons has acquired his fief by marriage with the heiress of an Old English family. There was at least a medieval tradition that Robert d'Oilli, the first castellan of Oxford, married a daughter of King Edward's kinsman Wigot of Wallingford and obtained with her a part of Wigot's extensive lands.[1] A less familiar instance of such a transfer is implied by the remarkable foundation charter of Monks Kirby Priory in Warwickshire.[2] In this charter, which is dated 1077, Geoffrey de Wirce, the first holder of the Mowbray fee in the midlands, states that out of the property which he has earned by his service from King William, he has given a number of villages and churches to St. Nicholas of Angers for the 'peace and spiritual welfare' of his lord King William and for the spiritual welfare of himself and his ancestors and of Alveva his wife and her predecessors. Alveva can only represent the Old English feminine name *Ælfgeofu*, and the probability that Geoffrey's midland lands had come to him with her is confirmed by the regard which he showed for the souls of her predecessors and by the fact that the whole of his estate in Warwickshire had belonged in 1066 to the same Englishman, a thegn named Leofwine. It is impossible to say how many Anglo-Norman marriages of this kind had taken place by the date of Domesday Book, but they agree with the Conqueror's normal attitude towards his English subjects, and the possibility that the number was considerable should not be ignored.

There is no reason to think that at any period of the Conqueror's reign Englishmen were expropriated on account of their race alone.

[1] The chief facts bearing on this tradition were collected by Freeman, *Norman Conquest*, iv, Appendix G.
[2] *Monasticon Anglicanum*, vii. 996.

To the end of his life, so far as can be seen, the Conqueror was willing to allow a stake in the country to Englishmen on whose loyalty he could depend. Many Englishmen are known to have served under his command in his continental wars; to one of them, Toki son of Wigot of Wallingford, he owed his life at the siege of Gerberoi, early in 1079.[1] But the arrangement of Domesday Book indicates very clearly that the men who had thus come in to him had been unable to maintain the social position which had been theirs before the Conquest. By 1086, in England south of the Mersey and Humber, the thegnly class had ceased to form an integral part of English society. The class still existed in name, even in southern England. But the men whom Domesday Book assigns to it were regarded as inferior, not only to the barons who carried responsibility in war and council, but also to the knights whom these great men were planting on the soil. In the survey of county after county the thegns who held land directly of the king himself are relegated by the Domesday clerks to an appendix which they share with the king's servants of foreign race and with women and poor persons holding land of him in alms.

The same impression of a race which had fallen upon evil days is given by the earliest writer who attempted to describe the condition of the English people in the Conqueror's later years. Early in the twelfth century, Ailnoth of Canterbury, an Englishman living in Denmark, wrote a life of the Conqueror's enemy, King Cnut II. In order to explain the wish of many Englishmen that Cnut should invade England in 1085, Ailnoth remarks that some of the English magnates had been slain, others imprisoned, others deprived of their inherited wealth and position, others driven from their native land, and the remainder oppressed by what he describes as 'public servitude'.[2] This description is rhetorical and it is impossible to attach any precise meaning to the phrase with which it ends. Nevertheless, the expression 'public servitude' is not inappropriate to the state of general depression to which Englishmen of the landholding class had been reduced by the Conquest. Their existence depended on the extent to which their alien king could control his alien followers. Many of them were holding lands once

[1] *Anglo-Saxon Chronicle*, MS. D, under 1079.
[2] *Historia Sancti Canuti Regis*, ed. Langebek, *Scriptores*, iii. 347.

their own in economic dependence upon a stranger. The Domesday clerks were not interested in the sorrows of individuals, but even they were moved by the sad case of Ailric of Marsh Gibbon who had held his land freely in the time of King Edward but in 1086 was holding it of William son of Ansculf 'at rent, heavily and wretchedly'.[1] It is also probable that many Englishmen of quality had fallen even lower in the social scale than Ailric of Marsh Gibbon. Later history suggests that the uniform terminology of the Domesday survey of southern England conceals under the heading of *villani* a large number of men who before the Conquest had held small estates — a hide or less — with the rank of thegn and the power of choosing a lord at will. Without assuming the existence of such people it is difficult to account for the subsequent appearance, even in Wessex and southern Mercia, of substantial landowners bearing English names, whose properties had come to them by inheritance. Landowners of this type are much more numerous in the east, the north midlands and the north, and many families which rose to great prosperity in the middle ages could trace descent from such ancestors. It is in every way probable that the number of Englishmen who retained at least some part of their lands throughout the confusion which followed upon the Conquest was far greater than would be gathered from the number of those whom Domesday Book identifies by name.

It is also probable that the English aristocracy as a whole reached the lowest point of its fortunes in the twenty years on either side of the year 1100. King William had been compelled to abandon his original design of governing England, so far as possible, through Englishmen. Between 1067 and 1070 Englishmen in considerable numbers attest his charters. Many of his earliest writs are addressed to English sheriffs, and were plainly intended to be read in local courts of which the composition had changed little since King Edward's day. After the English revolts of 1069 his policy changed. Englishmen fall into insignificance at his court and are replaced by Normans in the administration of the shires. The lands which had been forfeited by English rebels were granted out to foreigners in return for knight service. The Old English aristocracy had never adapted itself to the changes in the art of war from

[1] Domesday Book, i, fo. 148b.

which the institution of knighthood arose, and a considerable period must generally have elapsed before the sons and grandsons of pre-Conquest thegns had acquired the training which would give them an effective place in the new military order. By the middle of the reign of Henry I there are signs of a change in their condition. The king himself had owed much to English support at the beginning of his reign and had married a descendant of the Old English kings. There had arisen a new generation of Englishmen qualified by education to serve in war as knights. Englishmen were becoming prominent once more in local government. There is some reason to think that the king regarded his English subjects as a counter-balance to the Norman lords who had come to power in the time of his father and brother. For English families which had survived the shock of the Conquest the way to influence was once more open. The wars which had destroyed the Old English State had passed beyond living memory and there was no obstacle beyond a fading tradition to keep Englishmen and Normans from full co-operation in the king's service.[1]

Even in their unhappiest years, English thegns in the king's peace had been entitled to seek his court for protection against their adversaries. The clearest indication of the king's attitude towards them comes from a writ of William II or Henry I preserved in the 'Rydeware Cartulary' and published by the William Salt Society.[2] By this writ, the king orders Nicholas of Stafford, as sheriff of Staffordshire, to allow 'this Atsor the Englishman' to have his land of Edingale honourably for the service by which his father had held it, and to see that no one does him wrong therein.[3] Nicholas sheriff of Staffordshire, a member of the great Norman house of Tosny, was a baron of the first importance, and his appearance in the writ as a mere official is a good illustration of the way in which the higher Norman baronage had come to accept

[1] Cf. D. M. Stenton, *English Justice 1066–1215*, pp. 31–2.

[2] Vol. xvi, p. 284. The manuscript omits the initial of the king who issued the writ. It is assigned to William II in Davis' *Regesta regum Anglo-Normannorum*, p. 112, where an abstract is given. It was pointed out by Round, *English Historical Review*, xxix. 354, that the writ may equally well belong to the reign of Henry I. But in any case it cannot be later than 1107.

[3] His name represents the Old Norse name Ozurr, which was very common in the medieval Danelaw.

administrative service under the English crown. It is of greater interest that the king can clearly rely on a magnate of this class to use the royal authority for the protection of an Englishman's inheritance. Nothing more is known directly about Atsor the Englishman, but the medieval lords of Ridware, who held Edingale, claimed him with good reason as their ancestor. The possessions of the family were never great, but it acquired much influence in the late twelfth century, when a great-grandson of Atsor, who possessed a holding under Earl Ferrers, became seneschal of the earl's vast honor of Tutbury.[1] It is a striking illustration of the latent strength which remained to the smaller English families in their greatest depression, that within a century, a descendant of such a house had become the chief administrative officer of one of the greatest baronies in feudal England.

In many ways, administrative service under a great feudal lord resembled administrative service under the king. Among the multitude of officials employed by the Angevin monarchy, there are a few whose English descent is certain. Henry of Oxford, for example, who was sheriff of Oxfordshire in 1154 and 1155, was the son of an Englishman named Eilwi son of Godwine.[2] But from the standpoint of genealogy, the most interesting of these men is Nigel son of Alexander of Ingolds-by, a Lincolnshire knight who was much occupied in public business in the last years of Henry II. He was sheriff of Lincolnshire from 1185 until 1189. He was often employed in the management of estates which had come into the king's hand and he was a justice of assize in the eyre of 1188. By the combination of charters from various sources his descent can be traced through his father Alexander and his grandfather Osbert to a thegn named Colgrim, who held in 1086 under King William most of a considerable estate in south Lincolnshire which he had once held under King Edward. He was also holding in Lincolnshire small estates under the abbot of Crowland and Robert of Stafford, and a large one under count Alan of Richmond. In Yorkshire, he or Osbert his son acquired a knight's fee at Wensley under the count of Richmond for which, and for his land of the same fee in Lincolnshire, his descendants

[1] William of Ridware, Atsor's descendant, attests, as seneschal, many early charters of William, 2nd Earl Ferrers.

[2] H. E. Salter, *Facsimiles of early charters in Oxford Muniment Rooms*, 42.

owed castle-guard at Richmond itself.[1] The family which had thus adapted itself to the acutest crisis in English social history remained in possession of its chief estates until the fourteenth century.

At the present time there may be a certain danger of underestimating the strength of the English element in English feudal society. The criticism which J. H. Round directed against a large number of pedigrees beginning with an English ancestor cleared the ground for further enquiry. But the severity of Round's language has to some extent created the impression that the Old English descent of a medieval house can hardly ever be proved and that there is the strongest of presumptions against the native origin of any family which was of consequence in the twelfth or thirteenth centuries. Most of the great families of which the English descent is beyond question — Greystoke, Stanley, Audley, Neville of Raby, Fitzwilliam of Sprotborough, Fitzwilliam of Hinderskelfe — belong to Northumbria or to the northern parts of Mercia which the Conqueror had laid waste — a country with few attractions for Norman settlers. Even in this country, there are few cases in which continuity of tenure can be traced from 1066 into the middle ages. In southern England, the evidence for continuity of tenure and descent is much scantier. In the history of all but the greatest houses, it is a piece of unusual good fortune when the descent of a family can be carried through the lost generation which followed the knights and barons of Domesday Book. Among the baronial families of the south there are few parallels to the unchallengeable descent of the lords of Berkeley from the Englishman Robert son of Harding son of Eadnoth. In the second rank of English lords, among the honorial barons of the twelfth century, the descendants of English thegns are the rarest of exceptions. But the total number of men holding by military service in twelfth-century England was vast, and there is always the possibility that an unexpected piece of evidence may emerge to prove the English origin of the family from which one or other of them had sprung.

One example of which there can be no question may be given from Oxfordshire in the late twelfth century. By a charter of which the

[1] The history of the family is traced from the Yorkshire standpoint by C. T. Clay, *Early Yorkshire charters*, v. 255–8.

original still survives, Robert of Astrop, an undistinguished tenant upon the honor of St. Valery, granted to Bruern Abbey the whole estate in Milton under Wychwood which had belonged to his grandfather Alewi son of Eilsi of Faringdon.[1] These names are enough by themselves to show the English origin of Robert's family. Their interest is greatly increased by the fact that in Domesday Book Aluui appears as the holder of land at Milton under Roger de Ivri, whose fief developed into the Honor of St. Valery.[2] The statement that Alewi was the son of Eilsi of Faringdon has a still greater interest, for the Berkshire Domesday shows that Eilsi in 1066 was holding land at Littleworth near Faringdon of Harold as earl of Wessex.[3] It is unusual for a charter of the late twelfth century to give the detail which is necessary to prove a descent like this. But it would be very dangerous to assume that Robert of Astrop stood alone among his equals and contemporaries as the descendant of an English family of King Edward's day.

The investigation of cases like this is more than an antiquarian exercise. One of the cardinal features of English medieval history is the extent to which men of all ranks above serfdom in normal times cooperated with the crown in the work of government. To this cooperation the English administrative system in the middle ages owed the solidity which enabled it to survive the recurrent shocks of rebellion and foreign war. In this respect the medieval English State closely resembles the Old English order which it replaced. There is an obvious similarity of function between the knights of the shire on whom the Angevin kings relied in the administration of justice and local government and the thegns who had been expected to obey writs sent down to them by the Old English kings. When all allowance has been made for the executive efficiency of the Conqueror's followers and their descendants, there remains an element in the Anglo-Norman scheme of government which can only be due to English tradition· The means by which it was handed on through the catastrophic

[1] Augmentation Office Miscellaneous Books, 46, no. 124.

[2] Domesday Book, i, fo. 161.

[3] *Ibid.*, fo. 58. This, and other passages in Domesday Book which show Eilsi holding land at Faringdon and elsewhere twenty years later, are discussed by Round in the *Victoria History of Berkshire*, i. 292–3.

changes of the eleventh century can only be dimly seen. But one factor in the process was clearly the transmission of English ideas and practices by Englishmen who retained under the new conditions of the Conqueror's time something of their former interest in local affairs. Among the many services which genealogical research can render to history, none is more important than the identification of a few among the many individuals through whom the English conception of the State passed into the substance of Anglo-Norman life.

F. M. STENTON

6 English Learning in the Late Twelfth Century[1]

The title of this paper may raise false hopes in the minds of many; and it will be well to explain what has been attempted. English writers of the later twelfth century have on the whole been neglected; and when I was investigating the life and works of Alexander Nequam, it was necessary, in order to keep a sense of proportion, to try to learn something about the schools of the time, and to look at the work of some of his contemporaries. One or two things of interest have come to light, which I have tried to set out here. But the picture is far from complete. Nothing, for example, is said about legal studies.

The history of the schools in England in the twelfth century is at present very imperfectly known. The sources are incidental, stray remarks in prefaces, casual allusions in chroniclers, letters of papal judge-delegates, witnesses in charters and so on. In a number of places we know that there were schools at one time or another, but it is hard to trace any sort of continuity, which would lift them to the dignity of institutions. We are scarcely out of the period when it is the influence of some one master that makes the school famous. If he goes away the students will probably follow him; and if he dies, he may have no worthy successor. It is equally difficult to say how much progress was realised in the course of the century. Alexander, prior of Canon's Ashby, in his tract on the art of preaching, says:

> At the time when I was a student, there were few such founts of learning. [He has just explained that these founts are masters who teach theology without exacting a fee.] There were scarcely any masters to be found whose aim was not ambitious, whose teaching was not mercenary and whose tongues were not venal. But now, by the grace of God, there are many who teach without a fee. Many are

[1] I have to thank Professor F. M. Powicke for criticisms and suggestions, and also Miss E. Rathbone and Mr. R. W. Southern.

the founts of the Saviour, ever open to those wishing to draw from them. Almost every city has such a fount, at Northampton Master [here unfortunately there is a blank in the MS.], at Oxford Master Philip, at Exeter Master John and others elsewhere.[1]

These masters have not been identified.[2] There is some evidence for the schools at Northampton and Exeter, but it is fragmentary. Of Oxford and Lincoln there is a little more to be said. We know that Alexander Nequam was teaching at Oxford in the last decade of the century, and though none of his works in their present form date from this period, some of them are almost certainly based on his lectures. We know the names of two masters *theologiam Oxonie legentes*, John Grim and Simon of Gloucester (1201–3).[3] In another document, dated 1201, John Grim is called *magister scolarum Oxonie*.[4] It is surely significant that we can point to two teachers of theology there at the same time.

At Lincoln there was one notable master, many of whose works

---

[1] *De artificioso modo predicandi*, Serm. 2, Cambridge, Univ. Libr., Ii. 1, 24, s. XIII, ff. 173vb–174ra: Tempus quo puer eram scolaris pauci erant in terra ista fontes tales; uix aliqui inueniebantur magistri, quorum non esset intentio ambitiosa, lectio institoria, lingua uenalis. Sed multi sunt nunc, dei gratia, qui gratis docent. Multi sunt fontes saluatoris qui omnibus haurire uolentibus semper patent. Fere unaqueque ciuitas huiusmodi fontem habet, Norhamptona magistrum . . . Oxonia magistrum Philippum, Exonia magistrum Iohannem, et sic alie alios. The first part of this tract without the sermons is in Oxford, Magdalen Coll. 168, s. XIII, f. 128v, there ascribed to magister Willélmus Ruffus. Extracts from the sermons in it are anon. in Cambridge, Trinity Coll. R. 14, 40(912), s. XIII, pp. 48a–49b, but this passage is omitted. Alexander was prior 'in the reign of John', *V.C.H. Northants.* II, p. 133. He is found as papal judge-delegate at Oxford 1197–1201, *Oseney Cartulary*, ed. Salter, O.H.S., XCVII, IV, p. 62.

[2] Dr. Salter has kindly informed me that the only master Philip is the vice-archdeacon, found *c.* 1174–5, *Oseney Cartulary*, II, pp. 224 f.

[3] *Eynsham Cartulary*, ed. Salter, O.H.S., LI, II, pp. 45–7. They are acting as delegates of Hubert Walter; A. B. Emden, *Biographical register of the University of Oxford to 1500* (Oxford, 1958), ii. 826, 774.

[4] Hist. MSS. Comm., *MSS. of the Duke of Rutland*, IV, p. 82. The meaning of such terms is ill-defined. Cf. Alexander Nequam, *super Cant. Cant.*. VI, 20, B.M. Royal 4 D XI, f. 196vb: Theologi rectores scolarum locum istum (i.e. Cant. 8. 7) sic explanauere: Aque multe non poterunt extinguere caritatem de facili.

have survived. When Gerald of Wales wished to resume his theological studies and was unable to go to Paris owing to the war between Richard I and Philip Augustus, he turned to Lincoln, where he knew that theology flourished in a sane and healthy manner.[1] The master was Willelmus de Montibus,[2] who had formerly taught on the Mount at Paris, and was Chancellor at Lincoln from about 1190 until his death in 1213. His works have as yet scarcely been touched. They appear to be mainly compilations. Some bear a resemblance to works of Peter the Chanter; and in the *Similitudinarius* there are pieces taken from the sermons of Alexander Nequam. They are rather elementary aids for the instruction of the clergy, alphabetical *distinctiones* and similes for the use of preachers, little works on penance and on mistakes to be avoided in the conduct of church services. It is true that he wrote *questiones*, which have not yet been recovered. But his speculative bent can hardly have been great. His main efforts were directed to driving home simple lessons, by any means possible. One of his works is a collection of glossed verses in alphabetical order.[3] The first few headings are: De primo aduentu, De utroque aduentu, Ascensio Christi, Angeli, Ascensus, Assumptio, Amor, Amicitia, Amor bonus et malus, De amicis Job, Abnegatio propriorum, Anachorita. Each significant word in the line is glossed, so that if you learnt the verse, the lesson would be remembered. It is perhaps worth adding that the distribution of the manuscript and of the mentions of them in library catalogues suggests that his influence was mainly felt in the Midlands and the East of England. After William's death the school becomes obscure; but his teaching was given wider currency by Richard de Wethringsette, the first known chancellor of the University of Cambridge.[4] He wrote a manual for priests, known from its opening words as the *Qui bene presunt*, which, to judge from the number of manuscripts that have survived, had a great success in the thirteenth century; but it is an avowed compilation from the works of William.

It would be rash and probably unfair to belittle the work that was

[1] *De gestis*, III, 3, Opp. ed. Brewer, R.S., I, p. 93.

[2] On him see G. Lacombe, *New Scholasticism*, 5, 1931, 141 f., 148–50.

[3] Cambridge, C.C.C. 186, f. 21r; London, B.M. Add. MS. 16164, f. 15r.

[4] Emden, *Biographical Register of the University of Cambridge to 1500*, Cambridge, 1963, p. 679.

accomplished by these schools; but the coming of the Friars does seem to be the decisive turning-point. Certainly at Oxford they built up a great tradition with the help of Robert Grosseteste. It still remains to be seen, when his works have been examined and sorted out, how far he can be linked up with his Oxford predecessors. Our knowledge of such men as John of London[1] and John Blund[2] is tantalisingly slight beyond the fact that they both taught at Oxford. On the scientific side there seems to be a native tradition, but as far as theology is concerned, if there is anything vital, it draws its life and inspiration from Paris. The two most able English theologians of the century, Robert of Melun and Stephen Langton, taught in Paris; and everyone who could afford it went there to study. When they returned they were apt to be swept into the service of royal or episcopal administration.

For the history of the theological development of the late twelfth century there is no need to look beyond Paris. It is the history of an attempt that was made to arrange and systematise and work out the implications of the patristic material. Hence we have a whole series of *Sentences* and *Summas*, among which Peter Lombard's becomes a standard textbook. The movement does not stop here: it is only just begun. Having something to start from, new questions emerge, the various doctrines are gradually filled out. It is a fascinating process to watch, to see among much that seems to be mere word chopping how new questions are put and answered, how the solutions of one master suggest some new approach to his successor.

In other spheres there were strong external influences. Contact was

---

[1] Johannes de Garlandia, *De triumphis eccl.*, ed. Wright, pp. 53 f., cited by L. J. Paetow, *Morale scolarium of John of Garland*, p. 83. This probably refers to a period immediately before the strike of 1209–14. Cf. Rashdall's *Medieval Universities*, ed. Powicke and Emden, III, p. 50 n.

[2] J. C. Russell, *Shorter Latin Poems of Henry of Avranches*, Medieval Acad. of America, Studies and docs. 1, Cambridge, 1935, p. 131; lines 78 ff.: Primus Aristotilis satagens perquirere libros, Quando recenter eos Arabes misere Latinis, Quos numquam fertur legisse celebrius alter, Aut prius, ut perhibent Oxonia Parisiusque. See D. A. Callus, 'Introduction of Aristotelian learning in Oxford' (*Proc. Brit. Acad.* XXIX), 1943, pp. 241–52, and *Autour d'Aristote. Recueil d'études . . . offert à Mgr. A. Mansion*, Louvain, 1955, pp. 471–95. Callus assigns his period of teaching the arts at Oxford to the years before 1209.

made with Greek learning in Sicily and Arabic learning in Spain. There is a flood of translations from Greek and Arabic works, scientific and philosophical. The work of Haskins[1] has shown how many Englishmen took part in this movement. We may mention four of them, Roger of Hereford, Daniel of Morley, Alfred of Sareshel and Alexander Nequam. Roger was a canon of Hereford and among other astronomical works compiled a set of tables for the meridian of Hereford in 1178;[2] and perhaps it is due to him that his fellow canon, Simon du Fresne, inviting Gerald of Wales to come to Hereford, can say that not only astronomy and astrology, but also geomancy are studied there.[3] Of Daniel of Morley we know a little more.[4] He left England in the 1170s to study in Paris and found law in possession. So he went to Toledo where he worked under Gerard of Cremona; and he gives a lively picture of an argument between himself and Gerard about the influence of the stars over human affairs. Invited by his friends to return to England, he came with a precious load of books. He was on his way to Northampton,[5] where he heard that his subjects were studied, when he met the Bishop of Norwich, who asked for an account of the teaching of Toledo. This he gave in his *Philosophia*, which is partly cosmological and partly astronomical. It is largely a compilation based on the work of

[1] *Studies in the History of Medieval Science*, Cambridge, 1927.

[2] *Ibid.*, p. 125. J. C. Russell, *Isis*, 18, 1932, 15, has found him as a witness in a Hereford charter as late as 1195.

[3] Cambridge, C.C.C., 400, p. 119, G. Cambrensis, poem XLII, ed. Brewer, Opp. I, pp. 382 f. The date of the poem is *c.* 1195–7. The description of the subjects taught is not in Brewer's text and will be found in Appendix I. It is an addition of 32 lines after line 36. Its genuineness is supported by the excellence of the manuscript, on which see Dimock, Opp. V, p. xiv, H. E. Butler, *Medium Aevum*, IV, 1935, 143, and the description in the Catalogue by M. R. James. Father Ziegler tells me it is much the earliest reference to geomancy in England.

[4] See the preface to the *Philosophia*, most of which is in O.H.S. *Collectanea*, II, 169 f. The whole work was printed by K. Sudhoff in *Archiv. für die Gesch. der Naturwissenschaften*, VIII, 6–40, from B.M. Arundel, 377. Cf. T. Silverstein, 'Daniel of Morley, English cosmogonist and student of Arabic science' in *Medieval Studies* 10 (1948), 179–96.

[5] This word is omitted in Sudhoff's text. It was restored by A. Birkenmajer, *ibid.*, IX, 47, from Berlin lat. qu. 387. On the schools at Northampton see H. G. Richardson, *E.H.R.* 56 (1941), 595–605.

twelfth-century French masters, with the addition of material taken from translations of Arabic astrological works. The quotations from Aristotle, with one exception, are derived at second hand from a work then recently translated from the Arabic.[1] Later Daniel appears as parson of Flitcham in Norfolk,[2] the only preferment he is known to have held. Alfred of Sareshel is a much more important person, but unhappily nothing is known of his life except that he was an Englishman who studied abroad.[3] Presumably he returned, since two of his works are dedicated to Englishmen, his translation of the Ps. Aristotelian *De vegetabilibus* to Roger of Hereford and the *De motu cordis* to Alexander Nequam. The *De motu cordis* is mainly biological and is of some independent value. It 'shows a wealth of Aristotelian citation such as we cannot find in any other Latin author of the time'.[4] Alfred is also the earliest known western commentator on any of the *libri naturales* of Aristotle. The scientific works of his friend, Alexander Nequam, were not written until after he became a monk; and he set out to convey moral instruction, so that his knowledge appears rather incidentally and, as it were, reluctantly. But it deserves emphasis for the following reason. There is a considerable time-lag between the translation of the new Aristotle and its diffusion and assimilation. As has recently been shown, the most important people in this process were the naturalists, and in particular the doctors of Salerno. Now Alexander has not only the distinction of being the first person in the West to know both the Greco-Latin and Arabic-Latin translations of Aristotle, but he was also

---

[1] This is the work known as *Ps. Avicenna, De celo et mundo*, printed in Avicennae Opera, Venice, 1508 (reprinted Frankfurt am Main, 1961), ff. 37–42ᵛ. P. Alonso has shown that this is a translation by Hunain b. Ishak of extracts from a commentary of Themistius. He gives a list of Daniel's borrowings in *Al Andalus*, 16 (1951), 44–6. The Latin translation is anonymous, but is probably Toledan work of the third quarter of the twelfth century; see M. T. D'Alverny, *Archives d'hist. doctrinale et littéraire du moyen âge*, 19 (1952), 344, 352.

[2] Russell, *Isis, loc. cit.*, 22 f.

[3] C. Baeumker, *Die Stellung des Alfred von Sareshel*, Bayerische Akad. Sitz. Ber., Phil. hist. Kl., Abh. 9, 1913. G. Lacombe, *Aus der Geisteswelt des Mittelalters*, Beiträge, Suppl. Bd. III, 1, pp. 463–71. He quotes a passage in which Alfred names his master, Solomon Avenroza.

[4] Haskins, *op. cit.*, p. 129.

acquainted with one at least of the Salernitan doctors. For some whole chapters of the *De naturis rerum* are lifted straight from the commentary on the *Aphorismi* of Urso of Calabria.[1]

The time-lag is still more marked among the theologians, and little wonder. Aristotelianism in its pure form and the doctrines of Avicenna were not at all reconcilable with the Christian faith; and more than one person must have come to grief by taking them over too uncritically. There has recently been published, or rather republished, for it lay hid in the edition of Avicenna's works, a *Liber de causis primis et secundis*,[2] apparently written about this time, in which Avicenna's doctrines are accepted without reserve, and in which the quotations from St. Augustine are 'bowdlerised', so as to remove any specific references to Christianity, and the authority of St. Augustine is invoked to prove that we can have no knowledge of God![3] Alexander Nequam is perhaps the first theologian to introduce into his *summa* a doctrine of Avicenna, very tentatively and without mentioning his name. In his discussion of the faculties of the soul, he first expounds the traditional view of the three faculties, and then gives one that derives from the *De anima* of Avicenna. In the end he decides unconvincingly for the traditional one 'ne uidear abrogare doctrinam maiorum'. Other Englishmen knew something of Avicenna. Gerald of Wales quotes the translator's preface to the *De anima*,[4] and John of London, whom we

---

[1] A. Birkenmajer, *Le rôle joué par les médecins et les naturalistes dans la réception d'Aristote au xiiͤ et xiiiͤ siècles* (Extrait de la Pologne au VIͤ Congrès international des sciences hist., Oslo, 1928), Warsaw, 1930, p. 5, called attention to the occurrence of Urso's name in Laus sap. div. (IV, 235, ed. Wright, R.S., p. 425). Both II, c. 59 and c. 79 are taken from the Comm. on Aph. 32, part of II, c. 98 (pp. 181–3) is from the Comm. on Aph. 26 and part of c. 153 (pp. 236–7) is from the Comm. on Aph. 38, ed. R. Creutz, *Quellen u. Studien zur Gesch. der Naturwissenschaften und der Medizin*, V. I, Berlin, 1936.

[2] R. de. Vaux, *Notes et textes sur l'Avicennisme latin*, Bibl. Thomiste, XX, Paris, 1934.

[3] *Ibid.*, p. 138.

[4] *Spec. eccl. proem.*, ed. Brewer, Opp. IV, p. 10 (written *c.* 1220): super librum Aristotilis quendam de Anima intitulatum. This preface is not in the printed edition of Avicenna's works. It was first published by A. Jourdain, *Recherches sur les anciennes traductions d'Aristote*, Paris, 1843, p. 449, and has been printed several times since.

have already mentioned, is said to have taught scientific doctrines according to Avicenna.[1]

Turning to literary works we find a different state of affairs. The glory is not yet departed, but there is little more to come. We are at the end of a century's endeavour. The humanism of the twelfth century somehow failed to take root, and literary studies were scarcely provided for in the university curriculum. Grammar as understood and taught by Bernard of Chartres disappeared; and we are left with the rudiments for boys on the one hand and with logical investigations of meaning on the other. It is an exaggeration to say that the classics were neglected in the thirteenth century. Poets and prose-writers were probably read almost as much as before; but they came to be read rather for the information they contained than as models to imitate. They were regarded as quarries for useful sayings and stories suitable for inclusion in collections of *exempla*. Thus we get all the later moralisations. At the end of the twelfth century, however, this development was still in the future. Gerald of Wales, it is true, began to sound warnings over the encroachment of logic and the decay of *litteratura*; but no one fresh from reading Joseph of Exeter's epic on the Trojan War could realise it. And were there not in England two of the leading professors of the poetic art, Geoffrey of Vinsauf and Gervase of Melkley? The *milieu* of these men is elusive. Joseph of Exeter was the nephew of Archbishop Baldwin and apparently a member of his household.[2] Geoffrey, who wrote the standard text-book on the art of poetry, the *Poetria nova* as it came to be called to distinguish it from the *Poetria vetus* of Horace, taught for a time at Northampton, but was driven out from there by a rival.[3] Gervase of Melkley is also hard to trace.[4]

[1] J. de Garlandia, *De triumph. eccl.*, p. 54.
[2] G. Cambrensis, *De gestis*, II, 20, Opp. I, p. 79. Cf. Stubbs, *Epp. Cantuarienses*, R.S., pp. xxxvi, 230.
[3] See the poem printed by E. Faral, *Studi medievali*, N.S. 9 (1936), 56–7, and the comments of H. G. Richardson, *op. cit.*, pp. 597–601.
[4] Faral, *op. cit.*, pp. 34–7. He is found as a witness to two charters at St. Paul's Cathedral, London; a grant by Godfrey de Lucy to Geoffrey de Lucy, dean of St. Paul's and the chapter, 1231–41; and a grant by Peter son of William son of Alulf to G. de Lucy, dean of St. Paul's, 1229–31. See M. Gibbs, *Early Charters of*

It is possible to obtain a clearer view of the aims and achievements of the monastic writers. For the most part their works can be called theological. They wrote elaborate and lengthy commentaries on the Bible that contain little that is original. Robert, prior of Bridlington, and Clement, prior of Lanthony, are typical examples. Clement put together a Gospel harmony and wrote an enormous commentary on it that seems to be nearly all taken from older writers. He also commented on Acts and on the Pauline Epistles. His *Harmony* became the standard one for England and later a translation was made. His commentary was useful enough to be made the basis of a new one by William of Nottingham in the early fourteenth century.

The monasteries had great attractions for scholars. When he was in the schools Alexander Nequam had made a pact with a fellow-student to enter one, and became a canon at Cirencester, though his friend became an official in the Exchequer. Other examples are not hard to find. Warin, abbot of St. Albans (1183–95), had studied at Salerno,[1] and his successor John de Cella, who had been a master at Paris, was 'in grammar esteemed a Priscian, in verse an Ovid, in physic a Galen'.[2] Thomas of Marlborough, who later became abbot of Evesham, had been a pupil of Langton at Paris and taught law at Exeter and Oxford, and entered the monastery bringing with him the books on grammars and canon and civil law which he had used in the schools, and also book, on medicine.[3] Another monk of Evesham, Adam Sortes, had for many years taught the liberal arts before he became a monk.[4] Abbot Samson of Bury had made his way in the world by the same road; and in the chronicle of Jocelyn one of the arguments put forward on behalf of choosing a scholarly abbot is that otherwise *clerici litterati* may disdain to take the religious habit at Bury.[5]

Such men in their new life sometimes ceased to care for learning.

St. Paul's, Camden 3rd Ser., LVIII, 1939, nos. 206, 331. These references were overlooked by his editor, H. J. Gräbener, *Forsch. zur Romanischen Philol.*, Heft 17, Münster, 1965.

[1] *Gesta Abbatum*, ed. Riley, R.S., I, pp. 194–6.   [2] *Ibid.*, p. 217.

[3] *Chron. abb. Evesham*, ed. Macray, R.S., pp. 232, 267.

[4] *Ibid.*, p. 147.

[5] *Memorials of St. Edmund's Abbey*, ed. Arnold, R.S., I, p. 323.

Alexander of Ashby in the dedicatory letter to his work on preaching, addressing an abbot whose name is not given, says:

> I have not forgotten your excellence in the schools, how quick you were in learning and teaching, your diligent labour, your eager study, your acute thinking and your moving eloquence. But after you had fled from the schools to the cloisters, you became as it were an unlearned man (*quasi homo illiteratus*) and a despiser of letters, *nec lectioni nec doctrine insistens.*[1]

Alexander goes on to urge his friend to undertake some preaching at least. Some scholars by their ability rose to high office in their house, and their cares in looking after its affairs absorbed all their energies. But not all were so diverted, and there were those who thought a monastery was the home of true wisdom. The case is well put by Alexander of Ashby in another work, addressed to a monk named Letardus:[2]

> You must not be negligent, but diligent in the exercise of good work, in cultivating your heart and in the study of wisdom, in the knowledge that the acquisition 'of it is better than the merchandise of silver, and the gain thereof than fine gold'. And I do not advise you to seek a school or a master elsewhere than in the cloister. For if the law [that is the divine law] is learnt in quiet and silence, what place is better suited to the study of it than the cloister, where a discreet silence and a disciplined quietness is especially observed? You have many masters among you, most skilled in divine and secular learning, who will be able to expound theological questions (*theologicas rationes*) all the better as they know them more truly, not only by their knowledge, but by their experience. I think that only they purely and rightly understand the holy writings, who by the purity of their life keep close to that spirit, by which the scripture was composed and expounded.

These men were apt to be hostile to the newer learning and methods of enquiry. Senatus, prior of Worcester,[3] writes to Master William of

---

[1] *De artif. modo pred.*, prol., Cambridge Univ. Libr. II, 1, 24, f. 166v.

[2] *Breuissima comprehensio historiarum uet. et nou. test.*, prol., York Cath. XVI. Q. 14, s. XIII, f. 56rb. The work is anon. with only a short piece from the end of the prol. in B.M. Royal 6 B. XI, ff. 54v–61, s. XIV in.

[3] On him, see C. H. Turner, *Early Worcester MSS.*, Oxford, 1916, App. II.

Tunbridge, probably a master at Oxford and later in the household of the Bishop of Worcester: 'A book is said to have issued forth from your schools, which in passing through the hands of many has invited criticism (*reprehensionis morsum*). When I examined it I found no title and no author's name.'[1] But fortunately he gives the opening words which enabled R. L. Poole to identify it as the *Sententiae* of Peter of Poitiers, chancellor of Notre Dame at Paris.[2] It is certainly a work in which the dialectical method is employed to the full; and Grabmann speaks of Peter's virtuosity in making subtle distinctions that throw darkness rather than light on the question at issue.[3] Senatus goes on:

> But whoever the author is he treats audaciously of the Trinity, he disputes irreverently about God. And he so involves the ineffable secret of the Deity by subtle objections, that scarcely a word can be said about God that does not require someone to explain it.

He proceeds to object to some specific passages. Now Senatus was far from being an ignorant or unlettered person. He wrote two saints' lives[4] and some sermons; and we have several letters written to people who had consulted him. There is one to Roger, bishop of Worcester, who had asked for explanations on some points about penance. In another letter we see him swelling with pride as he answers Clement, prior of Oseney:[5]

> It is an old saying you read in the book of Kings, 'Those who ask counsel, let them ask it at Abel, because that city had many schools!' And I say this to you on account of the city that lies close to you, in which there are many eloquent orators and men who can weigh the

---

[1] Holland, O.H.S. *Collectanea*, II, pp. 181 f. Holland doubted whether Oxford was referred to. But see Salter's note on the Vision of the Monk of Eynsham c. XXVI, *Eynsham Cartulary*, O.H.S., LI, II, pp. 325 f.

[2] Holland, O.H.S., *op. cit.*, p. 182.

[3] *Gesch. der schol. Methode*, Freiburg, 1911, II, p. 510.

[4] The suggestion of R. R. Darlington that he made the abbreviation of the life of St. Wulfstan (*Vita Wulfstani*, Camden 3rd Ser. 1928, p. xxi) is supported by a letter to Roger, Bishop of Worcester in Bodl. 633 (1966), f. 197v: Uitam quoque beatorum pontificum OSWALDI et WLSTANI etsi non quo decuit, quo tamen potui, stilo descripsi.

[5] Holland, *op. cit.*, p. 180.

words of the law and who bring forth from their treasure things new and old for everyone that asks. These you have passed over, and you consult me.

It must be admitted that such men were often a little out of touch. But they were solid. Dom Wilmart's judgement on Adam of Dryburgh, a Premonstratensian canon who later became a Carthusian at Witham, sums the matter up well:

> Erudite, richly endowed with natural gifts and shot through with fervour, he did not understand, perhaps was not even aware of the immense movement in philosophy and theology, which was taking shape at that time. . . . He found his own level and peace in the disciplines of the past.[1]

There were others, especially among the Augustinian Canons, who were more in sympathy with contemporary movements abroad. We may begin with Robert of Cricklade,[2] who belongs to the preceding generation. He had been a master in the schools, we do not know where, and then entered the new royal foundation of Cirencester, where he wrote his *De connubio patriarche Iacob*,[3] an allegorical exposition of the story of Jacob. It contains an interesting passage on William of Malmesbury that seems to have been overlooked. He is answering those who criticise him for writing at all and says there are some authors still left in the world:

> I have read all the works of the venerable abbot of Clairvaux that have come into my hands; and the excellent work of William monk

1 A. Wilmart, *Mélanges Mandonnet, Bibl. Thomiste*, xiv, Paris, 1930, II, p. 161.

2 On him, see Haskins, *op. cit.*, pp. 169–71.

3 *De connubio*, II, 22, Bodl. Laud. misc. 725, s. XII, f. 129va (immediately after the passage cit. below): Non enim inuideo monachis scribentibus, sed congaudeo, licet non sim monachus, sed indignissimus canonicorum ecclesie sancte dei genitricis Marie sub disciplina sancti et uenerabilis S(erlonis) primi eiusdem loci abbatis pro remissione peccatorum suorum deo supplicantium. Serlonis is written out in full in Hereford Cath. P. 4, viii. The date of the work is *c.* 1138, since Robert refers in III. I (f. 152) to the death of Godfrey, abbot of Winchcombe, news of which had just reached him. Godfrey died in 1138. The preface is in Holland, *op. cit.*, pp. 161 f. Hereford, P. 4, viii, adds Winchelcumbensi after Laurentio monacho and Geruasio et Achardo after sanctis fratribus.

and cantor of the church of Malmesbury, which he compiled on the Lamentations of Jeremiah I have not only read, but caused a copy of it to be put in our church. I have also read his little book on the miracles of the blessed virgin Mary, which is also in our church. What shall I say of his excerpts from the works of the most blessed pope Gregory?... Other works of his I have not yet read, but I shall, if it pleases God to lengthen the span of my life.[1]

Robert became prior of St. Frideswide's at Oxford about 1140 and remained in that office until his death about 1180. During that time he made three journeys to Rome, and on one of them he went as far as Sicily. We also find him on a visit to Paris, violently opposing Peter Lombard's Christological views.

> I remember [he says] that Roger, who is now Bishop of Worcester, came to our inn. I asked him with whom he was studying theology, and he replied, 'With Master Robert of Melun.' 'I am very pleased,' I said, 'I was afraid that that heretic — he means Peter Lombard — had you ensnared in his net.' One of his chief pupils (I pass over his name in silence), who had come with Roger of a set purpose, I believe, on hearing this, said: 'In what point is Master Peter a heretic?' 'In many,' I replied. 'Let one of them be propounded,' he said.[2]

[1] *Loc. cit.* Nam et que in manus nostras uenerunt scripta uenerabilis abbatis Clarisuallensis legi; et uiri summe eruditionis Guillelmi Meldunensis ecclesie monachi et cantoris preclarum opus quod super Lamentationes Ieremie compilauit non tantum legi, uerum ut et in nostra ecclesia scriptum haberetur exegi. Legi et libellum eius de miraculis beatissime dei genitricis et perpetue uirginis Marie, qui et in nostra ecclesia habetur. Quid dicam super deflorationibus eius ex opusculis beatissimi pape Gregorii? In quibus ita uiolentus procedit eradicator uitiorum et diligens edificator uirtutum, ut in eo quodammodo uideatur impleri quod scriptum est: *Ecce constitui te super gentes et regna ut euellas et destruas et edifices et plantes.* Alia eius opuscula nondum legi, sed legam, si deo placuerit et uite mee spatium protelauerit. William of Malmesbury's excerpts from Gregory escaped Stubbs. They are in Cambridge Univ. Libr., Ii. 3, 20, mentioned by M. R. James, *Two Ancient English Scholars*, Glasgow, 1931, p. 19.

[2] *Spec. fidei*, III, 5, Cambridge, C.C.C. 380, f. 62v. The text of the whole chapter will be found in Appendix II. The date of the incident is before the

They go on to discuss Peter's view of the nature of Christ, which was indeed condemned at the Council of Tours in 1163. The work from which this is taken, a sort of *summa* called the *Speculum fidei* is as a whole disappointing. Robert contents himself with collecting and discussing rather slightly the texts from the Old and New Testament supposed to refer to the Trinity and the Incarnation and so forth. Only in the chapters devoted to Peter's views does he try to grapple with anything deeper and makes an attempt at reasoning.

Another prolific Augustinian canon was Peter, prior of Holy Trinity, Aldgate, a Cornishman, who tells us something about his family in a story in his huge *Liber reuelationum.*[1] Before this he had compiled another enormous work called the *Pantheologus*, which is divided into four parts.[2] The first is dedicated to his teacher, Master Henry of Northampton, who was a canon of St. Paul's; the second and third to Ralph of Haute Rive, Archdeacon of Colchester, who died at the siege of Acre in 1191;[3] and the fourth to Godfrey de Lucy, Bishop of Winchester, a fellow student, where we do not know. In the prologue Peter gives an interesting account of the way he came to write the

---

death of Peter Lombard in 1160. Possibly the occasion was Robert's visit to Rome in 1158. He made other journeys there in 1141 (not quite certainly) and in 1151; for these dates, see C. H. Haskins, *Studies in the hist. of medieval science*, Cambridge, 1927, pp. 169 f. The passage shows that Robert of Melun did return to Paris, as R. M. Martin suggests (*Œuvres de Robert de Melun I*, Spicil. sacr. Lovaniense 13, Louvain 1932, p. ix). The Robert archdeacon of Oxford, mentioned by Martin, p. x, was Robert Foliot. The *Speculum fidei* is dedicated to a layman, Robert, earl of Leicester. A copy of it is in the catalogue of the library of the Abbey of Lyre (Cat. gén. des MSS., Départements, II, p. 381, referred to by Manitius, *Gesch.*, III, p. 241 n.) of which the Earls of Leicester were patrons.

[1] Lambeth 51. The text is printed in the Catalogue. A translation was given by G. G. Coulton, *Social Life in Britain*, Cambridge, 1919, pp. 218 ff.

[2] Pt. I is in Oxford, Merton Coll. 191, B.M. Royal 6 E. VIII, 7 E. VIII; pts. II–III, in Merton 192, Royal 7 C. XIII, 7 F. IV; pt. IV in Lincoln Coll. lat. 83, Royal 7 C. XIV. There are other MSS.

[3] Ralph is thanked for helping Peter to hire scribes to copy the work. Pt. I, prol. preter rem, Merton 191 f. ivb: Michi et scribendi et transcribendi et scriptores conducendi non minus uoluptaria quam necessaria uelud Thimotheus Paulo aut Damasus Ieronimo liberaliter inpendis.

work.[1] He was at a synod in attendance on Stephen, his prior,[2] and Gilbert Foliot preached the sermon. When he heard it he could not restrain his admiration and praise. 'The whole sermon was varied by certain *distinctiones*, adorned with flowers of words and sentences and supported by a copious array of authorities. It ran backwards and forwards on its path from its starting-point back to the same starting point.' He then gives an example. When Gilbert spoke of Christ as a stone, he brought forward the stone which the builders rejected, which is become the head of the corner, he brought forward the stone which Jacob set up for a pillar and on top of which he poured oil, he brought forward the stone that was cut out of the mountain without hands. Peter was so much struck with this method that he determined to write a work in which the *lector studiosus* might find all such passages collected together and arranged. This is really important because it is an early example of the *distinctio* method, which in its simplest form consists in taking a word according to its senses and attaching a quotation of the Bible to each. The germ of it is old. But it was not developed as a systematic method of exegesis until after the death of Peter Lombard, when it arose and spread with great rapidity. It is unusual to get such a close view of the way in which a typical medieval form was transmitted.

It will be noticed that a large proportion of the writers whom we have mentioned are Augustinian canons. This predominance has hardly been brought out sufficiently; and it is difficult to suggest reasons for it. The Augustinians are a very elusive order. They have no rule that is worthy of the name and their constitutions, of which few survived, are not very helpful. Yet we have this undoubted intellectual activity that springs up very gradually, only to disappear again in the course of the thirteenth century. Possibly an examination of the Victorine tradition would throw some light on it.

Though the material we have brought together is fragmentary and far from complete, it does in a way fit together and combine to give

---

[1] It is repeated in the prol. of pts. I, II–III and IV in almost identical terms. The text of the prol. of pt. I, which gives the clearest account of his aims, will be found in Appendix III.

[2] Stephen was prior from 1170 to 1197.

us an idea of some of the many-sided interests of the writers of the period. They are poised a little uneasily, as though not quite certain of their direction. They look back to the earlier and less perplexing time when all that could be hoped for was to master and consolidate what one had, and forward to the great and lasting achievements of the thirteenth century for which they are helping to prepare the way. None of them was of outstanding importance, and most of them have been forgotten; but if we are ever to be given a history of learning in England in the Middle Ages, they will have a secure place in it.

APPENDIXES

I. Extract from the Poem of Simon du Fresne

Flos et honos cleri, nostram te transfer ad urbem,
    sunt ubi philosophi, summus habendus ibi.
Urbs Herefordensis multum tibi competit, in qua
    proprius est triuii quadriuiique locus.
35 Floruit et floret, et in hac specialiter urbe
    artis septene predominatur honos.
Gramatice doctrina docet constructio que sit
    recta, loqui recte que sine nemo potest.
Ars logice dat scire quid est inductio, quid sit
40   entimema, quid est maxima, quidque locus.
Retoris hec laus est quod sic sua uerba leporat,
    possit ut eloquio quemque mouere suo.
Quis numerus solidus, quis planus, quis cubicus sit,
    quisue laterculus est ars numerosa docet.
45 Dina per alkidade geometra foramine spectans,
    quot pedibus turris alta sit arte probat.
Musicus ostendit que sit proportio uocum
    dissimilesque docet consociare modos.

Lambeth 236, f. 166r (*G. Cambr.*, Opp. I, 382 f.); Cambridge, C.C.C. 400, p. 119.
   37–68 *om. Lamb.*

Astronomia docet ubi sol, ubi luna mouetur,
50   solis et eclipsim precinit arte diem.
Astrologus notat hic horas arcumque diei,
    quo breuis est et quo tempore longa dies.
Cum solem recipit Aries uel Libra, sub illis
    esse parem nocti comperit arte diem.
55 Principium Cancri cum sol subit arte probatur,
    quod spatiosa dies longior esse nequit.
Oppositum Cancro cum sol subit Egloceronta
    nulla dies transit sub breuiore mora.
Hic geomanticus est formans ter quinque figuras,
60   iudicio quarum queque futura uidet,
quid uia, quid populus, quid carcer, quid capud altum,
    quid queat in quauis queque figura domo.
Omnia distinguit, tandem pronuntiat utrum
    femina, uir uotum possit habere suum.
65 His aperit fisis quid sint elementa, quid ile,
    que mundi causa primicialis erat.
Hic noua lex legitur, legitur uetus, hicque decenter
    causidice leges equidicensque canon.
Hunc ubi tot radiant artes de iure teneris,
70   cum sis artis honos, artis amare locum.
Huc ergo uenias, toti dominaberis urbi,
    seruiet urbs flexo poplite tota tibi.

           62 quead *Lamb.*

II. RODBERTI KRIKELADENSIS, *SPECULUM FIDEI*, III, 5

De hoc quod auctor huius libri Parisius perhendinans publice Petrum
hereticum denominavit, et cum quodam discipulo eius, de eo quod Deus et
homo una [*f. 62v*] *persona est contulit et ob mutescere fecit.*

    Sed dicet aliquis: 'Quis es tu, qui tantum virum persequeris
mortuum, cum quo conferre non auderes vivo?' 'Immo aude-
bam,' dico, 'et in sua civitate, id est Parisius, ubi docebat, hereticum eum esse patenter pronuntiabam'. Testes michi sunt domnus

           Cambridge, C.C.C. 380.

5 Achardus postea Abricensis episcopus, et domnus Rodbertus
Herefordensis, qui tunc temporis Parisius erant, quando ibi
perhendinans, eum hereticum esse publice affirmabam; et cum
potioribus discipulis eius contuli, ad me, ut didici, ab eo missis.
Meminit enim me domnum Rogerum, qui nunc est Wigornensis
10 episcopus, venisse ad hospicium nostrum. Quem cum interrogas-
sem apud quem in divina pagina studeret, et respondisset, 'Apud
magistrum Robertum Meldunensum.' 'Perplacet,' inquam, 'time-
bam enim, ne te teneret inviscatum hereticus ille.' Quod audiens
quidam de potioribus discipulis eius, (sed nomen taceo) qui cum
15 domno Rogero, ut opinor, ex industria venerat. 'In quo,' inquit,
'hereticus est magister Petrus?' 'In multis,' inquam. 'Unum,'
inquit 'proferatur.' 'Separat' inquam [f. 63r] 'hominem a Deo,
ut non sit una persona homo cum Deo in Trinitate, qui revera
filius Dei est.' 'Non intelligis' inquit 'quomodo hoc dictum sit.'
20 'Nec intelligam' inquam 'in vita mea quia hoc heresis est pessima
et detestabilis.' 'Audi' inquit 'me patienter, et ego reserabo tibi
veritatem.' 'Veritas' inquam 'audienda est et semper amanda.'
'Nosti' inquit 'albedinem esse in corpore, et non conferre corpori
ut substancia sit.' Et ego 'Scio' inquam 'quo tendas. Non hoc modo
25 michi exemplificabis. Loquimur enim de duabus naturis, divina
scilicet et humana, et tu inducis de natura exemplum, et de
accidente, quod nec inter naturas computatur. Si vis michi exem-
plificare, induc exemplum de duabus naturis, sicut loquimur de
duabus naturis. Quod si nescis, ego inducam. Sicut anima rationalis
30 et caro unus est homo, ita Deus et homo unus est Christus.' 'Ita'
inquit ipse 'quod nullo modo ita.' Et ego 'Si nullo modo' inquam
'ita Deus et homo unus est Christus, ut anima rationalis et caro
unus est homo, tunc non ita. Sed ita et non ita tantum sibi contra-
dicunt, quod simul esse non possunt. Itaque sancta Dei ecclesia
35 catholica canit cum plena fide per universum [f. 63v] orbem
terrarum, ita Deus et homo unus est Christus. Heretici vero in
conventiculis suis perstrepunt, dicentes non ita.' Hoc itaque con-
cluso sermone obmutuit ille confusus. Qui vero tunc aderant sane
sapientes congratulantur michi. Itaque fideliter firmiterque

9 Wgornensis *MS.*

40 credendum et confitendum est, quia dominus noster Iesus Christus,
secundum quod Deus est, filius Dei est et creator omnium creatura-
rum; secundum quod homo est, filius hominis est, factus creatura,
ut creaturam redimeret.

III. Petri de Cornubia

Prologus in primam partem *Pantheologi*

Magistro Henrico de Norhamtun suus ille Petrus, olim quidem
discipulus, nunc autem seruus in domino, hoc totum quod est opti-
mum. Uir desideriorum sollicitus agnoscere que circa discipulum
in claustro canonicorum agerentur studia, petisti sepe ut saltem
5 unum uel duos quaternos opusculi nostri nouiter incepti tibi
transmitterem. Quod quidem ne facerem pudor dissuasit, timor
prohibuit, ignorantia excusauit. Os enim tuum omnes attendunt,
pectus suspiciunt, utrumque admirantur; coram cuius iudicio
Ieremias puer est et nescit loqui; Moyses quoque omni sapientia
10 Egyptiorum eruditus incircumcisus est labiis et eloquens non est
ab heri et nudius tercius ex quo tecum loquitur. Preterea cum
omne inuentionis humane initium suam habeat imperfectionem
timui patere morsibus inuidorum, qui aliorum sapientiam cum
annorum numerositate metientes se non posse laudari autumant
15 nisi aliene felicitati derogantes carnes conferant ad uescendum.
Quid igitur? Numquid ulterius funis inobedientie est protrahendus
et non potius magistro parendum quam inuido per silentium
parcendum? Freno igitur pudoris et timoris longius abiecto, elegi
potius magistri iussionibus obtemperare et, ut aliquorum temperem
20 inopiam, opus laboris mei quod secreto solus habui in plateas foras
diriuare quam pecuniam domini mei, quantumlibet paruam michi
creditam, in terram fodere et abscondere. Qui enim super pauca
fuerit fidelis super multa constituetur, et qui abscondit frumenta
maledicetur in populis; benedictio autem super caput uendentium.
25 Panis enim egentium, ut sapiens ait, uita est pauperis et qui de-

Merton Coll. 191, f. 2r; Royal 6 E. VIII, f. 1r (A); Royal 7 E VIII, f. 1r (R).
  15 nisi]ubi *A*.   16 protrahendus *A*.

fraudat illum, homo sanguinis est. Paruula michi credita est
pecunia quam si ad mensam dedero ueniens dominus illam exiget
cum usura, et qui mercedem calicis aque frigide promittit nullum
relinquens bonum irremuneratum michi cum Ysaac seminanti
30 centuplum in anno benignitatis sue accumulabit. Si enim multum
non ualeam cum Zacheo, saltem minutum uel unum cum uidua
inferam in donariis domini, apud quem non res sed uoluntas que
operi nomen imponit mercedem accipit. Accipe igitur, magister
bone, non quaternum unum, sed ex quaternis multis laboris mei
35 opus primum, non ut quod imperfectionis plurimum habet
iudices, sed ut euellas et destruas et edifices et plantes. Quod enim
in prima sui conditione de perfectionis laude minus habuerit, si
foliis uerborum tuorum adumbretur, si flosculis et coloribus
prudentie tue rethoricis depingatur, si gratia correctionis tue
40 nobilitetur, omnis admirationis laude plus erit. In eo siquidem tot
inuenientur areole aromatum, tot cellule uinarie pigmentariorum,
ut comedant amici, inebrientur karissimi. Minus peritis erit
desiderabile, perfectis uero memoriale: actiuis erit utillimum,
contemplatiuis uero iocundum. Uiris quoque labilis memorie qui
45 precepta diu retinere non ualent, claustralibus etiam et ad clerum
uel ad populum sermones assuefacientibus in hoc opusculo maxime
prospectum est, quos de omnibus diuine pagine auctoritatibus que
ad sermonem faciendum magis sunt necessarie celeriter ditat et
instruit et uerbis et auctoritatibus copiosos facit. Que enim ab
50 occultis diuersorum librorum sinibus sparsim a peritis cum difficultate uix tandem post multam inquisitionis moram ad aliquam
rem pertinentia colliguntur, hec omnia etiam ab imperitis in huius
opusculi aliquo capitulo simul congesta sine aliqua difficultate
celerius dicto reperiuntur. Ecce enim capitulum de tabernaculo
55 proferimus in medium, ut unius uerbi exemplo que diximus
etiam de aliis uerbis sine ambiguitate clarius elucescant. Ubi enim
de tabernaculo tractauimus, quot modis et quibus rationibus
tabernaculum in sacro eloquio dicatur enumerauimus; eiusdem
quoque uerbi diuersarum significationum distinctiones anno-
60 tauimus. Singulas quoque distinctiones diuersis et copiosis auctori-

29 irrenumeratum *A*.   34 unum *om. A*.

tatum tam ueteris quam noui testamenti exemplis roborauimus.
Auctoritatum quoque singularum que exponi indigebant, singulas
a sanctis patribus inuentas tam morales quam misticas expositiones,
nunc uerbis patrum propriis, nunc illorum prolixitate amputata,
65 nostris compendiosius adnexuimus, ut non iam oporteat sermones
facientem circa dicendorum inuentionem laborare, sed potius ex
iam inuentis et ante oculos positis et expositis non tam sermonem
facere quam iam factum formare. Unde et conclaustralibus nostris
quorum cura est in sermonibus suis uerba multipliciter distinguere
70 et diuersarum auctoritatum suppositione que dixerant compro-
bare, placuit librum studii et laboris nostri Pantheologum nom-
inare, quia uidelicet de omnibus nominibus ad sermonem faciendum aptioribus et plus celebratis que per totius theologie libros
inveniuntur sermocinatur et racionatur.

75 Formam autem et modum hunc scribendi ab illo ore aureo
communis patris nostri uenerabilis Gilleberti Londoniensis episcopi
mutuaui. Qui cum in sinodo iam nouus canonicus ad uenerabilis
patris mei Stephani Sancte Trinitatis Londonie prioris pedes,
humilis et attentus auditor assedissem, formam et modum ser-
80 monis eius quem fecit ad clerum ut audiui, admirans obmutui et
laudans tacere non potui. Totus enim sermo ille quibusdam dis-
tinctionibus uariatus et flosculis uerborum et sententiarum depictus
et copiosa auctoritatum subiectione roboratus, a principio per
tramites suos ad idem principium decurrebat et recurrebat ut
85 areolas agrorum multiplicibus riuulorum tractibus uniformi
dissimilitudine exaratas et multiplici uernantis germinis fructu
inter carnalium decursus fecundatas cogitares nec hominem sed
super hominem esse, qui tanta auctoritatum copia per singulas
sermonis distinctiones superhabundare potuisset affirmares. Cum
90 enim inter cetera Christum lapidem diceret, protulit in medium
illum lapidem angularem ab edificantibus reprobatum, protulit et
in medium lapidem illum quem Iacob unxit leo et erexit in
titulum, protulit et in medium nichilomnius lapidem illum in

68 *Post* formare *add. prol. in pt.* II–III (Merton 192). Utilitate quoque huius
qui stilo ecclesiastico epistolas scribit gaudebit.
89 firmares *R.*

Daniele de monte sine manibus abscisum. Et cum circa hec et
95 similia sermo eius in longum protraheretur, pulcherrima uerborum
uarietate distinctus, tanta velocitate sine impedimenti inuidia
quocunque uoluit decurrebat, ut non iam excogitata recitare, sed
omnia ante oculos diligenti examinatione conscripta legere
putares. Tante igitur et tam preclare nouitatis dulcedine exhilaratus,
100 tanteque et tam desiderande omnium utilitatis intentione ad pre-
sumendum similia prouocatus, sepe et multum solus mecum
tacitus et sollicitus cogitare cepi, quibusnam certe legis loris fugax
memoria teneretur, et quo certe artis fine rerum ac nominum
incomprehensibilis infinitas comprehendi ualeret. Tandem uero
105 post diuturnas lugubrationum ignorantie nebulas lumen patuit
querenti et scientie ianua aperta est pulsanti, per quam inoffenso
pede ad interiora artis precepta percurrerem, et opus uotiuum per
metodum artis inuentam ad finem diu desideratum usque pers-
ducerem, in quo lector studiosus omnia, prout diximus, sine mora
110 que querit inueniet; et in morem corollarii se inuenisse que non
sperabat optata pro mercede accipiet.

Opus autem istud quod Pantheologum diximus pro magnitu-
dine sui in quatuor partes siue uolumina eundem scribendi stilum
et similem tractandi formam per omnes suos libros habentia
115 distinximus, ut delicatis qui parua degustant ex parte sufficeret et
auide sumentibus qui omnia possunt ex toto non deesset. Quelibet
autem quatuor supradictarum Pantheologi partium xiii continet
libros capitulis suis distinctos. Capitula autem cuiusque partis in
principio sui disposuimus ut in primo limine quisque modum et
120 progressum tractatus agnoscat, et sine difficultatis mora que querit
inueniat. Primam autem partem Dauid nominauimus, non quia in
ea soli psalmi Dauitici, sed in ea sola psalmi Dauitici tractantur.
Preterea omnia eiusdem partis capitula a libro psalmorum sumunt
initia et omnes eiusdem partis paragrafi de psalmis Dauiticis
125 emanant. Prime enim partis omnia fere capitula paragrafis et
maioribus apicibus distinximus, ut paragrafi omnes et principia
capitulorum Dauiticam pretendant auctoritatem. Apices uero
omnes et sub primo paragrafo conscribantur et undecumque et
aliis libris tam ueteris quam noui testamenti testimonia inducant.

130 Pars autem secunda solis paragrafis exaratur. Et quia ex solis
Salomonis libris auctoritates sumit, nomen Salomonis sibi iure
uendicauit. Libri autem a quibus auctoritates inducit et a nonnullis
omnes Salomonis dicuntur, eo quod mellifluum Salomonis stilum
redoleant. Sunt numero quinque, videlicet Parabole Salomonis,
135 Ecclesiastes, Cantica canticorum, Sapientia Salomonis, Ecclesiasti-
cus. Pars autem tercia similiter solis paragrafis distinguitur et ex
solis prophetarum libris auctoritates inducit. Unde et prophete
nomen sortita est. Prophete autem ex quibus testimonia assumit
sunt numero XVIII videlicet Ysaias, Jeremias, Ezechiel, Daniel et
140 XII reliqui prophete qui in eodem uolumine conscribuntur; Iob,
Apocalypsis Iohannis. Pars autem quarta sicut et prima nullorum
singulariter librorum arctatur angustiis, sed passim et sine delectu
ex omnibus tam ueteris quam noui testamenti libris testimonia
dictorum que relique partes dimiserant sollicite colligit.

R. W. HUNT

7 Experiments in Exchequer Procedure (1200–1232)

'Experiments in Exchequer Procedure' may suggest a series of unimportant financial developments, with only a remote interest for students of medieval history, and of no value to anyone else. But finance lies at the bottom of most medieval, as well as of most modern, historical problems: the complaints of the barons in 1215 are chiefly financial in origin, while the struggle over the Charters is the central point round which our enquiry is built. Moreover, in these years changes took place in exchequer procedure which laid the foundations for the new structure which gradually superseded the old in the thirteenth and fourteenth centuries — a structure different from its predecessor, though the old forms were maintained, a not uncommon feature in English administrative history.

A comparison of the Pipe Rolls under Henry II and at the end of the thirteenth century makes this point clear. In the twelfth century they were essentially simple, in the fourteenth exceedingly complex. In the first period, each debtor was personally responsible for the payment of his debt: by the second, an intermediary, the sheriff, had been interposed between debtor and exchequer. At the second date, he was responsible for the collection of all debts within his bailiwick: the debtors answered to him locally, he in turn accounted for them to the exchequer, making a series of lump payments in his own name, and being held personally responsible on the Pipe Roll for the amercements of a particular court in a certain year.[1] It is this change from direct to indirect responsibility which marks the difference between twelfth- and fourteenth-century procedure. There are, however, other points to be considered. The farm of the shire retained its old place, but in a new guise and with new shoots. The debts, formerly individually large in

[1] Cp. *The Pipe Roll of 1295, Surrey Membrane* (Surrey Record Society, 1924, vol. xxi), pp. xxiv–xxviii, 16–24.

amount and few in number, were now almost overwhelming in their numbers and generally quite small in value. Their origin was no longer feudal: they arose largely from arrears of accounts and from fines and amercements levied as a result of some process in the royal courts. The character of the debtor had also changed. Under Henry II he was normally a great baron, an important official, an ecclesiastic or the representative of a town. By 1300 the net had spread much wider, so that it included many quite unimportant people. But the really important change was that the sheriff became responsible for the collection of all debts in his shire (outside special liberties), the Pipe Roll formula being: 'The same sheriff renders account of ――.' The details were given on Originalia and Estreat Rolls.

This analysis has served its purpose if it proves that the exchequer system of the fourteenth century differed from its predecessor in the twelfth, the change being in the direction of an increase in the number of debts, a decrease in their individual value. We have here to trace the first steps in this direction, to ascertain the causes of the change, and what attempts were made to find solutions for problems which confronted the exchequer in the early thirteenth century. Before John's accession, little change had occurred: Peter de Rivaux's seizure of the sheriffdoms in 1232 marked a distinct stage in the journey, ending the experimental period.

Chronologically, our subject falls into three main divisions: the first deals with John's reign to the sealing of the Great Charter, the second with the struggle between king and barons, and the third with the early part of Henry III's reign (Martinmas, 1217-32). Until 1215, the exchequer was attempting to solve the problems created by Henry II's legal reforms, a complete breakdown followed, and then, after 1217, came determined efforts to re-establish order, to develop improvements begun at the earlier date. In each period the developments in both farm and summonses are examined.[1]

[1] I am deeply in debt to Professor Tout, *Chapters in Administrative History of Medieval England* (Manchester, 1920-33) (especially for Peter de Rivaux); to Mr. Hilary Jenkinson, 'Financial Records of the Reign of King John' (in *Magna Carta Commemoration Essays*, ed. H. E. Malden (London, 1917)), as well as for much help on many difficult points; and to Mr. Charles Johnson for his

I. With regard to the summonses the first question is how far they were affected by Henry II's legal reforms. Now these reforms drew an ever-increasing volume of business into the royal courts: they formed an ever-increasing barrier to the transaction of all business at the exchequer. A steady stream of writs issued from the chancery. Acting on these, the king's justices amerced officials, jury, plaintiffs and defendants for defaults of all kinds. The result was a vast body of small debts that had to be collected. The details of fines for the issue of writs, and of the consequent amercements were forwarded from chancery to exchequer on Originalia Rolls — though this term was later applied only to debts arising in the chancery, all others being entered on Estreat Rolls. Now fines for issue of writs were usually half a mark, while amercements of that value were normal: if this sum were divided among a number of people, each individual's share would be small. As the business passing through the royal courts steadily increased, the number of debts grew too. Even by the end of Henry II's reign, it must have been clear that new machinery was needed to cope with the new type of revenue. In the early thirteenth century the question of reform became urgent.

A Yorkshire account shows the nature of the problem. The sheriff owed roughly £610, collected on account of 972 payments of the whole debt, in addition to 122 partial payments, giving a total of 1094 tallies cut and entered on the Receipt Roll.[1] This was one year's payments on the amercements of a single eyre in one county — an extreme case — but examples of two or three hundred tallies to one eyre are not rare, a hundred are common.[2] There are several sets of these for each shire in a normal year. The full significance of this is only realised when

recent discoveries among the Chancery Miscellanea, especially for the draft of Pipe Roll 17 John, to which he first drew my attention. The chief record authorities are unpublished exchequer records, especially Pipe, Memoranda and Receipt Rolls. Many statements are based on detailed analysis of these, and it is, therefore, often impossible to give exact references, without overburdening the text with lengthy footnotes.

[1] *Pipe Roll 2 John* (Pipe Roll Society, New Series, vol. xii), pp. 101–18. Cp. Lincolnshire (p. 91), where 1018 tallies were issued.

[2] *Pipe Roll 24 Henry II* (Pipe Roll Society, vol. xxvii), p. 71, gives an early example; *Pipe Roll 2 John*, p. 85 (Lincolnshire), for 370 tallies.

it is known that every one of these debts had in theory to be entered on the Pipe Roll every year until they were paid in full: many of them were so entered.

The methods employed for collecting debts and paying them into the treasury were complicated. If the sheriff had to issue a private tally for each sum collected,[1] congestion must soon have become a pronounced feature of local organisation: it must have been even more serious, when all the sheriffs appeared at Westminster at Easter and Michaelmas to make their profers. There was only one writer of the tallies at the Lower Exchequer: several hundred tallies might have to be cut for each accountant. The sheriff, having received his tallies, normally carried them back to his shire. Whether he distributed them to the individual debtors is not clear, but the general trend of the evidence suggests that he did.[2] If so, they had again to be collected before payment could be proved. Once tallies came back to the exchequer, they had to be paired with their foils before the account could be cleared, the debtor declared quit.

Relief measures were obviously essential, and attempts at reform had already been made before Henry II's death. At the end of the reign desperate debts were twice removed from shire accounts to the beginning of the Pipe Rolls:[3] about the same time appeared the first marginal notes on the state of the debts,[4] and even earlier there are tentative efforts at grouping small debts under half a mark in value in a single entry under the sheriff's name.[5] At the end of Richard I's reign but little progress had been made: the real problem remained unsolved. But by then the scribe's burden was slightly relieved, since he no longer had to enter every debt on the roll: the relief was small and affected the Pipe Roll alone. Tallies still had to be cut, distributed, and reassembled.

---

[1] Cp. Memoranda Roll, Lord Treasurer's Remembrancer, 13, m.4d., where the men of Kingston profer a tally *contra Juelem de Sancto Germano* who had recently been under-sheriff. This is clearly a private tally.

[2] Orders to sheriffs to distrain debtors to have tallies allowed are common on the Memoranda Rolls (Compotus) at this date.

[3] *Pipe Roll 28* and *33 Hen. II* (Pipe Roll Society, vols. xxxi and xxxvii), p. 1.

[4] Pipe Rolls (Originals) 31 and 34 Henry II, *passim*. They are not shown in the printed rolls. Marks on earlier rolls appear to be modern.

[5] *Pipe Roll 24 Hen. II* (Pipe Roll Society, vol. xxvii), p. 71 (Yorkshire).

In John's reign, the number of debts increased out of all proportion to the amount of relief gained. By 1199 grouped entries were still only used for a few total payments under half a mark. Even later, if the number of tallies given in a grouped entry is divided into the total, the result shows that each debt was rarely worth more than a mark.

From 1199 the increase in the number of fines and amercements was rapid. On the Pipe Roll of 1200 long double-columned entries were already common: early in Henry III's reign long paragraphs of unpaid debts were used to save more space. In 1200 a double-columned entry of the debts of one eyre took up nearly the whole dorse of a Pipe Roll membrane.[1] It would be interesting to know the real cause of this rapid development. Was King John acquiring a real grip on the administration of justice throughout the country? Was it the natural result of Henry II's assizes? Whatever the explanation, the constant appearance of shire officials demanding innumerable small sums must have been a fruitful source of irritation throughout the country. It is true that the barons' complaints in 1215 were largely based on abuses in the collection of feudal revenue. But is it possible that these petty exactions were really the unending pinpricks which urged them on? Whatever the cause, by 1215 the Pipe Roll was hopelessly clogged with long lists of fines and amercements, of debts with which, in spite of strenuous exertions, the exchequer had utterly failed to cope.

The invention of the *tallia dividenda* in 1206 offered the real solution of the problem, though this fact was not realised until more than ten years later, if fully then. The fact remains that in 1206, perhaps slightly earlier, some official at the exchequer had a really brilliant idea, which, like all great inventions, was also extraordinarily simple. The sheriff brought in large sums of money at his profer. Why should he not receive a single tally for the total instead of one for each individual payment? This is the essence of the new system. At first two types of these new dividend tallies made their appearance: the earliest was based on the farm, the payment there being much larger than was necessary to cover the amount due, with the result that a large surplus remained to his credit. On the same roll against the debts of individuals, and against grouped entries, was then added the words: 'In the treasury nothing

[1] *Pipe Roll 2 John*, pp. 72–85 (Lincolnshire).

and in the above-mentioned surplus so much.' The total of these sums corresponds exactly with the surplus under the farm, or with the entry that £x had been allowed below, the remainder being usually used in the same way the following year.[1] In 1207 we find the first examples of the second type, the true dividend tally, which has no essential connection with the farm.[2] Examples of both types are found, but under Henry III the second gradually superseded the first. This is a simple, but a vitally important, reform, for on it, and on its successor the tally *de debitis plurium*, was built up the whole system of grouped entry and indirect responsibility which was so marked a feature of fourteenth century procedure. Grouped entries had to a small extent lightened the work of the Pipe Roll scribe: no extension was practicable under the old, cumbersome tally system. The dividend tally saved work in the shires as well as at both Receipt and Audit. Instead of 972 tallies for total payments, given above, only one or two dividend tallies had to be cut. The particulars were entered on Receipt Rolls,[3] but work was saved in cutting and writing tallies, in distributing them locally, in pairing them at the Audit. The sheriff now only issued a private tally to the debtor, so that payment could be proved either in full county court, or next day at the *retro-comitatus*.[4]

At the Upper Exchequer, the discovery of this new form of tally had far-reaching results, since, for the first time, the grouped entry could really be used effectively. The combination of dividend tally and grouped entry relieved the congestion all round, and the latter began to throw out new forms. More and more debts were paid under grouped entries, the record of individual payments being made on Originalia,

[1] Cp. *Pipe Roll 8 John* (Pipe Roll Society, New Series, vol. xx), pp. 46–54, 115–19 (Kent and Surrey).

[2] Amercements through the Archdeacon of Stafford, *Pipe Roll 9 John* (Pipe Roll Society, New Series, vol. xxii), p. 76 (Cornwall). The sheriff rendered account of 21 debts, worth £19 16s. 8d.: he paid £25 10s. in one tally, the surplus being credited to him for his debt on the farm. Another example is found in the same county under the tallage (p. 77).

[3] See entries beginning: 'De eodem vicecomitis de X——' in Receipt Rolls 4, 5, 6, 7. Also see Hilary Jenkinson, 'Medieval Tallies, Public and Private', *Archaeologia*, lxxiv (1925), pp. 300–2.

[4] W. A. Morris, 'Plenus Comitatus', *Eng. Hist. Review*, xxxix, 403.

Estreat and Receipt Rolls. The system of marginal marks (*t.* for total payment, *p.* for partial, and *d.* for money still owing) were possibly now extended to the Estreat Rolls, though there is no indication of such a change until Henry III's reign. In theory every debt was still recorded on the Pipe Roll: in practice more and more were left on subsidiary rolls the former containing merely a short grouped entry in the sheriff's name.[1]

In dealing with the summonses, we have now seen that the invention of the dividend tally, with improvements in the audit system, especially the grouping of debts under the sheriff's name without details and the system of marginal notes, have formed the first step in the direction of indirect responsibility, towards the interposition of the sheriff between debtor and crown, towards decentralisation in the collection of crown revenue.

On the other hand, the farm of the shire still remains in some respects an unsolved problem — one too which it is difficult to state clearly, because it is difficult to get definite evidence as to the exact components of the farm before 1236. After that date, the facts, at least in some shires, can be ascertained with certainty.[2] Before the Conquest, the crown lands apparently made payments in kind, which were presumably the agricultural produce of the royal demesne: Doomsday Book furnishes some evidence of this.[3] Under Henry II was the farm still derived from this source? Three possible sources exist. First, the king might receive the agricultural profits, either in money or in kind, that is profits from corn, cattle, and so on. Secondly, there would be the profits from manorial, hundred and county courts. Thirdly, he received certain fixed payments, in the nature of rent, including view of frank-pledge, castle-ward, sheriff's aid. Were all these sources included in the farm under Henry II? The *Dialogus de Scaccario* suggests that they were.

From 1236 onwards we have detailed particulars of the farms in the

---

[1] The holders of liberties who answered personally for their debts at the exchequer had the same duties in their liberties as the sheriff had in the county.

[2] From the Particule Proficui, Lord Treasurer's Remembrancer's Miscellaneous Rolls, Bdles. 5, 6 and 9.

[3] Cp. J. H. Round, 'The Domesday Survey', *V.C.H., Hants*, i. 401-2.

Particule Proficui. Though there are many gaps, sufficient rolls survive to show that they formed part of a series of annual rolls, going down at least to Richard II's time. At Cambridge Castle details of these annual payments were available for general reference at the beginning of the fourteenth century.[1] This list has a close connection with the Particule Proficui for these shires. The latter are the sheriff's accounts for farm and profits, and an entry at the end records the amount used to pay the farm, the residuum constituting the profits, unless the sheriff farmed the profits. Now these Particule Proficui prove that by 1236 agricultural profits were practically non-existent as part of the farm of the shire. They contain details of profits from hundred and county courts, and fixed payments such as those which I have referred to above. They vary from shire to shire, but are fixed sums based on land tenure. Agricultural profits form a very small item in some counties.

There was a general re-appointment of sheriffs in 1236, the king retaining the ancient demesne in his own hands.[2] The odd thing is that, though this source of revenue was taken out of the sheriff's hands, the profits did not depreciate to any extent, the farm remained the same. The solution possibly lies in the fact that under John the demesne was largely granted out to individuals, allowance being made in the *terre date* in the farm. Though, in some cases, these lands were subsequently liable for fixed payments, they were not again paid into the farm of the shire. If this is so, then the farm had altered fundamentally in our period, though there is little evidence of this on the Pipe Rolls. Further, the exact nature of some of the fixed payments mentioned above is unknown.

Now the increment and profits were clearly money left over after the sheriff had cleared his account of the farm. Under Henry II farms of shires were already fixed: Buckinghamshire alone paid an increment, namely £10 and three hawks: by 1199 seventeen counties were liable, the sum being over £780, an enormous increase in ten years. Under John the profits appeared, sometimes absorbing the increment, sometimes being additional to it. By 14 John the yearly value had risen to

[1] J. W. Clark, *Liber Memorandorum Ecclesie de Bernewelle*, 1907, pp. 238–81.
[2] M. Paris, *Chronica Majora*. iii, 363; Exchequer Miscellanea 24/14; *C.P.R.* (*1232–47*), pp. 140–8.

nearly £2,500,[1] twenty-one counties being liable. In addition, Nottinghamshire and Derbyshire were charged, but the amount was not entered on the Pipe Roll. Some fifteen shires paid in full, Yorkshire accounting for nearly £600, though it had paid neither profits nor increment in 1199. If John's exactions were often on this scale, they must have been an important factor in the baronial outcry against him. Though the value of the hundred and county courts may have increased, they can hardly have done it so rapidly, especially since the central courts were absorbing many cases which must previously have gone to these local courts. The exact position is obscure, but this was clearly an important grievance, for Magna Carta[2] prescribed that counties were to be at their old farms without any increment, except in the demesne manors[3] — a direct attack on the profits. The reference to demesne manors is puzzling, because these are just what were missing from the Particule Proficui. Yet under Henry III, when for a short time profits were dropped,[4] we find profits from demesne manors as a separate item on the Pipe Rolls — a fact which (with other evidence) suggests that they did not disappear from the farm until after that date. Whichever way we turn, profits and farm alike remain something of a mystery, presenting problems which have so far defied solution.

The history of the farm and of amercements arising from Henry II's legal reforms having been traced, it now becomes clear that new and irritating sources of revenue had been tapped by King John, the amercements being all the more irritating, because, though small in value, they were an unending series of pinpricks; and because the benefit derived from them had long been forgotten, when the amercement was levied. Moreover, the increase in the revenue from the farm must have seemed enormous at that date, and since the sheriff was normally drawn from the feudal ranks, the barons would be the first to realise

---

[1] *Pipe Roll 14 John* (Pipe Roll Society, New Series, vol. xxx), below the Farm; e.g., p. 27 (Yorkshire). Where more than one year is included, an average has been taken.

[2] Chapter 25. Cp. also Articles of the Barons, ch. 14.

[3] *Omnes comitatus, hundredi, wapentakii, et trethingii, sint ad antiquas firmas absque ullo incremento, exceptis dominicis maneriis nostris.*

[4] See p. 143.

this fact. The results are well known: Magna Carta was drawn up and sealed, war broke out, and after Henry III's accession, peace was made at Lambeth, September 1217.[1]

II. In our second period (1215–17) the chief interest lies in the exchequer's breakdown, and in the effect of the war on the collection of the revenue. Pipe Roll 16 John, the last complete roll of the reign, records the audit of revenue collected in the exchequer year 1213–14, that is the Easter and Michaelmas profers of 1214. The exchequer had ceased work before June 1215.[2] Thus, the audit beginning in the autumn of 1214 was the last before the treaty of Lambeth. Here our records stop.

When the exchequer reassembled on 12 November 1217, three years' accounts required auditing, namely the years 17 and 18 John and 1 Henry III. During part of this time the exchequer was in the hands of Louis of France.[3] For these years there are extant both Pipe and Chancellor's Roll for the first half of 17 John; further, for Hampshire there is an account for 17 John and for the first half of 18 John, and for Lancashire for the whole of 16 and 17 John.[4] The next extant roll is that for 2 Henry III. Hence for two and a half years the accounts are now missing. Were these ever enrolled? If so, when were they lost?

A careful analysis of Pipe Roll 17 John and of the first two Memoranda Rolls of his son's reign furnishes the solution of the problem. From internal evidence it is clear that this Pipe Roll, though it deals with the last half-year before the war, was not compiled until after the exchequer began work again in 1217. It cannot have been made up in John's reign. Conclusive evidence of this is found in the formula for the farms: in this year it runs, *de firma Comitatus de dimidio anno septimo decimo Regis Johannis*, or *de firma Comitatus de dimidio anno septimo decimo ante guerram*. The normal formula is simply *de firma* or *de firma de hoc anno*.[5] This change in itself implies abnormality, and assumes an interval

---

[1] G. J. Turner, 'Minority of Henry III', *R. Hist. Soc. Transactions*, N.S. XVIII, p. 267.

[2] M. Paris, *Historia Anglorum*, ii. 156.

[3] G. J. Turner, *op. cit.*, p. 288; Martène and Durand, *Thesaurus Novus Anecdotorum*, i. 857.

[4] An examination of the farms gives the dates.

[5] See under the farm of the county.

between collection and audit. The reference to King John, according to
Pipe Roll practice, proves him dead at the time of writing. Finally, the
sheriff of Buckinghamshire and Bedfordshire on this roll paid part of
his farm, owed £8 6s., paid it later, and was quit. But Pipe Roll 2
Henry III charged him with this sum, adding the note: 'but now he is
quit in the preceding roll of half the year 17 John'. This proves con-
clusively that (a) Pipe Roll 17 John was the last roll before that of 2
Henry III, for *in rotulo precedenti* always refers to the last account taken;
(b) *set modo quietus est* shows clearly that the two rolls were being compiled at one and the same time. Now the exchequer was in the hands
of Louis of France until September 1217, and was not reopened until
Martinmas that year. Between then and Michaelmas 1218, a Memoranda Roll was compiled,[1] and it is possible that Pipe Roll 17 John was
begun then.

From what has been said it is clear that the missing accounts were
never enrolled on a Pipe Roll, and it has been assumed that no audit was
taken. Does the evidence prove this? Memoranda Roll 1 shows that
during the remainder of this year strenuous efforts were made to
examine these missing accounts, special attention being paid to farms of
shires and towns.[2] This effort, continued in subsequent years, was only
partly successful. In some cases, however, not only were the accounts
for all three years heard, but some accountants proved payment, while
others, though lacking full proof, gave the names of persons to whom
money had been paid. In other cases, attorneys were appointed to
represent sheriffs at the audit. Yorkshire certainly rendered some
account, possibly for all three years, though the details are difficult to
follow. Several membranes of this Memoranda Roll show the position
of town farms. These include Cambridge and Huntingdon, which
claimed to have paid the whole;[3] of Norwich and Yarmouth, which
had paid Hubert de Burgh's bailiff, who proved payment into the
Wardrobe.[4] Other cases could be quoted. Thus, though accounts were

---

[1] K.R. and L.T.R., Memoranda Roll 1.

[2] Memoranda Roll, L.T.R., 1, ms.2–6; cp. also Pipe and Memoranda Rolls
2–8 Hen. III.

[3] Memoranda Roll, L.T.R., 1, m.6.

[4] *Ibid.* Cp. *Pipe Roll 17 John* (Pipe Roll Society, New Series, vol. xxxvii), p. 5.

only enrolled for six months, the rest were actually examined by the exchequer, proof of payment being given at least in some cases. Possibly an elaborate search might prove the account fairly complete, but the difficulty of the investigation would be very great.

The fact that no enrolment was made is easily explained. The country was in disorder; money, when paid, would go to the man in the neighbourhood sufficiently strong to enforce his will, whether rebellious baron, or faithful follower of King John; money once received would be immediately spent on necessities of war. But many barons changed sides on John's death: to demand a strict account of these would be most unwise, to require it from John's supporters even more so. Therefore, the account only being taken where practicable, no enrolment could be made, because, if it were, the exchequer would have to insist on recovery of money when proper expenditure could not be proved — an impossible proceeding. This being so, the Memoranda Roll was the obvious place of record.

Five subsidiary rolls, still extant, make the position clearer.[1] Of these, Exchequer Miscellanea 1/48, recently discovered by Mr. Johnson among the unsorted Miscellanea of the Chancery, is a draft of William Briewere's account as sheriff of Hampshire for the first quarter of 17 and first half of 18 John, the whole being enrolled on Pipe Roll 17 John. Exchequer Miscellanea 1/8B (a peculiar record, part roll, part file) was compiled about 5 Henry III. Its form is rougher than that of the draft Pipe Roll. It deals with the debts of a number of people, sometimes still owing from the end of John's reign. Though it forms part of an attempt to audit these accounts, it has proved impossible to assign it an exact place in the scheme. The debts of the two Marshals, father and son, and of Briewere's successor as sheriff of Hampshire in 1215 are included, but not the farms of the war years. A similar roll is Exchequer Accounts 505/2, dealing largely with Hampshire debts. The attempt to connect these subsidiary rolls exactly with either Memoranda or Pipe Rolls proved unsuccessful. This series of five rolls shows that problems existed

[1] Exchequer Miscellanea 1/8, 1/8B, 1/48; Exchequer Accounts 505/2, Sheriffs' Accounts 52/1. L.T.R. Miscellaneous Rolls 1/5 proved to be part of L.T.R. Memoranda Roll, 3–4 Henry III. Cp. also Foreign Accounts, No. 1, m.3d, and Exchequer Accounts 505/13, found since this paper went to press.

with regard to the accounts at this time; that special procedure was necessary to meet the peculiar position, which had arisen owing to the breakdown of the exchequer. Similar rolls do not exist for other periods.

Our draft Pipe Roll requires fuller treatment, because (*a*) it is unique, and (*b*) it is the draft of a peculiar account on a unique roll. Its existence does not imply that drafts were part of the usual procedure — rather the contrary. Fragments of early Pipe Rolls exist,[1] but they are fragments, not drafts. Our record is a single membrane, 17·3 inches long by 6·7 inches wide, completely covered with writing on one side, and having two four-line endorsements, the second of which is almost illegible. Handwriting and size prove that it could never have been part of a Pipe Roll. It corresponds closely with the enrolled account, but adds details not included on the Pipe Roll itself. If the intention was to draw up a draft to solve the problem of the missing accounts, the attempt was soon abandoned. The position of Hampshire gives additional importance to the discovery; the county had a close connection with the exchequer, of which William Briewere was a baron, and, when the draft was drawn up, Peter de Roches was sheriff of the county. This increases the probability of its being a preliminary attempt to solve the problem of the accounts. The original intention was to examine this record in detail, but this proved impossible, because the condition of some of the cognate documents is bad, but chiefly because our knowledge of exchequer technique in the early thirteenth century is not yet sufficiently advanced. We have, however, as a result of the attempt, obtained certain definite results, of which the most important is the position with regard to the audit of the revenue for the three years 1215–17. The gap in the Pipe Rolls is due not to the disappearance of the rolls, but to the fact that they were never compiled. It is significant that, in the circumstances, the exchequer was sufficiently powerful to insist on even a partial account. It wisely refrained from forcing the accountants to extremities.

III. Our third, and last, period shows that, simultaneously with the tentative audit of the war years, preparations were made for the normal collection of revenue in 1217–18. What difference had the struggle

[1] Exchequer Miscellanea 1/1c, 1/2, 1/4.

made? What changes were to take place in the next fifteen years? The story can be briefly told.

The machinery was already in existence for the solution of the problem which faced the exchequer, when it resumed its normal course. In the early years of Henry III, the volume of fines and amercements became so large, that the scribe abandoned the two-column arrangement, and, where possible, arranged the debts in solid paragraphs to save space. Other noticeable changes in the summonses were: (1) the increased number of grouped entries, due to the more frequent use of the dividend tally; (2) the omission of any mention of the number of tallies issued;[1] (3) various changes in the form of the grouped entry.[2] These first appeared in 4 Henry III, and soon became normal, though the older form was still used. As the new form depended on the dividend tally, when the latter fell out of use in 7 Henry III, the former also disappeared. The Pipe Roll in this year shows a curious reversion to old forms: amercements are few, and there is a marked tendency to enter debts again under the names of individuals.[3] The next year this became more marked, even marginal notes being only sparingly used. In one grouped entry a hundred tallies were again cut. By 10 Henry III enormous blocks of amercements had replaced grouped entries, and as many as 347 tallies were again entered.[4] Throughout these rolls occasional examples of the new forms are also found. By 1228 the new forms referred to above were again in use, and from this point the movement went steadily forward. Now Pipe Roll 7 Henry III was begun at Michaelmas 1223, that of 12 Henry III at Michaelmas 1228, so that the period of reaction (if reaction it be) spread over roughly five

---

[1] The earlier formula was: 'The same sheriff renders account of £x of amercements . . . whose names and debts and the causes are noted in the roll which [the justices] delivered into the treasury. [The sheriff] delivered it into the treasury in z tallies'; the new form: 'The same sheriff renders account of £x of amercements of —— before whose names is placed the letter "t" in the preceding roll. He has delivered it into the Treasury.'

[2] These are common on Pipe Roll 64 (4 Henry III). None apparently occur in previous years.

[3] Pipe Rolls 67, under Essex and Hertfordshire (m.4), Norfolk and Suffolk (m.6d.).

[4] *Ibid.*, 70, under Lincolnshire (m.4).

years. It began about the date of the strengthening of Hubert de Burgh's power in 1223:[1] it ended approximately with the appointment of Segrave to three sheriffdoms — he had two more the following year — an appointment which anticipated Peter de Rivaux's *coup d'état* in 1232.

Though the clause forbidding profits of the shire was dropped in Henry III's reissue of the Charters, only profits from demesne manors, a quite separate item, appear on the Pipe Rolls at the beginning of his reign. As we have seen, the profits had increased in the quarter of a century before 1215 from £14 to over £2,500. When we remember this and the prohibition of all profits outside demesne manors in Magna Carta, their disappearance after 1217 becomes significant. From 5–7 Henry III, Buckinghamshire again paid the old increment, while only seven other counties made similar payments, the total being just over £220 as against £2,500 before 1215. Thus, up to 8 Henry III, this provision of Magna Carta was observed, but a marked change came then: the profits were suddenly restored to their old place. In this year eighteen counties were charged with profits amounting to £650 for three-quarters of a year only, while ten other shires were held liable, but no value was given. This sudden restoration of profits on such a large scale is really startling. Now the nine months in question cover the period January to September 1224, an important fact, if the political situation is examined. Moreover, in nearly every county concerned, the sheriffs were newly appointed that year, many of them between Christmas and the end of January.[2] Hubert de Burgh, who must be held responsible for this change of policy, had been himself for some time sheriff of Kent, Norfolk, and Suffolk. It is difficult to bring out the closeness of the connection between these new appointments and the reappearance of the profits, but an analysis brings out the fact that it was really remarkable. Now Hubert de Burgh's position was steadily improving throughout 1223, he was the moving spirit in a large number of these new appointments, while his follower Richard le Poer, Bishop of Salisbury, replaced Peter de Roches as sheriff of Hampshire. In view of the part played by the latter's nephew, Peter de Rivaux, in 1232, it is

[1] T. F. Tout, *Chapters in Administrative History of Medieval England*, i. 191.
[2] *Calendar of Patent Rolls (1216–25)*, pp. 417–21.

significant that his seven years' disappearance from our history on his removal from the Wardrobe at the end of 1223[1] should coincide so closely with this change of policy in regard to the profits of the shire, and with the return to the old form of grouped entry. It is easy to overstress the significance of these facts: on the other hand it is improbable that the coincidence in dates is purely accidental. In the summonses the change of policy apparently began a year earlier, but this is not really the case: the reaction began on the account audited in the year 1223–4, so that most of the audit would take place after the reappointment of sheriffs, after the removal of Rivaux from the Wardrobe. Now there is this important difference between the change in summonses and in profits: the money for the latter could only be collected after the change, in the case of the former the change lay not in collection, but in audit. This means that in actual fact both changes of policy occurred in the exchequer year 1223–4. This proves that Hubert de Burgh's acquisition of power had an immediate effect on exchequer policy, an effect which produced definite results on the Pipe Rolls.

The reaction ended about the year 1228, the new form of grouped entry being again introduced. After 1232 — the dividing line between old and new procedure — enquiries were held into the value of the profits. In June and July of that year Peter de Rivaux seized most of the sheriffdoms in England, while nearly all the remainder were in the hands of Peter de Roches, Stephen Segrave, and the two stewards of the Household. A discussion of their policy is outside the scope of this paper, but the general results of work already done on the succeeding ten years must be briefly stated in order to bring the present paper into its true perspective. Peter de Rivaux's counties rendered account at the Upper Exchequer through the sheriffs actually administering these counties under Peter, who could not render account to himself, as treasurer. Moreover, other local accounts for which he was responsible were also audited.[2] The position at the end of the audit in 1233 was certainly not worse than in an ordinary year. In 1234, Peter de Rivaux was banished from court, only to reappear in 1236, though he did not

[1] Tout, *op. cit.*, i. 191.

[2] Rivaux seems to have been in a much better position than Hubert de Burgh in this respect.

regain his old position. Now, between then and 1242 important reforms were introduced into the system of collecting the revenue, and a
detailed study of Pipe and Memoranda Rolls suggests that these reforms
were a direct result of the seizure of the sheriffdoms in 1232. The farther
this investigation goes, the more clearly does this fact stand out: it is not
obvious on a first examination of the rolls.

Thus, to sum up, Henry II's legal reforms, with the consequent
development of fines and amercements, threw an almost unendurable
burden on the exchequer. The solution of the problem was first the
grouping of debts under the sheriff's name, secondly the invention of
the dividend tally: the two combined led ultimately in the fourteenth
century to decentralisation in the collection of debts. Meanwhile, there
was a steady increase in the amount of farm demanded from the shire,
the extra payment being known as the profits. Both processes played
their part in the struggle over Magna Carta: they formed an important
section of King John's extortions. About June 1215, the exchequer
ceased work for two and a half years, but after Martinmas 1217, an
effort, at least partially successful, was made to audit the accounts of
these missing years. Between 1218 and 1223 the clause of Magna Carta
forbidding the profits was carefully observed, the reforms in the collection of the summonses being increasingly employed. Then, with the
growth of Hubert de Burgh's power, came a change in exchequer policy
which lasted until 1228, during which period the profits were restored,
and reforms in the collection of summonses remained in abeyance.
With the return of Peter de Roches and Peter de Rivaux in 1232, the
reform movement again came to the front, a policy which led to the
reorganisation of the shire accounts (1236–42) — a reform which, once
established, formed the basis for their collection until the middle of the
fourteenth century. Thus developments in exchequer procedure in the
first forty years of the thirteenth century are important, because in
these years were laid the foundations on which was erected the later
exchequer system. It is in these years that it obviously diverged from
the rules laid down in the *Dialogus*.

Mabel H. Mills

8 The Origins of Parliament

I. THE WORD

The antiquities of the word *parliament* have not been neglected either by lexicographers or by constitutional historians. The latter usually mention Jordan Fantosme and various thirteenth-century chroniclers; while the articles *parlamentum* in the Glossarium of Ducange and *parlement* in Godefroi's Dictionary are instructive although meagre in their references to record sources. But after he had studied all the references of historians and dictionary-makers, the enquirer might well be puzzled to know why certain sessions of the English king's court should in particular be called parliaments by the royal clerks. We may, however, get some way towards a plausible explanation by filling in a few of the gaps in the chain of references. For a full explanation we need to look at the working of parliamentary institutions; but that is a further step.

The earliest document in which the word *parlement* is preserved seems to be the Chanson de Roland, which comes to us from the latter part of the eleventh century. The emir Baligant says to the dying king Marsile: 'Ne pois a vos tenir lung parlement'[1] — 'I cannot hold long parley with you.' This meaning of 'parley', 'conversation', long clung to the word: but about the same time as the Chanson was first sung in England, *parliament* was being used with a different meaning in Italian cities, for a general meeting of the citizens, a folkmoot as Englishmen, or at any rate Londoners, would have called it.[2] We are here a step, it may be only a little step, nearer the meaning of parliament in the rolls and writs of thirteenth-century English kings: for in those early days the *parlamento* of an Italian city was an assembly with some real functions;[3]

[1] Line 2836.
[2] The earliest instance of the use of the word with which I am acquainted occurs in Caffaro, *Annales*, s.a. 1101 (*Monumenta Germaniae Historica, Scriptores*, XVIII, 13); later instances will be found, s.a. 1147 (*ibid.*, p. 36), and in *Annales Pisani* (1158–60) (*ibid.*, XIX, 244 f.). This general assembly of the commune had a variety of names: cf. Pertile, *Storia del Diritto Italiano*, II, i, 50 f.
[3] Cf. Pertile, *op. cit.*, II, i, 168 ff., VI, 53.

it was, like the folkmoot, a court, a tribunal, as fully representative as possible of all the citizens.

In the second half of the twelfth century the word was being used for other assemblies, for meetings of an emperor's or a king's court. So we find it used by Otto Morena when speaking of the diet of Roncaglia held by Frederick Barbarossa in 1154,[1] by Guernes de Pont-Sainte-Maxence when speaking of the council of Northampton in 1164[2] and by Jordan Fantosme when speaking of a council of William the Lion in 1173.[3] So also it is used by Wace to describe a meeting between Richard I, duke of Normandy, and Lothaire, king of France,[4] as well as the assembly in which Harold took his oath to duke William.[5] Wace, it should be remarked, employs *parlement* also in the sense of conversation,[6] and Guernes de Pont-Sainte-Maxence applies the word to interviews between Louis VII and Henry II and between Henry and Becket.[7] Here, however, it might be suggested, and perhaps correctly, that an interview between Louis and Henry takes place in the French king's court and an interview between Henry and Becket in the English king's court and that each meeting is a very special and solemn one.

Guernes, Jordan and master Wace were writing history, albeit in verse. A more considerable poet, Jean Renart, was writing a deal of verse about court life at the end of the twelfth and the beginning of the thirteenth century:[8] he often found it convenient to use *parlement* to end a line. So he uses it several times for an imaginary diet of an

---

[1] *Mon. Germ. Hist. Scriptores*, XVIII, 591. On these diets, which were held at irregular intervals throughout nearly the whole of the twelfth century, and ceased in 1194, see A. Solmi, *Le Diete imperiali di Roncaglia*, pp. 52 ff.

[2] *La Vie de Saint Thomas le Martyr* (ed. E. Walberg), p. 56.

[3] *Chronicles of Stephen, Henry II and Richard I* (Rolls Series), III, 226.

[4] *Roman de Rou* (ed. Andresen), I, 168, 172 ff.

[5] *Ibid.*, II, 257 f.

[6] *Ibid.*, II, 256, l. 5652. The word 'parliament' in any sense does not occur in any of Wace's written sources.

[7] *La Vie de Saint Thomas le Martyr*, pp. 128, 134–7.

[8] On Jean Renart's life and works, see Ch. V, Langlois, *La Vie en France au moyen âge . . . d'après des romans mondains du temps* (1926), pp. xxvi, 36 ff., 72 ff., 341 ff., and the introduction by L. Foulet to *Galeran de Bretagne* (1925).

imaginary emperor at Mainz and for another imaginary assembly at Rome. In the former meeting, which has been primarily summoned to enable the emperor to obtain the approval of his barons to his marriage, the heroine of the tale demands justice of the emperor's seneschal:[1] and in the other meeting the Romans assemble after the death of one emperor to choose another in the person of the hero.[2] But not only does Jean Renart apply the word *parlement* to the emperor's court, he applies it also to the court of a very humble lord, who, he says, held parliament just as if he had been a man of exalted rank.[3] A little earlier we have been told that the emperor convened parliaments for the pleasure of having a crowd of barons around him:[4] we must not forget that a parliament may have its festive side.[5] Jean Renart, it should be remarked, does not use *parlement* exclusively in the sense of a meeting of a court: he uses it also to mean 'parley' or 'conversation'.[6]

It will be convenient next to examine the use of the word in four chronicles, all written by contemporaries of Jean Renart and all dealing with contemporary history: the continuation of William of Malmesbury's *Gesta Regum* found in the *Liber de Antiquis Legibus*, written in Latin;[7] the history of William the Marshal, in French verse;[8] the history of the kings of England[9] and the chronicle of the kings of

---

[1] *Guillaume de Dôle* (ed. Servois: Soc. des Anciens Textes Français), pp. 135 ff.

[2] *L'Escoufle* (ed. Michelaut and Meyer: Soc. des Anciens Textes Français), p. 256.

[3] *Guillaume de Dôle*, p. 55.   [4] *Ibid.*, p. 18.

[5] See the testimony of Geoffroi de Beaulieu to Saint Louis' hospitality: in parliamentis et congregationibus militum et baronum, sicut decebat regiam dignitatem, liberaliter et largiter se habebat (*Historiens de la France*, XX, 12; so also Joinville (ed. N. de Wailly), p. 394).

[6] *Galeran de Bretagne*, pp. 78, 104; *Le Lai de l'Ombre* (ed. Bédier: Soc. des Anciens Textes Français), p. 35.

[7] *Liber de Antiquis Legibus* (Camden Soc.), p. 197. I incline to think that this was written not much later than 1217; one passage, which looks like an insertion (p. 204), refers to 1225.

[8] *L'Histoire de Guillaume le Maréchal* (Société de l'histoire de France, 1891–1901).

[9] *Histoire des Ducs de Normandie et des Rois d'Angleterre* (Soc. de l'histoire de France, 1840).

France,[1] both perhaps by the same author[2] and both written in French prose. The first of these writers gives the name of parliament to the meeting which was held at Bonmoulins in 1188 between Philip Augustus, Henry II and Richard.[3] Again he uses the word for the meeting at Staines in August 1215, where the bishops and barons waited in vain for king John: perhaps we can perceive in his choice of words the implication that it is in parliament that a king should meet his barons.[4] The historian of William the Marshal also gives the name of parliament to meetings between the kings of England and France,[5] as well as to a parley between Louis of France and the Marshal and their parties,[6] and to a parley or conversation between four people.[7] But he uses the word further for an assembly of the knights and men of the earl in Ireland,[8] and for the meeting at Worcester in March 1218, at which Llewelyn did homage and which was attended by the legate, bishops, earls, barons and sheriffs.[9] The usage of the writer of the *Histoire des Rois d'Angleterre* is similar to that of the other two writers. It is however notable that the assembly of barons at Soissons called by Philip Augustus in April 1213, is termed a parliament,[10] as is also the meeting at

[1] *Chronique française des Rois de France par un anonyme de Béthune* in *Historiens de la France*, XXIV, 754 ff.

[2] The same author appears to have written both the *Histoire . . . des Rois d'Angleterre* — the *Histoire des Ducs de Normandie* is borrowed matter — and the *Chronique des Rois de France*. See *Mon. Germ. Hist., Scriptores*, XXVI, 699, and *Historiens de la France*, XXIV, 751 ff.

[3] *Liber de Antiquis Legibus*, p. 199.

[4] *Ibid.*, p. 202: apud Stanes captum est parlamentum, ubi predictus Archiepiscopus et fere omnes Episcopi Anglie et predicti Barones convenerunt et fecerunt ibi moram per tres dies continuos. Idem vero Rex absentavit se et noluit ibi venire.

[5] *Guillaume le Maréchal*, I, 301, 322 (meetings between Philip Augustus and Henry, May 1188, July 1189); II, 46 f. (proposed meetings between Philip Augustus and Richard, 1198–9), 68 (meeting between Philip Augustus and John, 1201).

[6] *Ibid.*, II, 273, 277.

[7] *Ibid.*, II, 191: N'ont que ces quatre al pallement.

[8] Summoned by Meiler fitz Henry the justiciar; *ibid.*, II, 129, 131.

[9] *Ibid.*, II, 279. Cf. p. 282, l. 17872, where the word is applied to an assembly held after Michaelmas, 1218; see the note to this passage, *ibid.*, III, 252.

[10] *Histoire des ducs de Normandie et des rois d'Angleterre*, p. 120.

Staines in June 1215, at which king John 'gave his charter to the barons'.[1] The word is applied too to a meeting at Reading in December 1213, 'entre le roi et le clergie',[2] a meeting which seems to have been attended by the magnates,[3] and also to a meeting of king and barons early in 1215.[4] *Parlement* is equally used for meetings of the barons opposed to John,[5] for meetings between Louis and the legate,[6] for various meetings for negotiating peace,[7] and for a final gathering at Canterbury where the legate imposed penances upon Louis and his followers.[8] As we should suppose, the *Chronique des Rois de France* shows a similar usage: the assembly at Soissons in 1213 is a parliament,[9] and a meeting at Winchester between Louis and the legate.[10]

Another contemporary chronicler, Geoffroi de Villehardouin, employs *parlement* for an assembly of crusaders[11] and a similar usage is found in Arnold fitz Thedmar's chronicle written fifty years or so later.[12] We also find the word used in the same period for a legatine council in 1240[13] and a meeting of convocation in 1264.[14] And one who was writing early in the fourteenth century but whose mind and language were formed in the thirteenth, Jean, sire de Joinville, was still using *parlement* with at least three meanings. He speaks of the parliament held by the barons at Corbeil in 1227, a meeting which was certainly not held with any legal authority.[15] And when he is relating how, to escape the jealousy and vigilance of queen Blanche, king Louis and queen Marguerite used to meet secretly on a privy stair in the palace at Pontoise, Joinville says that they held their parliament there —

---

[1] *Histoire . . . des Rois d'Angleterre*, pp. 149 f. This is, of course, the 'parleamentum de Runemede' of the Close Roll (*Close Rolls (1242–7)*, p. 242).

[2] *Ibid.*, p. 125.   [3] Wendover, *Chronica* (ed. Coxe), III, 276.

[4] *Histoire . . . des Rois d'Angleterre*, pp. 146 f.

[5] *Ibid.*, p. 145.   [6] *Ibid.*, pp. 176 f.

[7] *Ibid.*, pp. 197 ff.   [8] *Ibid.*, p. 205.

[9] *Historiens de la France*, XXIV, 765.   [10] *Ibid.*, p. 772.

[11] *La Conquête de Constantinople* (ed. Bouchet), pp. 10, 30.

[12] *Liber de Antiquis Legibus*, p. 131.

[13] *Annales Monastici* (Theokesb.), I, 116; this may not be strictly contemporary.

[14] *Bishop Bronescombe's Register*, p. 218.

[15] *Histoire de Saint Louis* (ed. N. de Wailly, 1874), p. 42.

'il tenoient leur parlement'.[1] But he also speaks of parliaments which are undoubtedly judicial sessions of the king's court.[2]

It is clear, of course, that behind these varied meanings there is a common concept: where there is parliament there is conversation, discussion, debate. And a parliament which is at the same time a court is one at which, originally at all events, there is discussion or debate, at which there is something like free speech and free speaking. Such a court is of a very exceptional kind: and if it looks very much like a modern parliament, it looks rather unlike the ordinary court of law, modern or medieval, or such a parliament as is described for us in the *Stilus Curie Parlamenti* of Guillaume du Breuil, the *parlement* of Paris as it existed in the third decade of the fourteenth century.[3] But by that time the *parlement* had developed into something different from what it had been in the days of Saint Louis. There was much that was patriarchal about Saint Louis' justice: the descriptions that his contemporaries have given us leave no doubt of the intimacy of king and subject in his parliaments;[4] and there is still intimacy, or at least informality, in the parliaments of Edward I[5] and, it is to be supposed, in the parliaments of Henry III, however much charged these parliaments may be with legal and administrative business. But already these parliaments have a long history behind them; the forces which were to change the parliaments of Louis IX and Henry III almost out of recognition had already been at work for many years. The parliaments of Philip Augustus, of Henry II

---

[1] *Histoire de Saint Louis*, p. 332.   [2] *Ibid.*, pp. 370, 394.

[3] This treatise was completed by May 1332; see Introduction, p. vii, to Aubert's edition.

[4] Besides Joinville's well-known description (*Histoire*, ed. Wailly, p. 370; Langlois, *Textes relatifs à l'histoire du Parlement*, pp. 80 ff.) and Geoffroi de Beaulieu's statement of how Louis entertained his barons at his parlements (*Historiens de la France*, XX, 12), we have such anecdotes as that told by Guillaume de Chartres of the overdressed lady who, on the occasion of one parlement, with a few others went with the king from the *curia* to the *camera* (*ibid.*, XX, 33), and that told by Guillaume de Saint Pathus of the arrest of the comte de Joigny 'en un plein parlement' at the king's order (*Vie de Saint Louis* (ed. Delaborde), p. 148).

[5] Cf. *Parliamentary Writs*, I, 131 f.: a petitioner hands a petition to Edward himself; *Year Book 3 Edward II* (Selden Soc.), p. 196: Bereford's story of a parliament of Edward I.

and their contemporaries, had been great councils, plenary meetings of a feudal court, called for the purpose of discussing matters of exceptional importance: so much at least the chroniclers tell us. If perhaps justice was administered at these assemblies, it was, we may be sure, justice of a very exceptional kind.[1]

The word parliament slowly made its way into formal and official documents. At first it was regarded as vulgar or at least inelegant, a bad substitute for *colloquium*,[2] and therefore, however frequently poets or chroniclers might use the word, it is not to be expected in official documents of the highest class until men had become accustomed to its use. It will not, however, have been overlooked that writers about the year 1200 seem to have taken it as a matter of course that lords of every degree might hold parliaments — not only parleys but parliaments that were, in the formal sense, courts. And the earliest official documents which use the word with this meaning come from minor lordships.

About the year 1210 William de Hauville confirmed to the abbey of St. John at Colchester certain lands and their appurtenances: the boundaries were delimited by dikes and marks and these had been formally pointed out in a parliament held by the abbot and William. This parliament looks like a court: there are prud'hommes, *probi homines*, present who are expressly mentioned. It may be the court of the abbot or a joint meeting of the abbot's court and William's; but the scribe had very little Latin and he is not very successful in conveying his meaning.[3] Not many years earlier or later William the Marshal was

---

[1] Cf. Stubbs, *Constitutional History*, I, 645 ff. For a case under John see p. 161 below. For France, see the cases collected by Langlois, *Textes relatifs à l'histoire du Parlement*, pp. 21 ff.; but not all of these seem to have come before plenary meetings of the court. Cf. Luchaire, *Histoire des Institutions Monarchiques*, I, 310. The story of the wicked seneschal told by Jean Renart (above, p. 148) also suggests that it was in exceptional cases only that judicial functions were exercised in parliament.

[2] 'Colloquium quod vulgo dicitur parlamentum': Iohannes de Ianua, *Catholicon*, s.v. colloquium. Note that here the word is equated with both *consilium* and *concio*.

[3] *Colchester Chartulary* (Roxburghe Club), II, 355. Since William fitz Fulc, 'vicecomes Essexe', is a witness, the charter must be dated 19 May 1208-

granting a charter to his burgesses of Haverford, and in it he requires them to come in a body to his parliament or to his host whenever he or his bailiff shall hold the one or summon the other: the burgesses may leave behind only sufficient men to keep the town safely.[1] And not many years later again Gilbert de Clare, earl of Gloucester and Hertford, was granting a charter to the abbey of Margam, and again there is mention of parliament and host. It seems that those coming to the one or the other had imposed upon the hospitality of the abbey; henceforth the abbey was to provide bed and board only according to the ancient customs and assizes as they had been observed in the time of the earl's ancestors.[2] Fortunately we know something of this parliament in the time of Richard de Clare, Gilbert's son. It was a meeting of the court of the county (we cannot call it a county court) and clearly a specially full meeting of the court at which the earl is likely to be present as well as other exalted persons. At one such meeting the earl had ordered a local baron to be arrested on a charge of treason, and it is because of that quarrel, which came into the king's court, that we get some detailed knowledge of the earl's parliament.[3]

It is of interest to compare these local Welsh parliaments and the duty imposed upon the burgesses of Haverford to go 'ad parliamentum vel in exercitum' with the contemporary local parliaments in Italy and the duty imposed upon Italian townsmen in almost identical words.[4] And

---

29 September 1213, between which dates he acted as substitute or under-sheriff for Aubrey de Vere.

[1] *Cal. Charter Rolls*, IV, 327; see also *Archaeologia Cambrensis*, 4th Series, X, 96 f.; *ibid.*, Original Documents, II, xxxviii.

[2] *Cartae de Glamorgan*, II, 360 (No. ccclxi).

[3] *Curia Regis Roll*, No. 159, mm. 2, 10 f. Partly printed *Cartae de Glamorgan*, II, 547, and *Archaeologia Cambrensis*, 4th Series, IX, 241, from a partial transcript in Cott. MS., Vitellius C.X. See also *Cartae de Glamorgan*, II, 543, 562.

[4] Cf. A. Theiner, *Codex Diplomaticus Dominii Temporalis S. Sedis*, I, 35 (No. xliii): tam vos quam omnes qui sunt de vestro districto, nobis et successoribus nostris et ecclesie Romane fidelitatem curabitis universaliter exhibere, expeditionem, parlamentum, pacem et guerram ad mandatum nostrum et legatorum et nuntiorum nostrorum per totam Marchiam bona fide iuxta proprias facultates vestris expensis facere. . . . This is dated 23 November 1200. For later documents see *ibid.*, 41, 129; *Mon. Germ. Hist.*, *Epistolae Saeculi xiii e*

it is well to realise that we have to do with a development common to Western Europe, to such widely different environments as the Welsh marches and the states of the Church.[1]

It was not long before the word parliament began to creep into royal records. In 1234 it appears in accounts of royal officers in France.[2] In 1237 it appears on an English plea roll,[3] in 1242 on the English close roll[4] and in 1248 on the memoranda rolls of the exchequer.[5] In all these cases parliament has the meaning of the king's court. In 1247 it appears in the accounts of the count of Poitiers[6] for he had a parliament re-resembling that of king Louis his brother. By the middle of the thirteenth century *parliament* was well on its way to make its fortune. It appears, in the technical sense of a special meeting of a king's court, more and more frequently in official records and more and more frequently in chronicles.[7] Nevertheless for some time *colloquium* was preferred by the fastidious. It is probable that in this way we can explain the curiously fluctuating usage of the English chancery in the latter

---

registris Pontificum Romanorum, I, 507; III, 107, 499, note 5. Cf. A. de Boüard, *Le Régime politique et les institutions de Rome au Moyen Âge*, p. 214.

[1] I do not, of course, suggest that there were close similarities in detail. For an account of the *parlamento* of Friuli see Pertile, *Storia del Diritto Italiano*, I, 342 ff. For the *acta* of this parliament see P. S. Leicht, *Parlamento Friulano* (R. Accademia dei Lincei): the first mention of *parlamentum* in these documents seems to be in 1290 (No. xxvi).

[2] *Historiens de la France*, XXI, 233, 238.

[3] For this entry and its significance see *English Historical Review*, xxxii. 747–50.

[4] *Close Rolls (1237–42)*, p. 447.

[5] E. 368/20 (L.T.R. Mem. Roll, 32 Hen. III), mm. 4, 13.

[6] *Comptes d'Alfonse de Poitiers* (ed. Bardonnet, *Archives historiques de Poitou*, IV), pp. 158, 160, 170. Cf. Borrelli de Serres, *Recherches sur divers services publics*, I, 292 f.

[7] Among the St. Albans chroniclers Wendover scrupulously employs the word *colloquium*: his successor Matthew Paris has no hesitation in using the more popular word, although he seems never to have translated Wendover's *colloquium* into *parlamentum* in the chronicle he took over and revised. See the fifth volume of Coxe's edition of Wendover where Paris's alterations and additions are set out; see also *Modern Language Review*, IX, 92 f., for some remarks by A. B. White upon Paris's use of the word.

years of Henry III. On the same close roll the parliament of Oxford is
parleamentum and *colloquium*.[1] Similarly it was not possible for the
English chancery to speak consistently of the Scottish king's parliament
either as *parleamentum* or *colloquium*.[2] Again it is but rarely in the thirteenth century that parliament is mentioned in a writ of summons to
parliament: of all the writs issued for the Hilary parliament, 1265, only
those to the Cinque Ports appear to have contained it.[3]

But despite the objections of the old-fashioned, *parliament*, as we
know, not only won its way into favour but became particularly
attached to the *curia regis*. This transition we may illustrate by some
rather curious London documents. In 1267 Henry III had forbidden
that any should assemble parliament, conventicles or congregations
whereby the king's peace or the peace of the city might in any wise be
disturbed.[4] From two cases in the mayor's court in 1299 we may learn
unmistakably what such a parliament was that the king reproved: in
the first case, a carpenter is charged with gathering together a parliament of carpenters at Mile End, the purpose being to oppose a city
ordinance touching their craft;[5] in the second, seventeen smiths were
charged with making a parliament and confederacy in contempt of the
king and to the harm of the city. The purpose of this latter confederacy
seems actually to have been that of an ordinary craft gild and the defendants were discharged, but for our purpose this is the significant
fact: the prosecution founded their case upon the custom of England
whereby no parliament relating to the kingdom can take place without
the king and his council.[6]

But while it is true that by parliament, men by the fourteenth

[1] *Close Roll*, No. 73 (42 Hen. III), mm. 7, 8 (*parleamentum*), 7*b* (*colloquium*).
Similar variations will be found in writs connected with the Easter parliament
1260 (*Close Roll*, No. 76, mm. 1, 1*b*, 2, 2*b*).

[2] See *Scottish Historical Review*, XXV, 300 f. Add to the references there cited
a letter to the sheriff of Yorkshire which speaks of 'parleamentum suum
captum apud Edeneburg' (*Close Roll*, No. 73, m. 8*b*).

[3] *Lords' Report on the Dignity of a Peer*, III, 32 ff. For the later usage, see
Bulletin of the Institute of Historical Research, VI, No. 17.

[4] *Liber de Antiquis Legibus*, p. 98.

[5] *Calendar of Early Mayors' Court Rolls*, p. 25.

[6] *Ibid.*, p. 33.

century came naturally and usually to mean special sessions of the court of a king or some great lord,[1] yet this was not its sole meaning even in official documents. We may note in passing the employment of the word for the general assembly of the moneyers of the oath of the Empire, a corporation that for authenticating its official acts used a common seal with this inscription, 'Sigillum Magnum Comune Parlamenti Generalis Constituti':[2] and we may think how, but for the jealousy with which the name was reserved for the king's parliament, our city corporations might be calling certain of their meetings 'parliaments'. Another official usage very widespread, if not universal, was to give the name of parliament to meetings of potentates or representatives of different states or communities, especially meetings in a march or on the border. This usage certainly dates from the middle of the thirteenth century, since we find the word applied to the meetings between Alexander II of Scotland and Richard, earl of Cornwall, in 1244,[3] and to meetings between Llewelyn and the justice of Chester and other English representatives from 1256 onwards.[4] Later we hear of *dies parliamenti* in the Welsh march which are also called *dies amoris* or *dies Marchiae*, that is meetings for the purpose of composing differences between marcher lords.[5] About the same time the kings of France and Castile are stated to have held their parliament solemnly for six days and more.[6] In Ireland parliaments are held between English lords and

[1] There were, of course, several such in Italy. Besides those instances mentioned above (pp. 153 n. 4, 154 n. 1), parliament *eo nomine* is found in Monferrat in 1305 (A. Bozzola, *Parlamento del Munferrato* (R. Accademia dei Lincei), p. 3). In France there was the rather curious episode of the parlement of Charroux, instituted by Charles the Fair after he became comte de la Marche in 1314. It disappeared on his accession to the throne in 1322. See A. Thomas, 'Les Archives du comté de la Marche' (*Bibliothèque de l'École des Chartes*, XLII, 40 f.) and *Le comté de la Marche et le parlement de Poitiers*, p. lix.

[2] *Revue Numismatique* (1844), pp. 104 ff.; *Annuaire Soc. française de Numismatique*, XIX, 108 ff.

[3] *Close Rolls* (1242–7), p. 221; *Cal. Patent Rolls* (1232–47), p. 434; *Cal. Docs. Scotland*, I, 300 ff.

[4] *Foedera*, I, 339, 526; Shirley, *Royal Letters*, II, 329; *Liber de Antiquis Legibus*, p. 95.

[5] *Abbreviatio Placitorum*, p. 226; *Cartae de Glamorgan*, III, 869.

[6] Historical Manuscripts Commission, *Report on Various Collections*, I, 257.

Irish chieftains under march law.[1] These are but a few examples out of a large number that could be cited, since the usage continued into the sixteenth century.[2] It is easy to see how the usage originated from the examples which had been given from twelfth-century and early thirteenth-century writers. It is easy also to see the affinities between these solemn meetings for the settlement of disputes and the solemn meetings of the king's court consecrated to the settlement of internal discords and disagreements in the widest sense.[3] Nevertheless we are not to suppose that there was necessarily confusion in the medieval mind between distinct institutions as they evolved and emerged in the thirteenth and fourteenth centuries. Nor can we impose our own categories upon medieval institutions and give and refuse the name of parliament because some assembly fulfils or fails to fulfil some fancied requirement imagined by a later age. Taken in its context medieval usage, at least in official records, is as a rule sufficiently precise and technical. Chroniclers, it is true, are more loose in their terminology, but we do not rely upon chronicles for legal technicalities if we are wise.

II. THE COURT

Stress has often been laid upon the differences between the parliaments of different countries in Western Europe and in particular between the parliament of England and the parlement of Paris. Differences did indeed become marked in the course of the fourteenth century, but certainly in the thirteenth century contemporaries do not seem to have been struck by the differences between parliament and parlement.[4] We cannot perhaps lay much emphasis upon the manner in

[1] *Cal. Judiciary Rolls* (33–35 Edw. I), p. 385; Historical MSS. Commission, *Tenth Report*, App. V, 257, 260; *Early Statutes of Ireland*, pp. 378, 448.

[2] A. F. Pollard, *Evolution of Parliament*, p. 32 note.

[3] A letter from archbishop Giffard to the Pope in 1271 is very pertinent: 'quinimmo parliamentis secularibus oportebit frequentius intendere, iracundie tempora mitigare, reconciliare discordes et que pacis sunt, cum ordinatione regni, pro viribus procurare' (*Letters from Northern Registers*, p. 36).

[4] Very early in the fourteenth century Pierre de Saint Pol, a citizen of Bayonne, is saying that he has 'sui ceste besoigne . . . iiij ans a touz les parlementz d'Engleterre et de France': Ancient Petitions, No. 14,432. For this

which the name of parliament was caught up and applied to one body after another, although this has some significance. But when we find such a man as Humbert de Romans, Master General of the Dominican Order, the contemporary of Saint Louis and Henry III, grouping all parliaments together and prescribing the same kind of sermon to be delivered before them all,[1] we are justified in believing that they all looked very much alike. It is the custom, he says, for great kings to hold parliaments at appointed times every year at which assemble many counsellors and many of the worldly great and many prelates. These parliaments are held for three chief purposes: that the more important public affairs may then after more searching consideration be the more wisely resolved; that account may there be rendered[2] by the ministers of the realm; and that order may there be taken for the good government of the realm.[3] He goes on to review the shortcomings to be found in parliament against which sermons may be preached: the crookedness of counsellors, biased judgements, the difficulty of obtaining justice, the denial of audience to the poor, the protection of evildoers and, in particular, evil ministers, the corruption of gifts, favouritism and malice. 'Nay, how shall such a court correct the ills of the whole realm, unless it shall first be itself corrected?' Doubt has been cast upon the historical value of this passage on the ground that it

---

important case which illustrates the conflict of jurisdiction arising out of the Treaty of Paris of 1259 and the difficulty of the position of the French subjects of the English king, see *Cal. Chancery Warrants* (1244–1326), p. 398; *Cal. Close Rolls* (1313–18), p. 181; (1318–23), p. 390.

[1] *De Eruditione Praedicatorum*, lib. II, tract. ii, c. 86, in La Bigne, *Maxima Bibliotheca Veterum Patrum* (1677), XXV, 559.

[2] 'Ut ratio ibi reddatur': on this passage see Borrelli de Serres, *Recherches sur divers services publics*, I, 337. He argues, against Lecoy de la Marche and Ch. V. Langlois, that this has reference not to a financial account but to a report, *compte rendu*, by public servants of their administration. However little this passage may fit the parlement of Paris, if *ratio* is taken in the former sense, it might be argued that it would apply to the parlements of Alfonse of Poitiers which synchronised with the *compoti* (Molinier, *Correspondance administrative d'Alfonse de Poitiers*, II, pp. liv–lv), and to English parliaments until the meeting of which the settlement of accounts was not infrequently adjourned from 1248 onwards (below, p. 162).

[3] 'Ut ibidem ordinetur de Regno quod fuit ordinandum.'

is simply a subject-head for a sermon:[1] but, as we shall see, friars were busy in thirteenth-century parliaments[2] and passed from one to another. And parliaments were public assemblies which gave opportunities for such things as the preaching of sermons and the publication of sentences of excommunication, and men saw no incompatibility in the intermixture. As evidence there may be vouched, on the one hand, the instructions addressed by Pope Clement IV in 1266 to the papal legate, Simon cardinal of St. Cecilia's: when it shall befall that he is present in solemn parliaments at Paris or elsewhere he is to publish the sentences of excommunication against those who have taken up arms against the king of England or in other ways disturbed that realm.[3] On the other hand, we have the entry in the diary of Eudes Rigaud noting his sermon at the parlement at Paris[4] and the well-known practice of preaching in the parliaments of fourteenth-century England.[5]

We can then, I suggest, safely accept Humbert de Romans as a reliable witness, the more so since there is a considerable amount of evidence from record sources testifying to the similarity of thirteenth-century parliaments of different countries even in points of detail.[6]

Now whether he was writing, as seems to be assumed, towards the close of his career in the sixties or seventies of the century, or whether his treatise for the instruction of preachers was written at some earlier

[1] Borrelli de Serres, *loc. cit.*, calls it 'sujet d'homélie, qui ne peut d'ailleurs guère passer pour une source historique'.

[2] Humbert himself seems to have sat as a member of the court in the parlement of the Nativity of Our Lady, 1258: Echard, *Scriptores Ordinis Praedicatorum*, I, 148.

[3] Summaries will be found in *Registres de Clément IV* (ed. E. Jordan), p. 125, No. 426, and *Cal. Papal Letters*, I, 434. A transcript is in Add. MS. 15362, No. 92. I quote the relevant passage (f. 344*b*): 'Quocirca mandamus quatinus huiusmodi excommunicationum sententias in sollempnibus Parlamentis, quibus Parisius et alibi te interesse contigerit per te ipsum sollempniter publices, et per alios in omnibus locis in quibus expedire videris et precipue in locis marittimis, seu mari uicinis facias publicari.' Similar instructions were given to the archbishop-elect of Reims and the archbishops of Rouen, Tours, Bourges and Sens.

[4] *Registrum Visitationum* (ed. Bonnin), p. 312.

[5] Stubbs, *Constitutional History*, III, 442 f.; *Modus Tenendi Parliamentum* (ed. Hardy), p. 31.

[6] See below, pp. 172 ff.

period of his life,[1] there is no doubt that Humbert was describing a new thing — very new if the book was the fruit of his early maturity: for parliaments, in the form in which he presents them, were unknown in the earlier decades of the thirteenth century.

Throughout Western Europe it had been the custom for kings to hold solemn courts at the great festivals of the Christian year: there they wore their crown and there they took counsel. In England the multiplication of crown-wearings by Henry III appears to have brought the ceremony into disrepute and the practice was finally discontinued under Edward I.[2] In France the custom ceased earlier, but in 1182 it still seems to be contemplated that the bishop of Beauvais may go annually to three courts of the French king.[3] Perhaps too it was the strength of this tradition which determined Philip Augustus a few years later, on his departure for the crusade, to provide that three times a year during his absence a special court should be held at Paris by the queen and the archbishop of Reims, when the complaints of the people should be heard. It is quite clear that what were contemplated in especial were complaints against the *baillis* who were to be present to report upon the affairs of their districts.[4] But although we have here an institution which in some respects resembles the later parlement, no direct connection can be traced. The arrangements were purely temporary and provisional during the king's absence, and such notices as we have of meetings of the king's court in the early thirteenth century do not suggest the continuous existence of an organisation of the kind.[5] In England the

[1] Mortier (*Les Maitres Généraux*, I, 659) states definitely that most of his works were written after his resignation, i.e. between 1263 and 1277. This is probable, but direct evidence seems lacking.

[2] *Traditio*, XVI, 126–35.

[3] *Actes de Philippe Auguste* (ed. Delaborde), No. 53. It is, however, to be noted that the clause dealing with this point is, like others, repeated from a charter of Louis VII, of 1144–5: see Antoine Loisel, *Mémoires . . . de Beauvais* (1617), pp. 271 ff.; Luchaire, *Actes de Louis VII*, No. 138. Cf. Luchaire, *Histoire des institutions monarchiques de la France* (1891), I, 263 f.; Pfister, *Études sur le règne de Robert le Pieux*, p. 149.

[4] *Œuvres de Rigord et de Guillaume le Breton* (Société de l'histoire de France), I, 101.

[5] Cf. Borrelli de Serres, *Recherches sur divers services publics*, I, 290. See also the cases collected by Ch. V. Langlois, *Textes relatifs à l'histoire du Parlement*,

position was similar: from time to time specially full meetings of the king's court were summoned, but, so far as we can perceive, upon no definite plan and at no stated terms, and principally it would seem for political business.[1] But very early in the thirteenth century we have evidence to show that such afforced meetings of the *curia regis* might not only deliberate upon political questions but hear also actions at law which the court ordinarily attendant upon the king had not ventured to determine. In 1204 there was a dispute between William the Marshal, the countess of Meulan and the earl of Devon concerning the ownership of the manor of Sturminster. Perhaps it was because the parties were important people that the action was heard before the king himself, but the story was a tangled one and a decision was difficult, so the king adjourned the parties until the morrow, when they were to have right by counsel of his court. The Marshal appeared on the morrow (2 July) and again on the fifth day; the others did not appear. The king turned to his counsellors for advice, but they protested that they were so few and the circumstances so unusual that it would be better to defer the whole matter until the morrow of the Assumption (16 August) when the archbishop and the other great and wise men of the land would be able to be present. Finally a day seems to have been given to the parties for Thursday after the Assumption (19 August).[2] Now upon that date there was an important meeting at Worcester, which apparently lasted several days, and to it came Llewelyn, prince of North Wales, and Madog ap Gruffydd under safe conduct in the company of the Marshal and the earl of Salisbury.[3] There can be little doubt that here we have an example of the conjuncture of political and legal business at a plenary meeting of the *curia regis*.

---

pp. 30 ff. Minor cases did undoubtedly find their way to the king's court, but not apparently in any systematic way nor presumably especially for consideration at a solemn or plenary meeting of the court: cf. *Historiens de la France*, XXIV, 284 f. (case in 1237), 389 (case in 1239–41). On the distinction between the ordinary and plenary sessions of the king's court, see Luchaire, *Histoire des institutions monarchiques*, I, 310.

[1] Cf. Stubbs, *Const. Hist.*, I, 612.   [2] *Curia Regis Rolls*, III, 124, 147.

[3] *Rotuli Litterarum Patentium*, p. 44. See also *Law Quarterly Review*, XLIV, 116 f.

As early as 1242 we have a writ upon the close roll in a form which later in the century will become very familiar: the writ permits John de Nevile to hold the bailiwick of Shotover and Stow Wood until the forthcoming parliament at London.[1] This writ was perhaps not exceptional even at that time; but we seem to have no more writs of the kind recorded until 1248, when we may find a writ upon the close roll directing that a distress is to be respited until the parliament on the octave of Candlemas,[2] and also writs in similar terms noted on the memoranda rolls of the Exchequer.[3] Such writs are not, however, very frequently recorded for a good many years.[4] But these documents, however infrequently they may be enrolled, do point to a growing practice of referring to specially full meetings of the king's court, meetings that are coming to be termed parliaments, legal and administrative matters of detail as well as broad questions of politics or legislation.

This, of course, is a feature which was preserved in the organised parliaments of the later thirteenth century, but when we seek to draw the links closer between these parliaments and the institutions of the twelfth century and early thirteenth century we find that the chain of evidence is difficult to complete. Partly, doubtless, this is due to the carelessness of record-makers and to the disappearance of many records that were made, but chiefly perhaps because some new elements were necessary to create an institution which, however much it might owe to the ideas of the past, owed much more to the circumstances and genius of the thirteenth century.

The step to be explained is the transition from the occasional plenary sessions of the king's court held at no regular intervals to the regular and ordered meetings described by Humbert de Romans, to which the name of parliament is applied and which we find in existence from the middle years of the thirteenth century. The explanation has been advanced that in France this step was taken deliberately by Saint Louis with

[1] *Close Rolls (1237–42)*, p. 447.   [2] *Ibid. (1247–51)*, p. 104.
[3] E. 368/20 (L.T.R. Mem. Roll, 36 Hen. III), mm. 4, 13.
[4] They appear to have been enrolled very unsystematically and do not appear in any large number until after the accession of Edward I: cf. *Bulletin of the Institute of Historical Research*, V, 129 ff.

a view to checking the corruption and misgovernment of the *baillis*, the evils of whose rule were disclosed in the great inquisitions of 1247 and 1248. According to this view the oversight which the king's court had exercised over local administration was no longer to be merely occasional and spasmodic but regular and ordered. Hence the regular sessions of the court, at first usually four times a year, to which the name of parliament becomes affixed.[1]

This may not be the whole explanation of the development of the parlement, but it seems to be a very large part of it. And the explanation appears to apply *mutatis mutandis* to England as well as to France. The first demand for regular parliaments in England, so far as we know, appears in the Provisions of Oxford of 1258,[2] where it is to be found side by side with a scheme for redressing the evils of local misgovernment. Although the actual task of redressing these evils fell upon the justiciar, yet he found it necessary to refer a number of difficult cases, perhaps a considerable proportion of cases, to parliament.[3] The same idea that parliament exists to redress the evils which the ordinary courts cannot redress occurs again in the early years of Edward I. The statute called Rageman conceives of parliament as the centre of a system for repressing lawlessness and especially the abuse of power by 'bailiffs'. The general scheme of the statute is to give immediate relief to those who have been wronged, by sending justices on a special commission and by devising a special procedure outside the common law, and further to provide for bringing the offenders before the king in parliament when the justices also will have presented the results of their

[1] Borrelli de Serres, *Recherches sur divers services publics*, I, 290 f.

[2] Cf. Bémont, *Simon de Montfort* (1884), p. 351:'Le conte dit que en la commune porveance fete par le roy et par son conseil est porveu que trois parlemanz soient tenuz par an.' The inference is that this requirement of the Provisions of Oxford was a new departure.

[3] I have drawn attention to this point in *Transactions of the Roy. Hist. Soc.*, IV Series, v, 56 ff.: other cases, besides those there mentioned, will be found in Assize Roll, No. 873, mm. 6, 7. I strongly suspect that cases marked 'Loquendum cum Rege' or 'Loquendum', where there is no specific reference to parliament, not infrequently found their way there: Mr. E. F. Jacob believes such cases went to the council (*Studies in the Period of Baronial Reform and Rebellion*, p. 53), but this does not exclude a decision in parliament.

enquiries.[1] This statute is of uncertain date but comes from the period 1276 to 1278.[2] It was followed in 1285 by the statute of Winchester which required the justices to report to the king in parliament breaches of the provisions for maintaining the peace.[3] The idea reappears under Edward II. In December 1309 special commissioners are appointed in each county to enquire into cases of tortious prises and gifts exacted from those spared from prisage: they are to hear complaints and to submit reports to the council in parliament the following February, when also those found guilty are to appear.[4] Again the Ordinances of 1311 lay stress upon the hearing in parliament of wrongs done by the king's ministers and of breaches of the law committed by them.[5] It is very dubious whether any of these measures was very effective. By the fourteenth century, perhaps already in the closing years of the thirteenth, such a conception of parliament was obsolescent: but the idea and its persistence are important when we are considering the origins of parliament.

There is no doubt that in France regular sessions of the parlement on an ordered scheme began about the middle of the thirteenth century. The number of sessions gradually diminished with the pressure of business: session ran into session until finally in the fourteenth century one single session covered the whole legal year. This regular order was liable to be disturbed during periods of warfare or when there were other distractions such as a royal marriage, but it was always resumed.[6] In England also there is no doubt that parliaments were held on a regular scheme of Easter and Michaelmas sessions in the early years of Edward I,[7] and there is little doubt that this arrangement was founded

[1] *Statutes of the Realm*, I, 44.

[2] Cam, *Studies in the Hundred Rolls*, pp. 41 f.

[3] *Statutes of the Realm*, I, 98. Cf. Ryley, *Placita Parliamentaria*, pp. 451 ff.; *Cal. Patent Rolls (1281–92)*, pp. 264 f.; *Bulletin of the Institute of Historical Research*, V, 134 f.

[4] *Parliamentary Writs*, II, ii, App. 24 f.: *Cal. Patent Rolls (1307–13)*, pp. 248 ff., where the reference to parliament is omitted.

[5] *Rotuli Parliamentorum*, I, 285 f., Nos. 29, 40.

[6] Langlois, *Textes relatifs à l'histoire du parlement*, pp. 229 ff.; Ducoudray, *Les origines du parlement de Paris*, pp. 50 ff.

[7] *Bulletin of the Institute of Historical Research*, V, 133 ff., 151 f.

upon the tradition of Henry III's reign, although the years of civil strife and the difficulties of settlement after Evesham were not favourable to the maintenance of a regular uninterrupted sequence of parliaments. Still, broken as the sequence might be, there is no question that in the later years of Henry III's reign it was the rule to hold several parliaments a year.[1]

It is not at all unlikely therefore that in its origin the English parliament owes something to ideas borrowed from France, although it is of course true that like problems in countries sharing a common civilisation may suggest like remedies. There cannot, however, be much doubt that other parliaments which were held periodically at regular sessions owe a great deal to conscious imitation, whatever differences in detail there may be. It is inconceivable that the parliaments of Alfonse of Poitiers do not owe much to the parliaments of his brother Saint Louis, however many may be the minor differences.[2] The parliaments of Ireland are unquestionably modelled upon those of England:[3] and the parliaments of Scotland not improbably owe a great deal to the same source.[4] But we cannot perceive any feature in the parliaments of the Empire — even although there are close similarities in detail[5] — which we can suppose to have been borrowed from elsewhere. Why then, we may ask, was the word parliament ever applied to these assemblies which we more usually term 'diet' and the Germans 'Reichstag'?

Now, not only was parliament a court wherein personal wrongs were righted, but it had more general functions. This is well brought out in a letter addressed by Henry III in February 1260 to the council in England when he protested against a parliament being held in his absence. He refused his consent, but added that the justiciar to whose keeping the kingdom had been committed might, with their counsel,

[1] *Handbook of British Chronology*, 2nd edn., 1961, pp. 505–6.

[2] As against Boutaric, Molinier insists upon the differences between the parlements of Saint Louis and Alfonse (*Correspondance Administrative*, II, pp. xxvi ff.): he concludes (p. lxv) 'ce parlement d'Alfonse est bien plutôt un corps administratif qu'un organe judiciaire'.

[3] See now Richardson and Sayles, *Irish Parliament in the Middle Ages* (1952).

[4] Cf. *Scottish Historical Review*, XXV, 300 ff.

[5] For the Imperial parliaments of this period, see Ehrenberg, *Der deutsche Reichstag, 1273–1378*; see also below, p. 172.

dispense universal justice (*iustitia communis*) to all and singular, provided that no new departure or law (*noua mutatio siue ordinatio*) was made in the kingdom without the king's presence and assent.[1] Obviously it was recognised at that time that parliament had a dual function: the dispensation of the highest justice on the one hand; on the other, changes or reform in administration and law. It is possible that in requiring three parliaments a year the framers of the Provisions of Oxford had in mind a periodical review of administration, but in point of fact the burden of supervising administration fell upon the council and there is no evidence that parliament was greatly concerned with questions of detail, while it is clear that broad questions of policy and legislation were brought before it.[2] This concern with what we may call politics was a feature common to all parliaments which have any claim to be called national, a characteristic to be discerned very much earlier than any attempt to use parliaments as a regular and ordered means of providing remedies for wrongs which would otherwise fail of redress or of obtaining counsel on difficult questions of administration.[3] This is a feature which the Reichstag shared in common with other national assemblies.[4]

It may be objected that the parlement of Paris was not a deliberative and political assembly, but was primarily and almost exclusively judicial in its functions: this indeed appears to be the view that holds the field today.[5] But I venture to suggest that this view is mistaken and derives

---

[1] Shirley, *Royal Letters*, II, 155.

[2] For the activities of the council, see Powicke, 'The Baronial Council (1258-1260)' in *Essays in Medieval History presented to T. F. Tout*, pp. 119 ff. For the position which parliament was intended to occupy our best evidence is provided by the Provisions of Westminster (*Annales Monastici* (Burton), I, 477; cf. Jacob, *Studies in the Period of Baronial Reform*, p. 373).

[3] This is not, of course, to say that legal decisions were not taken or administrative questions considered in exceptional cases at plenary meetings of the king's court: cf. Stubbs, *Constitutional History*, I, 401; Luchaire, *Histoire des institutions monarchiques*, I, 265 ff.

[4] Ehrenberg, *Der deutsche Reichstag*, 61 ff.

[5] Borrelli de Serres, *Recherches sur divers services publics*, I, 296. Cf. Langlois, *Revue Historique*, XLII, 90 f. But see Ducoudray, *Les Origines du Parlement de Paris*, pp. 316 ff.

really from the method employed in drawing up the surviving records of the parlement, those ancient registers which we know as the *Olim*. The *greffiers* responsible were interested only in legal precedents, and we can show from documents surviving in England that they could on occasion overlook entirely a session of the parlement at which political business was transacted. If we examine a table, such as that constructed by M. Ch. V. Langlois[1] or M. Ducoudray,[2] of the sessions of the parlement, we shall notice that in the year 1263, at a period when it was customary to hold four sessions a year, only three are recorded. Thus in the year 1261 there are sessions following Candlemas, Whitsun, the Nativity of Our Lady and Martinmas, and so also in the years 1260 and 1259.[3] In the year 1262 the Whitsuntide session was put off because of the celebration of the marriage of the king's son, and instead a session was held on the octave of the Assumption (22 August) which served also for the customary session in September after the Nativity of Our Lady. But in the year 1263 the session which should have taken place in September is altogether wanting.[4] Now it so happens that in that year Henry III was summoned to a meeting of the parlement of the king of France on the quinzaine of the Nativity of Our Lady: the session was held at Boulogne, apparently to suit Henry's convenience, for in the days of Saint Louis the parlement was not tied to any one town.[5] At that meeting there were discussed, so an English chronicler says, the details of a proposed crusade and the coronation of the French

---

[1] *Textes relatifs à l'histoire du Parlement*, pp. 229 ff.

[2] *Origines du Parlement de Paris*, pp. 50 f.

[3] In this year the parlement sat at All Saints as well as at Martinmas: possibly the two sessions were continuous.

[4] A table of the sessions of the parlement may make the position clearer: all sessions were probably at Paris except that of the Nativity, 1263:

1259	Candlemas	Whitsun	Nativity B.V.M.	All Saints and Martinmas
1260	Candlemas	Ascension	Nativity B.V.M.	Martinmas
1261	Candlemas	Whitsun	Nativity B.V.M.	Martinmas
1262	Candlemas		Assumption	Martinmas
1263	Candlemas	Whitsun	[Nativity B.V.M.]	Martinmas

It is possible that there was a special session late in Lent, 1261: Eudes Rigaud, *Regestrum Visitationum*, p. 398; see below, p. 171, note 5.

[5] *Foedera*, I, 432.

king's son:[1] and it was to this meeting that Simon de Montfort was summoned in a vain attempt by Saint Louis to effect a settlement of the differences between the earl and Henry.[2] Such business, however, did not interest the *greffier*, and no note of the Boulogne session is to be found in the *Olim*. Again, if we may trust an English chronicler, it was at an otherwise unrecorded parlement of the Assumption in 1269 that Edward entered into his agreement with Saint Louis concerning the crusade.[3]

It is of course unlikely in any case that when Henry III or Edward attended the French parlement, either spent much time in hearing the trivial cases that fill the greater part of the registers. There is a well-known story telling how Henry III kept the parlement waiting while he heard mass at every church in Paris on the way from his lodgings:[4] however true this may be[5] it is unlikely that the normal routine of the parlement would have been suspended to await the English king's arrival: if the parlement was kept waiting, some other business must have been afoot. We must admit the possibility that, under Saint Louis and perhaps under his immediate successors, the business of the parlement was, like the business of other contemporary parliaments, a mixture of the judicial, the administrative and the political.[6] The re-

---

[1] *Liber de Antiquis Legibus*, p. 57.

[2] So Guillaume de Nangis: rex Franciae Ludovicus. . . . Simonem comitem ad parlamentum suum apud Boloniam super mare convocavit (*Historiens de la France*, XX, 414). Cf. Shirley, *Royal Letters*, II, 249.

[3] *Liber de Antiquis Legibus*, pp. 110 f. Parlements were held at this term 1262, 1273, 1274. Cf. *Olim*, I, 765, No. 32, where there is what seems to be an adjournment to this term in 1269.

[4] This 'Historiola de pietate Regis Henrici III' has been printed from Rymer's transcript (Add. MS., 4573, fos. 57 f.) of the destroyed Vitellius D. XVI, by Champollion-Figeac, *Lettres de Rois*, I, 402 ff., and E. A. Bond in *Archæological Journal*, XVII, 317 ff.

[5] The story is written round Henry's one recorded *bon mot*, and perhaps quite correctly, and certainly quite naturally, appears in several contemporary or subcontemporary versions which do not mention parliament. One will be found in a collection of *exempla* (*Speculum Laicorum* (ed. J. Th. Welter), p. 10), another in the continuation of Matthew Paris (ed. Wats (1640), p. 1009), repeated in Trevet's *Annales*, p. 280, and yet another in the St. Albans *Opus Chronicorum* (Trokelowe, *Chronica*, p. 36).

[6] There seems no reason for doubting that the 'pallamentum' in 1261 to

striction of the parlement to the dispensing of justice, the shedding of the heterogeneity of the ancient *curia regis*, was a development of later years.

Parliament then added the periodical redressing of wrongs not righted by the ordinary process of law to certain of the ancient functions of the *curia regis*, those functions for which special solemnity and a specially full attendance were deemed necessary, not excluding important or difficult judicial decisions. In the process of time the balance of functions — a balance never perhaps too closely reproduced in any two countries — changed under the pressure of events or as the result of deliberate policy. It is noteworthy that in Germany the name of parliament was not given to the Reichstag until the very closing years of the thirteenth century, more than a generation after the great period of the organisation of parliaments elsewhere:[1] and by that time every national parliament was developing along its own lines and differences were becoming marked. Looking back from the twentieth century and influenced, as we must be, by our knowledge of the developments of the fourteenth and fifteenth centuries, the parliament of the Empire seems to have been distinctly more like the later parliaments of Edward I

---

which the clergy of the province of Rouen sent representatives to treat concerning a crusade was a 'parlement' (see Eudes Rigaud, *Regestrum Visitationum*, p. 398, and Bonnin's note, p. 399). See also *Grandes Chroniques de France* (ed. Paulin Paris), V, 150, 167, where 'parlements' of 1303 and 1304 are mentioned. I feel considerable difficulty in following Borrelli de Serres in dismissing these assemblies — the one the first of the 'États Généraux', the second a meeting for treating of peace with Flanders — as having no connection with the parlement of Paris (*Recherches sur divers services publics*, I, 288 f.).

[1] The earliest use of the name known to me is in a letter of January 1294 from Adolf of Nassau to Edward I (Bart. Cotton, *Historia Anglicana*, p. 434; *Mon. Germ. Hist.*, *Constitutiones et Acta publica*, III, 434), the next in 1296 (*ibid.*, 523 f.: cf. Ehrenberg, *Der deutsche Reichstag*, pp. 3 f.). It is perhaps not without significance that Richard of Cornwall did not, so far as we know, call his one general Reichstag in 1269 a parliament but *colloquium* (*Mon. Germ. Hist.*, *Constitutiones et Acta publica*, II, 488, 616: cf. J. F. Boppart, *Richard von Cornwall*, p. 115). In the account of this assembly to be found in Wyke's *Chronicon*, pp. 223 f., and apparently furnished by a follower of Richard's, it is called 'principum et magnatum Alemanniae convocatio'.

in England, Scotland and Ireland[1] and distinctly less like the contemporary parlement of France. But nevertheless we must remember
that well into the fourteenth century the parliaments of these islands
continued to resemble the parlement of France very closely indeed,
and we cannot be at all sure that the differences which we see would
have been plain to contemporary observers.

That there were contemporary observers well qualified to compare
the functions and procedure of different parliaments is a point worth
emphasising. First let us consider the large number of people attending
the English parliament who must have had some acquaintance with the
French parlement. After the treaty of Paris of 1259 it was necessary for
the king of England as duke of Guyenne to be constantly represented
by proctors in the parlement. The number of proctors appointed from
then until the Hundred Years War was very large. Not only was
Edward I represented by such men as Francesco Accursi, a civil lawyer,[2]
and the seneschal of Gascony,[3] but from time to time we find such
appointments as those of Stephen of Penchester[4] and Thomas of
Sandwich[5] — both of whom acted as justices in England and the latter
of whom filled the posts of seneschal of Ponthieu, of escheator and of
constable of the Tower — of Nicholas Segrave[6] a baron, of William of
Blyburgh[7] a wardrobe clerk, of Otho de Grandison[8] who had been
styled the king's secretary and was later keeper of the Channel Islands,
of the archdeacon of Winchester,[9] of sundry friars on occasion, as well

[1] For Edward I's Scottish parliaments, see *Scottish Historical Review*, XXV,
300 ff. For Edward I's Irish parliaments see now Richardson and Sayles, *Irish
Parliament in the Middle Ages*, pp. 57–70.

[2] *Foedera*, I, 516, 524; Langlois, *Textes relatifs à l'histoire du Parlement*, p. 92;
Chanc. Misc. 3/21, No. 2; *Statutes of the Realm*, I, 42; *Parliamentary Writs*, I, 6.

[3] Langlois, *op. cit.*, 124 f., 133: cf. Maitland, *Memoranda de Parliamento*, pp. 3,
300.

[4] Chanc. Misc. 4/5 (Wardrobe Account, 1289–1290), ff. 12*b*, 16, 17, 22*b*;
Parl. Writs, I, 8, 16, 19; *Rot. Parl.*, I, 3*b*, 98*a*, 126*b*.

[5] Chanc. Misc. 4/5, ff. 16, 22*b*; Langlois, *Textes*, p. 102; *Rot. Parl.*, I, 3*b*.

[6] Chanc. Misc. 4/5, f. 12*b*; *Parl. Writs*, I, 15, 20, 29; *Rot. Parl.*, I, 93*a*.

[7] Chanc. Misc. 4/4, f. 13; Langlois, *op. cit.*, pp. 103, 124: cf. *Parl. Writs*, I, 62.

[8] Chanc. Misc. 4/5, ff. 11, 23, 29; *Parl. Writs*, I, 2, 81 f., 136; *Rot. Parl.*, I, 76*a*.

[9] Exch. T.R. Misc. Books, E. 36/201, p. 23; *Rot. Parl.*, I, 44*b*.

as of very distinguished persons such as Edmund, earl of Lancaster.[1] These are but examples of the personal links between the parliaments of England and France. Information about the Scottish parliament at this period is hard to come by, but we know that it was attended from time to time not only by such men as the Bruces and Balliols, but also by others familiar with the English parliament who came either as representatives of the English king or as suitors. Thus William of Blyburgh paid not only a visit to the parlement of France but also the parliament of Scotland:[2] and the abbot of Reading may be found petitioning not only in the English parliament but also in the parliament of John Balliol.[3] Again we have such an example as that of Jean, sire de Picquigny, vidame of Amiens, who is found acting as proctor for the count of Flanders in the parliament at Stirling in August 1293:[4] unquestionably he was familiar with the procedure of the parlement of Paris.[5]

The journeys of certain English friars exemplify most strikingly perhaps this coming and going between parliament and parliament. For instance, William of Gainsborough, then Minister General of the Friars Minor, was present at the assembly at Norham in June 1291, called to consider the question of the Scottish succession. This meeting

[1] *Foedera*, I, 793 f.

[2] Chancery Misc. 4/5 (Wardrobe Account, 1289-1290), f. 25. For Blyborough see Tout, *Chapters in Administrative History of Medieval England*, ii. 160, 163, 170-81.

[3] *Acts of the Parliaments of Scotland*, I, 445 f.; *Rot. Parl.*, I, 61a.

[4] *Acts of the Parliaments of Scotland*, I, 448.

[5] He appears as a litigant on several occasions between 1257 and 1296; on the first occasion he was presumably a minor (Boutaric, *Actes du Parlement de Paris*, I, Nos. 79, 2304, 2410, 2574). Relying upon a document printed by Dutillet in his *Recueil des rangs des Grands de France*, F. I. Darsy (*Picquigny et ses seigneurs*, p. 36) stated that in 1298 Jean de Picquigny sat as a member of the court: this document is a French translation of the list in *Olim*, II, 423, No. xiii, printed also by Langlois, *Textes*, p. 169, and renders 'Vicedominus Priviconii' as 'Le Vidame de Piqueny', but no such Latin form of the name is to be found elsewhere. Darsy stated also (*op. cit.*, p. 37) that he visited England in the same year. He was certainly in favour with Edward I: *Cal. Patent Rolls* (1281-92), p. 321; *Cal. Chancery Warrants* (1244-1326), p. 32.

was not a parliament, but it will serve as a starting-point.[1] In October 1292 he is at Edward I's Scottish parliament at Berwick when the same business is under consideration: his stay is prolonged, for he is still there in November.[2] In 1294 he, with a Dominican friar, Hugh of Manchester, is acting as proctor for the king of England in the parlement of Paris.[3] In August 1295 he is at a parliament at Westminster,[4] and again in September 1297.[5] In 1302 he is raised to the see of Worcester and thereafter as bishop attends the king's parliaments.[6] His companion in Paris, Hugh of Manchester, is found attending the September parliament in 1297,[7] and the September parliament in 1305.[8]

These personal links between parliament and parliament are to be taken into account when we consider the likenesses between the procedure of different countries. There were similarities even in little things. It is not perhaps surprising to find a traditional forty-days' summons to parliament common to England and Scotland, but it may strike us as curious to find it in Germany also.[9] The writs of summons in England and in Germany look as though they might have been derived from a common formula.[10] That absentees from parliament should be liable to a money penalty both in Germany and in Ireland is a coincidence which also may strike us.[11] These likenesses we may ascribe to

---

[1] Palgrave, *Documents illustrating the History of Scotland*, Illustrations No. 4; Prynne, *Exact Chronological Vindication*, III, 504; *Foedera*, I, 766.

[2] Rishanger, *Chronica*, pp. 255, 260.

[3] Pierre de Langtoft, *Chronicle*, II, 204 ff.

[4] E. 36/202 (Wardrobe Account, 23 Edw. I), p. 44.

[5] *Parliamentary Writs*, I, 55, No. 10.

[6] *Ibid.*, I, 137, 139, 158 ff., 182 f.   [7] *Ibid.*, I, 55, No. 10.

[8] *Ibid.*, I, 159 ff., Nos. 54–6, 59; Exch. Parliament and Council Proceedings, 1/20.

[9] Stubbs, *Constitutional History*, III, 394; *Modus Tenendi Parliamentum* (ed. Hardy), p. 3; Hannay, *On 'Parliament' and 'General Council'* in *Scottish Historical Review*, xviii, 158; Ehrenberg, *Der deutsche Reichstag* (1273–1378), pp. 10 f. In Germany as in England the custom of a seven weeks' summons was not maintained: much shorter periods are found in the fourteenth century.

[10] Cf. the summons to Lübeck in 1310: *Mon. Hist. Germ., Constitutiones et Acta publica*, IV, 332.

[11] For Germany, see Ehrenberg, *op. cit.*, pp. 23 f.: for Ireland, Richardson and Sayles, *Irish Parliament in the Middle Ages*, pp. 137–44.

accident or to some remote legal heritage. They may indeed be regarded as trivial resemblances, but we may find similarities in procedure of a much more arresting character.

There has come down to us a great deal of detailed information regarding the parlement of Alfonse of Poitiers which we can compare with the detailed information we possess of the working of the English parliament of Henry III and Edward I. On the one hand we have certain financial accounts which contain references to the parlement, a large number of writs, various records of parliamentary proceedings, in particular a large roll recording the proceedings at the parlement held at Toulouse in 1270 just before the departure of Alfonse for the crusade.[1] On the English side we have chancery and exchequer enrolments, various memoranda of parliamentary proceedings, petitions and miscellaneous documents.[2] Without attempting a detailed analysis, attention may be drawn to the close similarity of the writs issued in the name of Alfonse and those issuing from the chancery and exchequer of Henry III and Edward I. There is the same mixture of administrative, judicial and purely feudal business in the two parliaments. Homage is rendered in the count's parlement as in the English parliament.[3] The results of inquisitions of various kinds are reported to either parliament.[4] Debts are respited and lands and goods replevied until parliament.[5] There are appeals from lower courts.[6] And intermixed are matters which concerned the count personally rather than public administration, just as a large part of the petitions presented at a parliament of Edward I were concerned with gifts and rewards and other personal

[1] Now printed by Fournier and Guébin, *Enquêtes administratives d'Alfonse de Poitiers* (1959), pp. 289–354.

[2] For references to these, see *Bulletin of the Institute of Historical Research*, V, 129 ff., and *Handbook of British Chronology*, pp. 499–513.

[3] *Correspondance administrative*, I, 3, No. 4: *Enquêtes*, see index p. 469. For some account of corresponding English documents, see *The Early Records of the English Parliaments* in the *Bulletin of the Institute of Historical Research*, V, 129 ff., VI, 71 ff.

[4] *Correspondance administrative*, II, lxiii, and references there cited.

[5] *Mandements inédits d'Alfonse de Poitiers* in *Annales du Midi*, XII, pp. 307, 313; *Correspondance administrative*, I, 64, No. 100: cf. p. 23, No. 35.

[6] *Correspondance administrative*, II, lxii, and references there cited.

matters.[1] And if we compare the entries on the parlement roll of 1270 with the parliament rolls of Edward I, we cannot fail to be struck by the likeness both in form and substance.

There are very close similarities between the procedure of the parlement of Paris and that of the English parliament. The mass of petitions presented in either parliament is an obvious point of similarity, as well as their trying by *maîtres des requêtes* in France, by receivers or auditors of petitions in England. Again a great deal of the detailed work of the parlement in France was performed by commissioners.[2] This is also a feature of the parliaments of Edward I. Thus in 1275 auditors are appointed in the Easter parliament to examine the contentions between the citizens of York on the one hand and the abbot of St. Mary's and the dean and chapter of St. Peter's on the other.[3] In the Michaelmas parliament of 1278 the contentions between the king of Scotland and the bishop of Durham were first heard before certain commissioners and afterwards before the king and his council: the business is later remitted to the same commissioners to determine.[4] An instance of a rather different kind is one where the king in council charges the seneschal of Gascony and Adam of Norfolk, constable of Bordeaux, to conduct an inquest into the disputes between the bishop and city of Bayonne: this was to be completed in time for the Michaelmas parliament of 1290.[5] A similar procedure was apparently contemplated when in October 1289 auditors were appointed to hear complaints against the king's ministers and their replies — the enquiry which resolved itself into the 'trial of the judges'.[6] The English parliament did not develop any permanent organisation resembling the *chambre des enquêtes*, but to discuss the reason for this and other differen-

---

[1] *Correspondance administrative*, II, lxii f.: cf. *Enquêtes*, *passim*.

[2] On this subject, see P. Guilhiermoz, *Enquêtes et Procès* (1892): the section on 'Commissions à enquérir' (pp. 27 ff.) affords a succinct view of the main features of the French system, which it is thus easy to compare with the system, if such it can be called, in England, as it appears in documents of the kind here cited.

[3] *Cal. Patent Rolls (1272–81)*, p. 120.

[4] *Foedera*, I, 565.

[5] Champollion-Figeac, *Lettres de Rois*, I, 280 f.

[6] *Foedera*, I, 715.

ces between the parliaments of England and of France would take us far from the question of origins. It is important, however, to remark that in the thirteenth century there was in England a rudimentary system of local and special enquiries which might well have led, as it did in France, to a distinct and organised branch of parliamentary procedure.

As the English and French parliaments developed in different directions, so the procedure and organisation of the English and Scottish parliaments diverged widely. But in the thirteenth century the similarities were still very close. No one who examines side by side the surviving parliament rolls of John Balliol and those of Edward I but must be struck by the close correspondence. Particularly is this marked in the form of petition, in the proceedings upon petition, in the adjournments to future parliaments.[1]

Nor is there need to dwell upon the similarities between the parliaments of Ireland and England. Since the Irish parliament was, like all the courts that served the Pale, purely English, it is but to be expected that it should be in nearly all respects similar.[2]

In discussing and comparing the parliaments of the thirteenth century no reference has been made to the presence or absence of representatives of the commons. It is from the standpoint of the modern age that the feeble beginnings of popular representation have any importance in parliamentary history. In the thirteenth century the popular element is of little significance, so far at least as the competence, jurisdiction or procedure of parliament is concerned. Popular representatives may be needed to give the appearance of popular support, and they may be summoned to a session of parliament in much the same spirit as they are summoned to welcome Henry III home from France[3] or to take oath to a new king and to receive orders to keep the king's peace[4] or to grace a coronation.[5] If the advice of representatives of the commons is

---

[1] The surviving enrolments for two parliaments of 1293 are printed in *Acts of the Parliaments of Scotland*, I, 445 ff.

[2] Richardson and Sayles, *Irish Parliament in the Middle Ages*.

[3] *Close Rolls* (1242–7), pp. 129 f.

[4] *Annales Monastici* (Winton.), II, 113.

[5] *Parliamentary Writs*, II, ii, 17 f.

seriously required it is likely that they will be summoned to a special meeting.[1]

Nor does the discussion of parliamentary origins necessarily entail an enquiry into the source of representative institutions. That source has been sought in many directions, but indeed popular representation is an idea so widespread that we hardly need to seek for sources and affiliations. It is found among the revolting Norman peasantry of 997,[2] and certainly quite independently among the burgesses of Irish towns in the thirteenth century.[3] Representation is so marked a feature in the medieval Church, and particularly in certain religious orders, that we have been invited to see here a source of inspiration for the British constitution.[4] The list could be indefinitely extended. The real problem, however, is not to explain the occasional association of popular representation with a session of parliament in England or elsewhere, but to explain why popular representation became an essential and inseparable feature of English parliaments. The explanation is not to be found by any examination of the origins of parliament, however far-reaching or ingenious.

---

[1] This is more particularly the case with town representatives who were summoned several times by Edward I to discuss such matters as town planning and customs duties (*Parliamentary Writs*, I, 49 ff., 134 f.): in France under Saint Louis they were consulted about coinage (on this see Ch. V. Langlois in Lavisse, *Histoire de France*, III, ii, 259).

[2] William of Jumièges, *Gesta Normannorum Ducum* (ed. J. Marx), pp. 73 f.

[3] In 1252 the articles of confederation between Dublin and Drogheda provide for common counsel between representatives of the towns (Gilbert, *Historical and Municipal Documents of Ireland*, p. 131): in 1285 the confederation embraces Dublin, Drogheda, Cork, Limerick and Waterford and the articles provide that two or three citizens or burgesses from each town are to meet triennially at Kilkenny on the morrow of Trinity (*ibid.*, p. 196). It is possible that the court of the Four Burghs in Scotland has its origin in a similar confederation (cf. *Acts of the Parliaments of Scotland*, I, 724: an earlier reference to the Four Burghs will be found in *Rot. Parl.*, I, 108). Another parallel is afforded by the moneyers of the oath of the Empire who had a representative parliament, meeting every four years, but the evidence does not go beyond the first half of the fourteenth century: see *Revue Numismatique* (1844), pp. 105 f.; *Annuaire Soc. française de Numismatique*, XIX, 108 ff.

[4] E. Barker, *The Dominican Order and Convocation*, pp. 72 ff.

In conclusion it may be well to summarise the suggestions I have to make. The difficulty is to explain how the occasional plenary meetings of the king's court in the early thirteenth century became transformed into the organised parliaments later in the century. We must, I suggest, assume some definite plan, some grafting of new ideas upon the stock of an ancient institution common to Western Europe. A beginning seems to have been made in France and to have been associated definitely with a scheme for bringing the royal *baillis* and local administration generally under control. Similar ideas, arising a few years later, are to be found in England. Although here regular parliaments may have been devised in some measure as a curb upon the king, it is likely that the recent reorganisation of the parlement in France had considerable influence on the measures taken in England. In turn the English parliament was imitated in Ireland and influenced the parliament of Scotland. Nor did the influence of the French parlement soon cease: the constant intercourse between the French parlement and the English court may explain in some measure at least the similarities in procedure to be found in the English and French parliaments in the later years of the thirteenth century. It is possible too that such influences were even more widely diffused owing to the presence, for example, in the Scottish parliament of suitors familiar with the procedure of the parlement of Paris. It is not clear that Germany was affected by the example of foreign parliaments, although the name was borrowed late in the thirteenth century. Nor does there seem reason to suppose that Italy was influenced from the North and West,[1] although the popularity of the name parliament about the year 1300 may be due to imitation from abroad rather than to native influences.

There is space but for a brief postscript. It was not to be expected that the similarities so evident in the later thirteenth century would continue for long. England soon became cut off by war from France. Not only so, but the legal systems of the two countries determined that there must be wide divergences in procedure. France had no such organisation

[1] Compare, however, Pertile, *Storia del Diritto Italiano*, II, i, 319. But the French model which is supposed to have been adopted in Savoy seems to be the *états généraux*.

of royal courts of law as had been created in England in the twelfth century and perfected in the thirteenth. The parlement of Paris had ultimately to perform many of the functions of the king's bench, the common bench and the justices in eyre. The parlement in consequence became increasingly a professional body of lawyers, while in England the judicial work of parliament receded more and more into the background. Scotland also was cut off by war from England and the Scottish parliament developed in its own way little influenced by ideas from over the border. It was only between England and Ireland that the old links subsisted and there only parliamentary institutions retained a close similarity.

H. G. RICHARDSON

9 The Black Death in Wales

The epidemics of the fourteenth century have been the subject of much discussion by eminent scholars, whose investigations have been supplemented by detailed studies of various localities. No considered attempt, however, has been made to trace the course of the disease within Wales, which, by reason of its isolated position and mountainous character, is frequently regarded as having largely escaped the visitation. The study of the effects of such an agent upon a society predominantly pastoral offers a subject of special interest.

The obscurity of conditions within Wales during the years of the Pestilence is primarily due to the paucity of evidence available from the usual sources. Contemporary chronicles throw no light upon the situation with the exception of Geoffrey le Baker's reference to the spread of the disease to Wales by the year 1349. Ecclesiastical evidence, to which Cardinal Gasquet attributed much importance in dealing with England, is conspicuously lacking, while parliamentary and legal evidence is, as a rule, inapplicable beyond the border. We are, therefore, driven to examine documents of a fiscal nature, but the less adequate machinery of record in Wales, particularly in the lordships of the March, constitutes a further obstacle. Not only is evidence scanty, but the manner in which the information for a large part of the country is presented, makes it difficult to obtain definite statistics. This was due to the complex conditions, political, economic and social, which had arisen in Wales after a conquest extending over some two hundred years. That conquest had the effect of creating a number of distinct political units, lordships or baronies of the March, each comprising one or more subordinate lordships, based on the original Welsh divisions, but in the lands of the Crown and in other parts conquered during the last Welsh War, the old divisions continued to be known as commotes. Each lordship now came to be regarded theoretically as a manor, but was not necessarily a unit of cultivation.

Where conditions were favourable, agriculture was introduced and manors on the English model established. These naturally developed in the lowlands, the castle forming the nucleus of foreign settlement. The lands of the lord formed the demesnes, English followers together with the Welsh of the lowland 'vills' being incorporated within the manor as Free or Customary tenants. This area, therefore, came to be administered as a distinct section of the lordship known as the 'Englishry', the resources of which were directly drawn upon for the support of the new administration. In contrast, the inhabitants of the upland 'Welshry', the remaining portion of the lordship, continued, in the main, undisturbed by the newer influences of the valleys, the lord contenting himself with receiving the dues and services which had formerly been rendered in accordance with tribal custom. In the Welshry, therefore, tribute based upon communal obligations continued to be paid, while the feature of the Englishry was the payment of rent or the performance of service in return for direct and individual tenure of land. Any attempt to analyse the effects of the Death in Wales must take cognisance of this very real economic division.

Owing to the nature of the country, agriculture could assume serious proportions only along the border and on the coastal plains of the south where manorial development was most marked and where the Englishry often occupied the major part of the lordships. These conditions were also to be found inland along the valleys, but beyond the mountain rim the Englishries were of very limited extent. In West and North Wales in particular, they were frequently confined to the immediate vicinity of the castle, but at more accessible points some features of a manor might be found on the limited demesnes of the lord. Little or no development, however, is perceptible, and before the close of the thirteenth century even these few acres of demesne had usually been given over to the customary tenants to hold 'at will' as rent-paying 'gabularii'. The commotes were mainly made up of free and unfree 'trefs', each of which participated in the use of the extensive mountain wastes and contributed its quota to the ancient dues of the commote. Tribesmen here held their land according to kindred principles, but by the early fourteenth century disintegration was proceeding within the kindred system, leading to a gradual extension of the practice of individual tenancy. This was especially the case in South

Wales and in those districts more closely in touch with English influences.

The large manors were making rapid progress during these years, but signs of coming change were not lacking. Hired labour was being substituted for the services of the customary tenants; the lord was becoming a stranger to his Welsh possessions so that the produce of the manor was less directly necessary. Portions of the demesne were, therefore, let to freemen or to customary tenants, making for a considerable class of 'gabularii' on the manors of South Wales. Attempts were being made to bring the elaborate organisation of the manor within more moderate proportions and to make up the revenue by less burdensome methods. The expedients of renting and 'farming' were being applied wherever opportunity offered. In spite of these incipient changes, however, the manor in the early part of the reign of Edward III was still flourishing in Wales but the outbreak of epidemics after the middle of the century immediately arrested development and hastened dissolution.

The spread of the Black Death into Wales would seem to have been by way of the lower Severn valley into the border counties and into the lordships of the south-eastern March by way of Caldicot. Prior to the winter or spring of 1348–49, records betray no sign of any untoward happening. By March 1349 the plague was raging in the eastern, and indeed in the western, portion of the lordship of Abergavenny, the lord of the former district falling a victim early in the month. By the middle of the following month, wholesale destruction had been wrought among the inhabitants here, the extent of which loss can best be gauged from an examination of the rents.[1] In each of the hamlets, an average of one-third only of the original rents could be obtained; at some of the villages, e.g. Wernyrheolydd and Trefgoythel, much greater losses occurred, pointing to almost complete extinction.[2] In the

[1] Evidence of reduction in rents must necessarily be regarded as of doubtful value unless such reduction is recorded as being due directly to the pestilence. The writer has endeavoured to keep this in view throughout this paper.

[2] E.g., Werneryth: *There used to be of rents of assise £13 10s. 3½d. and now remain £1 14s. 6d. because of mortality.*

Trefgoythel: *Rents of assize used to be £3 10s. 6¾d. but now only 6s. because of the mortality.*

manor of Penrhos, only £4 of a total of £12 could be collected 'because many of the tenements lie empty and derelict for lack of tenants'. So disastrous had been the effects through the whole lordship that the guardian of the heir petitioned for a reduction of £140 in a rent of £340, 'by reason of the mortal pestilence lately so rife in these parts'.[1] As a result of an enquiry, arrears, allowed to the extent of £60, and £40 a year, were deducted from the rents as permanent loss. The Prior of Abergavenny, too, experienced serious financial difficulty at this time.

The neighbouring lordships of Usk and Llantrissent, Trelech, Monmouth, Skenfrith, White Castle and Grosmont were also very generally affected by what was termed the First or the 'Great' Pestilence, the changes in the manor of Raglan necessitating a new rental.

Westward along the plain of Glamorgan the plague cannot be traced at this early date although a detailed inquisition was made in the spring of 1349 into the Glamorgan inheritance of Hugh le Despenser who had died on February 8 of that year. Northward, the epidemic spread through the border counties of Hereford, Shropshire, and the County Palatine of Chester, where it raged during the spring, summer and early autumn. Of the border lordships north and west of Shrewsbury, Caurs with its hamlets was seriously stricken,[2] the rents of assise of the freemen of Yockleton falling from £8 to £1 10s. The mills, it is said, were rendered valueless 'for lack of grinding, because there was no suit, and this because of the Pestilence'. At Harlegh, in the same manor, the demesnes could not be extended and no one wished to hire. A similar condition was to be found in the neighbouring lordships of Whittington, Ellesmere and Whitchurch, and in the lesser manors of Roughton, Sutton, Wrockwardine, Moreton Saye, La More, Aldenham and Bradford.[3] Little or no revenue was available from such sources as the courts, the markets and fairs, while in one case only £7 could be collected of a possible sum of £40. The accounts of the manor of

[1] Rot. Orig. 24 E. III, m. 8.

[2] Inq. p.m., C. Edw. III, File 96 (14).

[3] Inq. p.m., C. Edw. III, Files 95 (7); 98 (2); 98 (3); e.g., Whittington: *Michaelmas, 1349, two watermills, formerly worth £2, now only £1 yearly because the tenants are dead in the present pestilence. Rents of freemen formerly £3, now only £1.*

Chester for many years after the first outbreak are eloquent of the disastrous consequences in that region.[1] Large tracts of the demesne lands and escheated tenements in the various vills were allowed to remain uncultivated, and could not be let owing to lack of tenants.

It may be presumed that the pestilence extended by way of the three important routes into the lordships of the eastern March but, on this, information is somewhat unsatisfactory. Detailed record of the Bohun lands of Brecon and Huntington offers no direct evidence of its presence, though the receipts show greater fluctuations than in ordinary years.[2] Interest attaches to the visit of the lord and his lady to the castle of Brecon in the latter part of the year 1348, when elaborate preparations were made for a long stay. Little record is forthcoming to throw light on events in the adjoining lordship of Builth, a fact which is, indeed, true of the greater part of the Central March, including the extensive domains of the Mortimers of Wigmore and Cleobury Mortimer.

We are more fortunate in respect of the lordships of north-eastern Wales, especially the districts on the coast route leading from Chester. The burgesses of Rhuddlan, because of the poverty of the people, were, in 1350, granted a rebate of one-fourth of their farm of £40 for certain mills. This was raised to one-third for the following years 'until the said mills were of more value'. Many of the lead miners of Holywell died, the survivors refusing to work there. Debts of the courts of Flint could not be levied, and offices became difficult to farm.[3]

The lordship of Denbigh[4] seems to have experienced the full force

---

[1] Ministers' Accounts, Bundle 783, Nos. 1, 15, 16, 17, including Escheators' Accounts.

[2] Min. Acc., Bundle 671, Nos. 10810 *et sqq.*

[3] Min. Acc., Bundle 783, Nos. 1, 15, 16, 17; e.g., Chelmondeston: *4s. 4d. issues of 1 place of land in the lord's hand because acquired without licence. Now the place lies uncultivated because of the pestilence, and is common.*

Min. Acc., Bundle 1186, Nos. 4, 5, 11, 23. Account of the Ringild of Hopedale: Park of Lloetcoet (Llwydcoed): *£1 5s. 10d. agistments of the Park, and no more because of the Pestilence in the previous year.*

[4] Min. Acc., Bundle 1182, Nos. 3, 5 *passim;* e.g., Uwchalet Commote: Account of Griffith ap Madoc, Ringild: *Allowed £2 14s. 1d. from the customs of*

of the plague. Even in 1354, the heirs of deceased tenants of the *villatae* of Barrog and Petryal (commote Uwchalet) were unable through poverty to obtain possession, the lord thereby losing 'tunk' and other customary payments attaching to the lands. Similar entries are noted in the remaining commotes, while the Escheator's accounts for the whole district continue to record long lists of tenements still vacant through death or poverty.

The unique collection of Court Rolls that have been preserved for the lordship of Ruthin[1] makes it possible to follow the course of the disease there during the year of the outbreak as well as in succeeding years. In the first five months of the year 1349, the court proceedings are recorded in the usual manner, only an occasional death occurring, probably from natural causes. With extreme suddenness, however, in the second week in June, 7 deaths took place within the jurisdiction of the Court of Aberwheeler. During the next fortnight, all parts of the lordship were seriously attacked. Within that brief period 77 of the inhabitants of the town of Ruthin died, together with several of the 'nativi' of the 'maerdref' there; in the neighbourhood of Llangollen there were 10 deaths; in Llanerch 13, in Dogfelen (Dogfeiling) there were 25, and in Abergwiller 14, figures which more than doubled in the next few weeks. Allowance, however, must be made for duplication in the entries in the few cases where tenants might have held more than one tenement. The epidemic somewhat abated by the last week of July or early August, but it broke out with renewed violence during the remainder of that month when the death-rate reached its highest. After this it fell rapidly, although a few deaths were ascribed to this cause throughout the following winter. The ordinary business of the courts almost ceased at these troublous periods, and the Rolls were mainly given over to the enumeration of vacancies in the holdings of deceased tenants and to the recording of transfers, the profits from

---

divers tenants of the 'villatae' of Barrok and Petrual, in the lord's hands because the tenants died in the time of the Pestilence and their heirs are unable to pay for the inheritance.

Min. Acc., Bundle 1183, No. 2, 3.

[1] Ruthin, Court Rolls, Portfolios 217, 218, 219.

such sources often amounting to large sums. In these writings of the courts, two brothers are stated to have taken advantage of the plague to rob stricken families of their household goods and even of their animals.[1]

Passing from the March into the Crown lands, we again find sufficient evidence of widespread mortality. It is difficult to determine whether infection was conveyed by land alone, or whether the sea also played a part. It may fairly be assumed that the latter is true in the case of Carmarthen where the two officials of the Staple were among the early victims — about the end of March. In fact, the Carmarthen district suffered severely at this first visitation, especially the small manor of Llanllwch,[2] where lay the main portion of the demesnes of the lord of Carmarthen, the Prince of Wales. These demesnes were held 'at will' by a dozen gabularii, who all died, so that the tenements were left in the hands of the lord. By 1353, courts were still suspended and strangers were renting portions of the vacated lands, and had set up new tenements, though a large part 'lay waste and unmeasured for lack of buyers'. Miscellaneous revenues of the borough of Carmarthen, such as the mill-tolls and fisheries, were seriously diminished and the fairs could not be held.

During the summer, the pestilence made serious ravages throughout the commotes of Ystrad Towy and Cardiganshire, but inasmuch as the communities were answerable as a body for the various dues, it is almost impossible to make any but very general statements with regard to these areas. Items of evidence do occasionally appear. In every district great difficulty was experienced in obtaining anyone to hire the local offices of beadle, reeve or serjeant. The advowry tenants and chensers, some of whom were to be found in most of the commotes, either died or fled. In the districts of South Cardigan, 97 of a total of 104

---

[1] Court Rolls, Portfolio 218, No. 4. *Also the jurors say that Madoc ap Ririd and Kenwric his brother came by night in the Pestilence to the house of Aylmar after the death of the wife of Aylmar and took from the same house one water pitcher and basin, value 1s., old iron, valued 4d. And they also present that Madoc and Kenwric came by night to the house of Almar in the vill of Rewe in the Pestilence, and from that house stole 3 oxen of John the Parker and 3 cows, value 6s.*

[2] E.g., Min. Acc., Bundle 1158, No. 2.

'gabularii' withdrew before midsummer for fear of the pestilence.[1]
The issues from escheated lands reached high totals; a marked rise is
noted in the fees derived from the Chancery seal, and the various towns
and bailiwicks were from this time forward very commonly farmed.
Accounts continued for many years to record deficits.

The documents of the Principality of North Wales offer a more
illuminating picture. It would seem that a heavier toll of victims was
exacted here than was the case in the South. In the Anglesey commotes,[2]
very large numbers of escheated tenements were still in decay in the
year 1351 either through death or through the poverty of the people.
Thirty-three such entries are noted for the hamlets of Trefdisteinydd,
Dyndrovel, etc., in the Commote of Malltraeth, equivalent to a total of
£6 13s. 2d. in rent. In Llifon Commote the decay of rents (mainly
from native land) amounted to £4 18s., in Talybolion, £9 8s. 3½d.,
and in Turkelyn £6 9s. 9½d. The demesnes of Beaumaris were let to
townsmen.

The Caernarvon records[3] also point to serious losses, particularly

[1] Advowry tenants = landless strangers dwelling temporarily in a commote
by payment of an advowry fee of 4d. a year.

Chensers = itinerant traders paying a licence *fee* or *cense*.

gabularii = tenants paying a single rent in lieu of services.

[2] Min. Acc., Bundles 1149, 1150 *passim:* e.g., Commote of Malltraeth:
*Decay of rents of Davydd Moil of the vill of Trefdisteinydd 5s. 4d.; Gronow With
3s. 4d.; Turlach 22s. 4d.; Cadwgan ap Jak of Trefithon etc. (30 other like entries)
whose land were in the lord's hands for lack of tenants and because the lord's tenants
in the same vills are incapable (impotentes et insufficientes) of holding the said lands.*

Commote of Turkelyn (Twrcelyn): *Allowed 11s. 6d. part of £2 12s. 1½d., rents
of the Villeins of Bodevyney in the extent of Bodenawyn because there are now only
two tenants there — one 'native' and one advowry.*

[3] Min. Acc., Bundle 1171, *passim.* E.g., Commote of Cruthy (Creuddyn):
*Account of the Rhingyll of the Commote, Michaelmas, 24–5 Edw. III. Advowry
8d. — Advowry of Blethin ap Madoc and David ap Madoc etc. . . . and no more
because the remainder are dead by the Pestilence.*

*Farm. — Farm of the Rhaglawry, used to be £2 3s. 4d. before the Pestilence. —
Nothing, because let by the Justice's Deputy and the Chamberlain to Madoc Blodeyth
for £1 6s. 8d.*

Commote of Cafflogion: *Allowed £8 2s. 2d., viz., £4 2s. 2d. for this year and
the last two years for the lands of divers freemen lying empty and uncultivated.*

Arllechwedd Isaf: *Remittance of 5s. 2d. annual rent of the customs and services of*

among the 'advowry' tenants and 'nativi', to the dearth of officials and to the higher receipts from the Seal. Almost all the villeins of Deganwy died, their lands being leased to a certain Glodyth for eight years. Tenements of the villein hamlets of Arllechwedd Isaf were, in the words of the account, 'handed over to oblivion' and new tenements established. The little manor of Hirdref in Dinllaen (Lleyn) was farmed for one year only, because assessment could not be made for a longer period owing to the great loss of tenants. Many escheated lands and tenements scattered throughout the various 'vills' of the same commote were farmed with the manor of Bodifan and other lands in the county of Anglesey for a sum of £50. The villein hamlet of Redemknelyn in Eifionydd yielded after the pestilence only 5s. for its dues of oatmeal and butter, instead of £1 8s. as previously. The heavy decays in the Anglesey accounts are not repeated in all the commotes of Caernarvon, although in Commote Cafflogion the uncultivated lands of freemen dying without heirs showed a loss of over £4 a year.

By the end of the year 1349 the epidemic had very generally subsided, but from the Court Rolls we learn that in Ruthin a few deaths were still being attributed to the same cause in 1351 and 1354. These occurred only occasionally during the period 1357-60. The winter of 1361-62, however, saw another, though milder, outbreak referred to as the Second Pestilence.[1] The disease then almost disappeared until the summer of 1369, after which time it is seen to have spent its force.

The later epidemics are also traceable in the adjoining County of Flint,[2] in the lordship of Denbigh,[3] and to some extent in Anglesey and Caernarvon. One-third of the farm of the town of Montgomery, also, had to be remitted. Many tenements in the 'patria' were vacant after 1361, and the 'cylch' payment of the Commote of Teirtref was much reduced owing to fewness of inhabitants.[4]

---

the villeins of the king for 13 *bovates of land with easements which were handed over to oblivion on the making of the extent.*

[1] Court Rolls, Portfolio 219/1. Ruthyn: *Edmund ap Madoc ap David qui tenuit unum Burgum in Novo Vico decessit in Secunda Pestilencia.*

[2] Min. Acc., Bundle 1186, No 23; Bundle 1187, Nos. 11, 12.

[3] Min. Acc., Bundle 1182, No. 5; Bundle 1183.

[4] Min. Acc., Bundle 1206, No. 3.

On turning again to South Wales, we find that the plague of 1361 visited the plain of Glamorgan, especially the lordship of Ogmore and its 'Welshry' of Eglwys Keynor (Llangeinor). The manor of Caldicot had by this time lost about 4 gafolmen, 14 customary tenants, 19 cottars, and several holders of assart land, a loss which resulted in a deficit of rents of £3 2s. 9¾d. from that source alone, while the custom of serjeantry only brought in the sum of 4½d., as the tenants who had been responsible for this particular payment had died.

In the Upper Gwent area, on the other hand, the outbreak which was sufficiently severe to be known as the Second Pestilence was that of 1369, while important changes, reflected in the issue of new rentals, occur again as late as 1382. The epidemic of 1369 was generally severe in south-eastern Wales, but it is impossible to estimate its extent since the documents group the losses to the lord from this plague with those still outstanding from the previous 'death'. Trellech borough lost nearly one-third of its burgesses, and there was a corresponding diminution in the rents of the tenants of Llangwm (Usk). The manor of New Grange (Usk) was badly affected, and certain of the customary tenants of Tisset died. This decay in the rents, caused directly by the pestilence, continued to be recorded for many decades in Usk manor and borough, in Tregrug, Troye, Caerleon and Edlogan the losses in the manor of Llantrissent being particularly heavy.[1] Similar effects are seen in the lordships of Monmouth and the Three Castles. During the same year the customary tenants of Caldicot were further reduced to four and the lands let to strangers. This formerly large and flourishing manor had within twenty years been reduced to insignificance as a direct result of the plague.

Along the plain of Glamorgan the epidemic of 1369 is traceable at Leckwith, at Ogmore and again at Llantwit Major, where 147 acres of villein land escheated to the lord.[2] The demesnes, before many years, were put to farm, as also were those of Oystermouth, Llandimore and other Gower manors. The manor of Bronllys (Brec.) also shows traces of having been affected, certain of the customary services having lapsed owing to the death of villeins. Several of the advowry tenants, too,

[1] Min. Acc., Bundle 928, *passim.*
[2] Inq. p.m., C. Edw. III, File 253.

died, though in the neighbouring manor of Brecon in the same year few signs of the disease can be observed.

This brief survey of these years would lead us to believe that the pestilence did not attack with equal force all parts of Wales. It is on the manors that the effects are most clearly seen. The seriousness of the blow to many made even the semblance of recovery difficult. The appearance of the disease at the critical sowing season brought about a heavy reduction not only in the rents, but in the total receipts of the manor. The problem of obtaining a revenue at once presented itself to the lord, who accommodated himself to the new circumstances by renting out his lands. Consequently, in succeeding years, the revenue of the manor was again noticeably on the increase, and occasionally, within a brief period, the original totals were even exceeded. But agriculture on the manorial pattern was no longer developed. No expenditure was incurred either in labour, implements, or in material. Sales of corn, stock, or miscellaneous products ceased. Such manors became solely units for the collection of rents. Others, less directly affected, were able to retain their organisation for the time, only to be involved in the economic disturbances which followed. The manors of Brecon, Bronllys, Roath (Cardiff), Llantwit Major and Ogmore still continued cultivation on a considerable scale, the first-named maintaining a vigorous existence even after the two pestilences.

It is a matter of surprise that sheep-farming was not widely adopted as an alternative for meeting the new situation that had arisen. This was possibly due to the fact that Welsh wool had a poor sale in the markets of the time. Only in the lordships of the middle-eastern March was there a considerable and rapid development in this direction, probably representing the expansion into Wales at this point of the wool-growing industry of Herefordshire and Salop. By the reign of Richard II the manor of La Royl (Clyro) and the neighbouring grange of Gabalfa in Elvael (Rads.) had between them a flock of over 1000 sheep belonging to the lord of Painscastle. The Bohun lordships of Brecon, Bronllys, Hay and Huntington are particularly noticeable in this connection. The manor of Huntington had over 300 sheep, Hay had 335, and at Brecon a flock of nearly 1000 is recorded in 1373, more than 400 being purchased in that year alone, though agriculture still flourished in these manors. The chief sheep-farm was at Bronllys, which had over 1000 sheep distributed among the hill-farms of Gwenddwr, Troscoed and Llaneglwys. These were formerly the grazing-grounds of the monks of Dore, but were now rented by the lord from the monks. The Bohun manors furnish the best examples in Wales at this time of the production of wool on a commercial scale, the amount derived from all the manors being considerable. The wool was either sold in the same year or allowed to accumulate. In the year 1373 it reached the high total of 18,500 fleeces, 3000 of which were packed and sent to Blanche Appleton,[1] 6000 were sold, and the remainder reserved for future sale.

During the succeeding years, notwithstanding the vitality thus displayed by certain manors, the practice of letting the demesne gained ground. Labour troubles were undoubtedly an important cause, but it is probable that the renting of the land proved both profitable and convenient. One by one the manors as agricultural 'units' were being reduced to the same stage of decadence, and that by the rapid extension of those processes which are noted in their incipient stages at a much earlier date. The miscellaneous elements of the manor were among the first to be involved in the change. The courts were held less frequently and their perquisites were reduced. The garden was let out as pasture; the dove-cote and the fish-stew remained unstocked or were farmed; the ferry-boat was hired out; the profits from pannage and timber declined, and the quarries were let. The letting of the mills became now almost universal, and these were often leased for life or for a period of years. In a lease of this character the suit of the customary tenants who remained was also transferred, and it was usual for the lord to undertake the heavier repairs to the building, to replace the millstones, and to reconstruct the weir in case of 'grand-breach'.[2]

The system of letting out the pastures was extended to every available plot for which offers could be obtained, including even the parks and old stubble or 'frisc' land. The hay of the meadows was sold in the fields, or the meadows were leased often on condition of being en-

---

[1] A Bohun manor in Co. Essex, convenient to the London market.

[2] E.g., Grosmont: *£4-farm of the Mill of Grosmont let to William atte Hulle, from Michaelmas 36 Edw. III for 12 years, the lord to find the heavy timber and millstones only for repairs and to pay half the expenses.*

closed. It is of interest to note that the prices at which these lands were let were, on the whole, the same as those which prevailed formerly. Presumably this was to avoid competing with the rents already ruling, so that land often lay idle for the year, though possibly it could have been let at a lower figure. Lands thus remaining vacant were not uncommonly given to manorial officers to supplement dwindling incomes. Far larger portions of the demesne soon came to be rented.[1] The demesnes of Hay were let in gross to a few of the enterprising townsmen; those at Penkelly (Brec.) were leased for twelve years to one man. At Marshfield (Mon.) they were let in plots to those tenants who wished to avail themselves of the same but on the neighbouring manor of Rumney they were rented for ten years to the whole body of villeins on condition that they maintained the buildings, walls and ditches in an efficient state. The letting of the demesne did not necessarily include the services of the villeins or the buildings of the manor, both of which were sometimes disposed of separately. The stock and implements were usually sold, and only in one instance, at Huntington, can reference be found to the expedient of leasing the stock with the demesnes. In contrast with the above arrangements, whereby the manor was let in portions, stands the policy adopted by certain lords of farming out the whole manor as a unit at a fixed sum. The seignorial rights of the lord were not, however, included in such transactions, advowsons of churches and all royalties, including the perquisites of courts, being reserved by him.

The manor of Caldicot affords some interesting evidence during the years succeeding the Black Death. In spite of the great loss of life there, the demesne continued to be cultivated. Several of the servants were retained and a few customary services employed. Labour, too, was being hired and the stock was still considerable. By 1367 the value of the demesne land let totalled about £6 13s., at which figure it remained until the second pestilence two years later, when it rose to £7 10s., and the whole of the demesnes were farmed some years later at about £8 for the year. Cultivation ceased and the numerous other issues of the manor were collected separately, the services of the few

[1] E.g., Min. Acc., Bundle 1209, Nos. 5, 11, 12, 13, 14; Bundle 1236, Nos. 4 *et seq.*

remaining 'nativi' being sold. Early in the following century all the villeins are stated to have died, with the result that there was no one available to become reeve. The office was therefore replaced by that of a salaried bailiff whose work consisted solely of collecting the rents. The death of customary tenants on so large a scale presented a serious problem and resulted in further disintegration of the manor. An immediate effect was experienced in the lapse of the services and customary obligations of those who had died, for it was found difficult to revive the same in the case of new holders. Services were, therefore, only continued for those villeins who survived.[1] The disposal of the escheated land in villeinage figures largely in the business arrangements of the manor. Where possible it was re-let, leased in tenements or broken up into smaller parcels, and sometimes a number of holdings were grouped and farmed as one tenement. Cases occur where freemen assumed villein status upon taking up a customary holding. It was far more common, however, for the rent of the tenement to be approximately assessed at an increase on the original rental *plus* the value of the services, or the prices of the demesne land might be taken as the basis of estimate. In certain instances the lord allowed the holdings to be let at a lower rent or, for 'lack of hirers', they remained vacant.

In view of the greatly increased supply of available land and the decrease in population, it would be reasonable to assume that the land would be obtainable at cheap rates. This was not the case. No one reading the records for South Wales can fail to mark the tremendous transfer of land that was proceeding within the manors, and that at increased prices. Portions of the demesne, as well as the tenements of deceased bond-tenants, were being acquired by freemen, by villeins and even by cottars and strangers, many tenements of considerable size being built up. The demesne itself might represent but one of several larger tenements and thus have lost its original character as the nucleus of a manor.

The release of so large a proportion of land, therefore, had the effect of creating a new position on the manor within a comparatively brief period. The distinction between the different classes of land was

[1] E.g., 2s. *increased rent of 2 acres of 'native' land late of Wm. Macy in decay, let to John Saith to be held freely by him and his heirs for ever.*

fast disappearing, as, moreover, was the distinction in practice between the classes of tenants. Bondage was becoming a less prominent feature though the lord continued his hold on a substantial remainder of his villeins. It is evident that a greater degree of independence was being displayed by the villeins themselves. The customary tenants in Leweston and Pelcomb (Pem.) compelled the lord to remit for a money payment the obligation of any of them to become reeve, threatening to withdraw unless he complied with their request. Facilities for liberation, too, were once again beginning to offer themselves. Apart from the escheated villein land which was regranted as free land, many customary tenants were permitted on payment of an increased rent to hold their land freely, for the lord no longer required their services.[1] On certain manors a portion of the tenements came to be held by burgage tenure, whereby the holders were freed.[2] Villeins, too, were allowed on payment of a small annual fine (*capitagium*) to leave the lordship and dwell elsewhere.[3]

A section only of the tenantry, however, had been able to avail themselves of the opportunities thus opening up, but the large proportion must have felt keenly the difficulties of the period. Lack of cultivation had resulted in higher prices of foodstuffs, as, indeed, of all other commodities. The wages of the worker were slightly increased but not in proportion to the cost of living, for while workers were fewer in number, the demand for labour had also fallen. The lord, the chief employer in the past, now that his demesnes were let, had little need of labour. The individual tenement holders who had taken his place worked their own land with the aid of their families and hired as little labour as possible. Again many of the holdings, having been converted into pasture, required fewer workers. The labouring class was also receiving additions from the advowry tenants who were settling upon the manor at this time in increased numbers. The

[1] Rentals and Surveys. 13s. 8d. *Jeuan ap Griffith holds 4 acres of free land by extent and when it was native land he rendered thence at Michaelmas 1s. 2d. and for works at Michaelmas 10½d.*

[2] Min. Acc., No. 9056. 11½d. *increase of rent of Jeuan Vachan for three parts of one rood of 'native' land of his own land to hold for himself and heirs in one burgage.*

[3] Min. Acc., 924/18.

equilibrium of labour which had at first been disturbed by the Black Death was largely restored as a result of the policy of the lord in dissolving his demesne.

The consequences of the Black Death in the Welsh lands in each manor are more obscure. As in the case of the manor, the lord necessarily experienced immediate loss in rents and customs,[1] a loss for which he was, to a great extent, compensated in other ways. Issues derived from miscellaneous sources show a decline in value but the practice of 'farming' was now extended in many cases to include almost every item of the accounts.

Some reduction in revenue was caused by the death of chensers and advowry tenants, though the goods of those dying intestate became the property of the lord, and a fine was exacted from any who wished to withdraw from the district.[2] The most serious difficulty was experienced as a result of the death of the tenants. Welsh freemen, though still adhering very largely to tribal principles in their occupation of land, were officially assessed, on a quasi-feudal basis, as individual holders,

---

[1] E.g., Min. Acc., Bundle 1182, No. 3; 1183, No. 2. Denbigh Lordship, Caemerch Commote: *Respited £1 4s. 6d. for this year and the two preceding years, viz., 8s. 2d. a year, for customs and services of 7 nativi, viz., for each 1s. 2d., because they are included in the 31 'nativi' above, and there are only 24. Respited 3s. 4½d. for the services of 9 freemen, viz., for the same years, 1s. 1½d., because they are included in the 45 tenants and there are only 36.*

Uwchdulas: *Decay of rents and services of various 'gavells' with other rents £4 17s. 5⅝d.*

Uwchalet: *Whence he allows (to the Computor) for 'tunc' and custom of butter from 2 'gavells' of land in Llechtalhaern, because they are in the lord's hands for lack of service of the tenants, £1 0s. 10d.*

Min. Acc., Bundles 1149, 1150; Min. Acc., Bundle, 1171. Commote of Eifionydd: *In decay of rents of the 'vill' of Redemknelyn which was in the hands of villeins, vacant since the Pestilence, extended at £1 8s. for 8 'crannogs' of oatmeal and 3 vessels of butter, for which the Computor is charged above 5s. Respited £1 8s. 1½d. part of £1 17s. 3½d. rents of lands and tenements of free tenants in the lord's hands because there are no heirs, neither could anything be raised from the same.*

[2] Min. Acc., Bundle 1171, No. 7. Caernarvon, Commote of Creuthyn: *8d. advowry fine of Blethin ap Maddoc and David ap Maddoc . . . and no more because the remainder are dead by the Pestilence. Of the reliefs of 'advowry' tenants dead, from whom the lord has from each half a mark, and from the goods of the same which the lord shall have if they die without heir.*

the obligations of the holder being interpreted as the rent of the tenement, or 'gavell'. It must be understood that such an interpretation
could only apply to the immediate share of the household in arable, and
not to open wastes or pasture grounds of the kin. Death on so large a
scale naturally resulted in the escheat of many tenements of this kind.
The accustomed payments of 'ebediw' (heriot) from the goods of the
deceased or the payment of 'relief' by his heir, brought to the lord a
considerable immediate return. When no heirs came forward or when
they were too poor to pay the requisite fine, the holding was if possible
rented to others, though lack of applicants often made this difficult.
Expedients of agisting or of selling the herbage might then serve to
diminish the loss in some measure.[1] It seems clear that here again, as a
general policy, a strong effort was made to maintain the original rents
in disposing of the escheated lands, and instances even occur when
these figures were increased. In some commotes the community
was able to establish their claim of common to certain escheated
lands.[2]

The effects of the Black Death upon the revenue of the commotes of
South Wales were much less marked. The totals of escheated lands
were much lower, a fact that would lead us to suppose that the fatalities
were few in comparison with those of North Wales. Again, notwithstanding that the chief rents such as the 'gwestfa' (food-rents) and
the Rents of Extent had come to be assessed in many cases upon smaller
groups and even households, the commote was still responsible for the
payment of the full amount. Indeed, the outstanding feature in these
districts throughout the period is the persistence at the original figures

---

[1] Court Rolls, Portfolio 217, No. 14. Ruthin, Court of Colyan (Coleion):
*Llewelyn Seys who held English lands died in the Pestilence, from whose death came to
the lord, 1 horse. And afterwards Jeuan his son came and sought to be admitted to hold
the said lands, to whom it was granted, . . . saving the rights of the lord, and he paid
for relief 9s. 2d. and for rent 9s. 7d. Jeuan ap Heylin who held from the lord hereditary
lands and lands 'in acres' died . . . from whom there came heriot and 'gobrestin'. (The
nearest heir claimed and paid relief £1). David ap Maddoc who held from the lord
'native' land and 3 acres of free land in Wernlydyr, died in the Pestilence. Because he
has no heirs, it was conceded that Wladus his widow should hold it for life, performing
the various services due therefrom. And she pays no heriot or relief.*

[2] E.g., Min. Acc., Bundle 1182, No. 4. Talabryn.

of the old common assessments. Certain early evidence tends to show that tenements in decay were exempt from such rents, though the best testimony points to a contrary view, a condition which would impose a heavier burden upon survivors.

On all sides the unfree tenants of the Welsh lands suffered very real hardship as a result of the pestilence, and their villages were seriously depleted. This class of tenant held almost invariably by the tenure of 'trefgyfrif', according to which, upon the death of a holder, the land was redistributed equally among the remaining members who were responsible for all the dues of the 'tref'. The heavy death-rate, therefore, threw an almost insupportable burden on the remaining tenants of the vills compelling them in many cases to surrender their holdings and to join the ranks of the advowry. Such examples as the following are constantly found among the records of North Wales: '£2 13s. 4d., part of £6 13s. 4d. rents of the tenants of the villata of Cotimot [in decay] because five villeins are unable to hold the vill and can scarce pay the £4 0s. 2d.'[1]

'Decay of land of Meredith Benhir, escheat in Llanbigail, 15s. 6d. because no *one* tenant could hold it.'[2]

In the Commote of Malltraeth, Anglesey, long lists of lands in certain of the vills are vacant 'because the lord's tenants in the same 'vills' are incapable of holding the same and are *insufficient*'.[3] Occasionally, tenants are seen to resume their tenement after an interval, as did a certain Llewelyn ap Madoc ap Howel, of whom it is said that 'he left his land during the Pestilence on account of poverty, but now came (1354) and was admitted by the lord's favour to hold the said land by the service due from the same'.[4] The position of some was temporarily relieved by respiting the rents, but the situation was so serious in the

---

[1] E.g., Min. Acc., Bundle 1149, No. 1 — Commote of Twrcelyn.

[2] *Ibid.* — Commote of Talybolion.

[3] Min. Acc., Bundle 1149, No. 1 (mem. 3) — Commote of Malltraeth.
Commote of Talybolion: '*Native*' *Land;* 14s. 6d. *herbage of Villein land in Aberalaw which Madoc ap Philip, Eynon ap Philip, and 3 others (named), nativi, held for £1 12s. 2d., because the nativi who were surviving after the Pestilence were not 'sufficient', on account of their inability to hold the said lands.*

[4] Ruthin, Court Rolls, Portfolio 218, No. 4.

northern Principality that in July 1352 a general order was issued on the advice of the Council of the Prince of Wales to the Justice's Deputy and Chamberlain of North Wales relieving the villeins and men of advowry of each commote from their obligation to contribute cattle for the munitioning of the castle (*staurum principis*). The terms of the order were retrospective, and were to continue until conditions improved.[1]

The reversion to the lord, not only of the land 'in acres', assarted land and native land, but also of the 'hereditary land', had important consequences. It enabled the lord to assume direct hold over the tenure of a far larger part of the lands of the commote. These lands were usually let on a yearly tenancy or on a lease to the highest bidder, although it is true that a proportion was still unoccupied even fifty years later.[2] As on the manors, however, much land changed hands about this time. Men who were able added to their own tenements or acquired others. New holdings were established, some on a considerable scale. Greater mobility is seen, and the opening up of opportunities

---

[1] Min. Acc., Bundle 1171, Nos. 7 and 8 — Commote of Creuddyn:

Store of the Prince (*Staurum Principis*): *5s. 4d., received from half of the value of 2 cows which the community of the Commote (viz. the Villains and men of advowry) used to give to the lord's lardar for munitioning the castle of Conway — a cow appraised @ 5s. 4d. this year. Nothing received from half the value of one ox which the lord was accustomed to have from the community for the same store, because it was remitted owing to the poverty and fewness of the tenants. Sum 5s. 4d.*

Text of Remission: '*Edward, etc., Prince, to the Deputy of the Justice of North Wales and to the Chamberlain there:*

'*Because of our especial grace and by the advice of the Council, We have respited to our bond tenants and the people of our advowry, the money for which our Auditors of Accounts have charged them to find for the "garnestures" of our castles in your bailiwicks, since the time of the pestilence. We ask you to cease to levy the said money until further command.*

Given under our privy seal, London, 30 July, 26, Edw. III.'

[2] Ministers' Accounts and Court Rolls during these years record long lists of lands and tenements transferred.

Min. Acc., 1182/3. Isalet: *Allowed 'Tunk' and other customs of $\frac{1}{4}$ part of 1 'gavell' of land of Cadarn within the parts of Lewenny which Thomas ap Lowarch held there and which came into the lord's hands. The lord gave it to John de le More to hold in the English manner for rent.*

for individual initiative seems to have encouraged the renting of larger tenements than had formerly been the custom, and members of kindreds frequently came to occupy lands irrespective of their fellows and additional to their kindred holding. The cumulative effect of such circumstances, therefore, is to be seen in the gradual breaking away from tribal customs and the establishment more and more of direct tenure and personal responsibility. The social cleavage between tribesmen and non-tribesmen based upon descent, was now giving place to an economic distinction. Greater inequality existed even among land-holders themselves, while the landless class was on the increase. That the latter experienced difficulty in obtaining employment may be gathered from references made to their leaving the 'Welshries' in search of work. In the 'Englishries' we are not able to trace any restrictions on wages, for English statutes did not apply over the border, but some restrictive measures had been in operation from the time of Edward I in the Commotes of the Principality. Servants were not permitted to receive more than a certain wage 'according to the Statute of the patria', and workers were from time to time fined in the commote courts for breach of the Statute. The whole community of servants of Mabelvew (Carmarthen) were on one occasion fined for this reason, but in the March lands no restrictions of such a nature appear. The renewed prominence given to the Statute in the late fourteenth century points to a rise in wages beyond the former limits, but the policy was hardly one of strict adherence to the regulation. The community of workers, upon payment of a fine, was tacitly permitted, at least in certain years, to break the Statute and wages would thus tend to find their natural level.

It cannot be supposed that the economic strain and a social upheaval, which frequently had the effect of estranging men from their inherited rights in land, could fail to give rise to serious unrest among a people subject to alien rule. Administrative evils and a system of exploitation served but to add to racial hostility, and before the effects of the Black Death had culminated in the new economy observable in the manors and 'Welshries', the situation was seriously complicated by the outbreak of the Glyndŵr rebellion, which was far more disastrous to the economic life of Wales than even the ravages of the Pestilence. The final consequences of the Black Death, therefore, are lost in the devastation of war.

[NOTE: The subject has been further dealt with by the Author in *South Wales and the March, 1284-1415 — A Social and Agrarian Study*, Oxford University Press, 1924, and in *Proceedings of the Royal Society of Medicine*, xvi (1923).]

WILLIAM REES

10 The Organisation of Indentured Retinues in Fourteenth-century England

The fourteenth century is an important period in the history of aristocratic retinues in England not only because it was a period of some considerable activity on their part but because it was one in which their leaders, adapting themselves to the general change in the structure of society, began to develop new forms of retinue organised on the principle of personal contract in place of the out-dated principle of tenurial loyalty.[1]

The development of these new retinues is traditionally regarded as a retrograde step in social organisation. They are criticised as a 'bastard' form of feudalism; the personal contract on which they were based is said to have lacked the 'stability of the tenurial relationship';[2] and they themselves, unlike the 'voluntary associations of lord and man which had prevailed in the tenth century', are described as having been 'unfettered by legal restrictions, and as time went on increasingly indifferent to right and wrong'.[3] In consequence, they helped in a large measure to break up late medieval society by loosening the ties of traditional loyalty and obedience, by dislocating the work of public assemblies, by laying violent hands on disputed property in the interests of their lords, and by giving them the opportunity, if not the motive, for civil war.

And as far as some of the new forms of retinue are concerned the

---

[1] I am indebted to Professor V. H. Galbraith for many helpful criticisms and suggestions in the preparation of this paper.

[2] H. M. Cam, 'The Decline and Fall of English feudalism', in *History*, xxv. 225.

[3] J. E. A. Jolliffe, *The constitutional history of medieval England*, p. 424.

truth of these charges cannot be denied. But there was more than one type of retinue based on the principle of personal contract. The statute[1] of 1390, which deals in greater detail than any previous legislation with the formation of these retinues, recognises three distinct types: first, resident household attendants; secondly, men who are bound by written indenture to serve their lord for life in peace and war; and thirdly, those whose attachment to the lord is shown simply by the acceptance of his fees and the wearing of his badge and livery. And it is against the third of these types that almost all contemporary criticism is directed.[2] It is they who are denounced as 'Maintainers, instigators, barretors, procurers and embracers of quarrels': and whom lords are eventually forbidden to engage, while the other two types are accepted as legitimate and are expressly allowed to wear their master's livery as the outward sign of their allegiance.[3]

In the case of the household attendants the reason for this distinction is plain. It was indispensable for men of property to have servants to administer their affairs, to maintain their state and dignity, and to protect their property and person from attack.[4] And household retainers had, from time immemorial, discharged these services without developing the undesirable characteristics of the purely liveried retainer. Having regular duties and specified rewards they were not under temptation to secure illicit patronage by illegitimate forms of service; living in their lord's immediate presence they could be effectively controlled; and enjoying a stable tenure of office they were not subject to those rapid changes of allegiance which contributed so

---

[1] 13 Richard II, statute 3 (*Stat. Realm*, ii. 75).

[2] *Ordinatio de Conspiratoribus*, statutes 20 Edw. III c. 1, 1 Ric. II c. 7, and 13 Ric. II statute 3 (*Stat. Realm*, i. 145, 303, 304; ii. 3, 75).

[3] *Ibid.*, ii. 75: though the right to give livery to retainers of both types is limited to laymen of the rank of banneret upwards, and indentured retainers who receive it must be of the rank of knight or squire.

[4] Public opinion had long recognised the right of magnates to give such retinues their livery, as is shown in the thirteenth-century reference, which Lady Stenton discovered, to the robber chief who clothed his band in uniform 'as if he had been a baron or an earl' (quoted by H. M. Cam, *op. cit.*, p. 224).

largely to making the purely liveried retainer a menace to ordered society.[1]

But why indentured retainers should have enjoyed the same approval is not so clear. They were not, like household attendants, old-established members of society in the early fourteenth century; and though the fact that they were retained by indenture implies that they had a more binding attachment to their lords than the purely liveried retainer, it tells us nothing more about their character and functions. And these are the less easy to ascertain because their numbers were never, in all probability, very large and they received, for the greater part of the century, very little public attention; no mention being apparently made in the legislature till the fifth year of Edward III's reign of even the limited group of such retainers who served the king,[2] and no specific legislation being enacted about the general body of indentured retainers till the century was almost over.[3] They were, therefore, at one time, regarded by historians as being essentially a development of the later years of the century when, in the words of Stubbs,[4] 'in the troubled times of Richard II . . . the necessities of private defence compelled the great households to revive the practice of private war'. But of late years an increasing number of much earlier examples of this form of contract has come to light[5] and we now have ample evidence of the existence of indentured retainers from the late thirteenth century onwards, in the text of some two hundred examples of the contracts, surviving either in the original or in registered copies, and in contemporary references to others whose full text is no longer available.[6]

[1] Mr. McFarlane has recently drawn attention ('Parliament and "bastard feudalism"', below 260-1) to the extreme instability of their allegiance and the undesirable results of that instability.

[2] *Rot. Parl.*, ii. 62, § 18, and *Cal. Close Rolls*, 1330-3, p. 390.

[3] Above, p. 201, n. 2.   [4] *Const. Hist.* (5th edn.), p. 559.

[5] E.g., H. G. Richardson and G. O. Sayles, *The Governance of Mediaeval England*, p. 464; J. E. Morris, *The Welsh wars of Edward I*, p. 278; N. Denholm-Young, *Seignorial administration in England*, p. 23, and J. Conway Davies, *The baronial opposition to Edward II*, p. 36. Mr. Conway Davies also calls attention to the very widespread use of written bonds and verbal oaths of alliance as a means of building up parties and confederacies for political purposes on the principle of personal contract.

[6] Considerations of space prevent the quotation of examples, but consider-

And from this evidence it seems clear that the indentured retinue played an important part in, and made a valuable contribution to, the working of two contemporary institutions: the contract army, increasingly used by Edward I in the closing years of the thirteenth century and brought to its full development by his grandson in the Hundred Years' War,[1] and the baronial household.

Co-operation between the indentured retinue and the contract army was, of course, made easy and natural by the fact that both were based on the same general principle and raised by the same methods. The king, that is, raised his army, as the barons did their retinues, by concluding personal and voluntary contracts with particular individuals to serve under agreed conditions in return for specified payments and allowances: the terms of the agreements being, as in the case of the private retinue, embodied in formal indentured contracts, written out in two identical copies, sealed alternately with the seals of both parties, so that each might have in his possession a permanent record of the terms to which he had bound himself, duly authenticated by the seal of the other. And it is clear from the indentures of retinue that most of the retainers so engaged were intended to find a place in the national system. For not only do the great bulk of indentures impose on the retainer the duty of serving under his lord in time of war, but the detailed conditions of this service, as laid down in the contracts, conform very closely to those obtaining in the national system. The retainers, that is, are to bring specified contingents to serve for given periods, they are to receive fees and wages according to their rank, compensation for their horses lost on service and the cost of shipping if the expedition goes abroad; while the lord, in return, enjoys a share

---

able numbers are in print in two of the volumes of John of Gaunt's Register published in R. Hist. Soc., Camden 3rd Series, xx. 288–350, and lvi. 13–26 (referred to below as Reg. I and III respectively). Other printed copies are referred to below and a number are fairly fully summarised in J. Bain, *Cal. of documents relating to Scotland*, ii, nos. 905, 1407, 1899; in the *Catalogues of ancient deeds*, iv, nos. A. 6404 and 8019, v. no. A. 11547, and in Dugdale's *Baronage*, i. 183, 780.

[1] See Morris, *Welsh wars*, and A. E. Prince, 'The indenture system under Edward III', in *Hist. essays in honour of James Tait*, pp. 283–97.

of the ransom of the prisoners they capture or other profits of war which they secure.[1]

And from this close association with the contract army the indentured retinue certainly derived considerable support. The king's use of indentured contracts for military service must have helped considerably to spread the use of the indenture of retinue among the aristocracy by familiarising all classes of the nation with the forms of contract organisation. The frequent levy of contract troops by the king enabled lords to increase the size of their retinues by giving them increased opportunities for employing the retainers in the national army and thereby recouping a part of the cost of their peace-time maintenance. It also facilitated the task of selecting new recruits by bringing lords into contact with potential retainers outside the limited circle of their own neighbourhood and tenantry, and by giving lord and retainer an opportunity of testing each other's quality and of acquiring the mutual loyalty and confidence necessary for the more intimate form of service. And quite possibly it was from the contract army that lords derived the practice of sub-contracting — of engaging retainers, that is, not only to serve in person but to raise by a series of sub-contracts a subordinate troop to serve the lord under their command, thereby greatly assisting him to develop and control his retinue by relieving him of the responsibility for selecting, equipping and commanding its rank and file.

The benefits of the association of the contract army and the indentured retinue are not, however, all on one side. In the matter of recruitment, for example, the contracts give no support to the suggestion sometimes made that indentured retainers were merely a selection of military subordinates, discharged after the war and re-engaged by their commanders for peace-time service. They were engaged, in the overwhelming majority of cases, not by a succession of temporary contracts to serve in war and then in peace, but by one permanent and all-embracing life-contract to serve in both;[2] and though lords may, in

---

[1] Most of these points are illustrated in John of Gaunt's contracts (above, p. 202, n. 6).

[2] There are a few temporary contracts for peace service only (e.g. the fifteen months' contract between the earl of Pembroke and Sir Robert Fitzpain (Bain *op. cit.*, ii, no. 1407)), and a certain number of contracts for limited periods of

some cases, have made their first contact with their retainers by commanding them in the contract army, far more often, it seems from a study of their personal careers, their association developed directly from the ordinary contacts of civilian life and brought recruits to the army who, if they had not entered into the peace-time bond, might not have engaged themselves for purely military service.

And this permanent, lifelong character of the military obligation imposed by the indenture of retinue, moreover, strengthened the contract army just at its weakest point. For the king rarely engaged the services of any purely military contractor for more than a single year at a stretch and very often for no more than six or even fewer months.[1] When the campaign was over the troops disbanded, and the king had no guarantee either that any particular commander would be prepared to serve or that his troopers would re-engage themselves with him. So that the contract forces had a fluctuating and somewhat unreliable personnel in comparison with that of the feudal army which they replaced. This defect was remedied, to some extent, within the framework of the military system by individual leaders who drew up purely military sub-contracts with some of their subordinates, engaging them for considerable periods, or even for life, to give military service whenever it might be required.[2] But such contracts are rare and, in the main, it was the members of the indentured retinues, retained to serve their lords for life in peace and war, who mitigated the instability of the contract army by providing a force always ready and under contract to serve whenever it was required. Its numbers may not have been large in proportion to the total size of any troop, but it was at least a nucleus round which the other less stable elements could collect, and the support which the indentured retinues gave in this way to the national military

---

service in peace and war (e.g. the earl of Hereford's contract with Sir Thomas Mandeville for a year's service (Ancient Deed, L. 1981)), but the vast majority of known contracts in which peace service is included are for life in both peace and war. No instance appears to be known of a retainer being engaged for war and then for peace, or vice versa.

[1] Prince, *op. cit.*, p. 291.

[2] The Black Prince, for example, entered into several such engagements (*Cal. Pat. Rolls, 1377–81*, pp. 192, 249 and 345).

system, both by bringing it recruits and by increasing its stability, supplies us with one reason for the favourable attitude to them of contemporary legislation.

A still stronger reason can be found in the relation of the indentured retinue to the baronial household which is revealed by the terms of the indentures. Contracts differ, of course, considerably in the particularity with which they state the terms of service. In some cases they merely lay down in general terms that the retainer shall 'serve' or 'stay with' or 'be retained in the service of' the lord. But in most cases it is clear that regular, personal attendance on the lord and in his household, not only in times of exceptional need but also on the normal occasions of both private and public life, is one of the essential purposes of the retainer's service. Most commonly it is laid down that the retainer shall come to the lord on his summons, and though, in some cases, this liability is limited to service in England or the British Isles, in others it is explicitly extended overseas, sometimes to service in the Holy Land and very often, as in most of John of Gaunt's numerous contracts, to service with the lord 'wherever he will'. And in many cases the nature of the occasions when the retainer may be required to attend is explicitly defined: he shall come to his lord at tournaments,[1] at parliaments and other assemblies:[2] sometimes he is to ride with the lord,[3] to take counsel with him[4] or to join him in his recreations:[5] and not infrequently it is explicitly laid down that he is to be 'menial with the lord',[6] to 'attend him in his court',[7] to 'be in the household' by the lord's command,[8] or, very

[1] Henry Percy and Ralph Neville: *Percy Chartulary* (Surtees Society, vol. 117), p. 274.

[2] The earl of Lancaster and Sir Philip Darcy: Ancient Deed, L. 3254.

[3] The earl of Nottingham and Sir Thomas de Clinton: *Patent Roll*, 1 Henry IV, pt. i, m. 15.

[4] See above, n. 2.

[5] The earl of Lancaster and Sir John Eure: Bodleian Library, MS. Dugdale 18, f. 39 v.

[6] The earl of Warwick and Walter Power: *Cal. Pat. Rolls, 1391-6*, p. 465.

[7] The duke of Gloucester and William Cheney: *Patent Roll, 1 Henry IV*, pt. iii, m. 8.

[8] The duke of Exeter and Thomas Proudfoot: *ibid.*, pt. vi, m. 18.

formally in one case, 'to be in the household at his will, to do him honour and service'.[1] So that though the indentured retainer was not, in general, permanently resident in his lord's household,[2] his regular duties were clearly those of a household and personal attendant. And even in the discharge of his military obligations he was simply continuing or reviving an older household tradition. For, as Professor Stenton has shown,[3] in the early days of the feudal régime in England, it was with knights retained in his household that the tenant-in-chief discharged his feudal service. The process of sub-infeudation no doubt relieved the majority of household knights of this form of service in due course, but it never, perhaps, entirely died out; and even as late as 1276 we find a tenant-in-chief, Maurice de Berkeley, proffering his

[1] See p. 206, n. 3.

[2] In one or two cases, as in that of John Darcy, who was retained in 1309 as a yeoman 'to serve diligently about the person' of the earl of Pembroke (Ancient Deed, L. 6404), it seems that the retainer must have been in more or less constant attendance. But the statute of 1390, as we have seen, makes a clear distinction between the indentured retainer and the resident household attendant (above p. 201), and in the great majority of cases the contracts also make it clear, either by laying down that the retainer shall come to the lord whenever he is summoned, or by specifying, as most of John of Gaunt's contracts do (p. 202, n. 6), that he shall have wages or travelling expenses from the time when he leaves his own home on the lord's summons, that normally he maintained his own household and came into residence or attendance on the lord, only for limited periods as and when he was required. And sometimes the lord is under obligation to give quite a substantial period of notice of his requirements — a month in the case of Hugh Despenser and Sir Peter Ovedale (*Cat. Anc. Deeds*, iv. no. A 8019).

But this intermittency of attendance was probably common among existing forms of household retinue. Knights and squires who had estates of their own must have had substantial periods of leave to attend to their affairs; and we find indications of an arrangement similar to that of the fourteenth-century indentured retainer, for example, in Walter Map's statement (*De Nugis Curialium*, Camden Soc. vol. 1. Dist. V, Ch. vi. p. 224) of Henry I of England: 'Quemcunque juvenem infra montes Alpium audiebat captantem boni famam principii ascribebat familiae . . . et quandocunque contigisset ab ipso mandari, suscipiebat in adventu suo singulis diebus a recessu residentiae suae singulos solidos.'

[3] *First century of English feudalism*, pp. 139–45.

feudal service of three knights in the persons of himself, his son and one of his domestic knights.[1]

The same identity with normal household service is equally apparent in some of the rewards which the indentured retainer received[2] — diet at the lord's table for himself and his subordinates, fodder and supplies for his horses, and the explicit grant of 'household wages'[3] being compatible only with personal attendance. In some cases also there are such obviously domestic allowances as that of candles for the retainer's room,[4] while in one contract, that of Sir Thomas Berkeley with the earl of Pembroke,[5] it is explicitly laid down that the retainer shall be provided with lodging in the household if there is surplus room when the regular attendants are accommodated.

It is clear, therefore, that in the nature both of his services and of his rewards, the position of the indentured retainer was almost identical with that of the already-existing household knight; and the only material difference between the two is that the lords, in their perpetual search for new ways of ensuring the personal loyalty of their followers, had imposed on them the obligation of giving a binding written acknowledgment of their undertakings.

[1] John Smyth, in his *Lives of the Berkeleys* (vol. i, p. 169), gives the names of the three knights and, relying presumably on a household account or other family record, states that the third member of the troop was a 'domesticke knight' of the leader. And as far as the names of the three are concerned he is confirmed by the official Marshal's register in *Parl. Writs.*, i. 212.

[2] These, like the exact extent of the services to be rendered, vary considerably from one retinue to another, and even between members of the same retinue holding the same rank and having the same obligations. And some of them, it is true, do not necessarily imply personal attendance. The commonest and most valuable of all, for example the fixed annual fee, paid generally in cash from a specified treasury or manor, or sometimes, as in the earl of Norfolk's contract with Sir John Segrave (N. Denholm-Young, *op. cit.*, p. 167), taking the form of an outright grant of land itself: or the equally common grant of robes and saddles, although normal forms of reward to the household attendant, are not necessarily proof of residence. But the other forms of allowance, which are compatible only with residence, are equally common and almost equally important.

[3] The duke of Exeter and Thomas Proudfoot. (Above, p. 206, n. 8.)

[4] The earl of Lancaster and Sir Philip Darcy. (Above, *ibid.*, n. 2).

[5] Exch. Accts., 68/1, m. 1: summarised by Bain, *op. cit.*, ii. no. 905.

This difference, however, is fundamental, because it brought a new element of stability into the retainer's relations with his lord. They had not, of course, the stability of the tenurial relationship but, on the other hand, they avoided the rigidity of the hereditary bond which must, at times, have strained the tenant's personal loyalty. Lord and retainer, in the indentured relationship, had complete freedom in their choice of each other and, normally, took full advantage of this freedom to make as sure as possible that the choice would be congenial enough to be enduring. Very frequently lords and retainers were men whose geographical proximity gave them considerable opportunity of realising each other's character and capacity. And it seems, further, that often enough the retainer would serve the lord, intermittently or continuously, for a considerable period before the binding indentured contract was entered into. In some cases the contracts themselves make this clear by stating that the retainer's fee is the reward, not only of the services he is undertaking in the future, but of the good service he had already given in the past,[1] and in some retinues we can find cases of retainers who seem to have done as much as fifteen years' probationary service before entering on their formal indentures.[2]

But once the indenture was concluded it was a very stable and a strictly binding contract. From the retainer's point of view the obligation it established was an exclusive and an over-riding one, binding him not only to serve his lord, but to serve him 'before all others'[3] and to serve him on all occasions within the scope of the agreement. Some relaxation of this absolute obligation might, it is true, be made in individual cases. Contracts, for example, sometimes exempt the re-

---

[1] E.g., Henry, earl of Lancaster and Sir Edmund Ufford (Ancient Deed, L.S. 155): the earl of Salisbury and Sir Edmund Doumer (*ibid.*, B. 4915): *Gaunt's Register*, i. nos. 802, 823, 835 and 849.

[2] Henry Green, for instance, whose name appears in the list of John of Gaunt's knights drawn up between 1379 and 1383 (Reg. III, p. 7), and who, as early as November 1379, was drawing a fee as 'nostre bien ame bacheler' (Duchy of Lancaster Misc. Books, 14, f. 20), does not seem to have been indentured till 1391 (*Cal. Pat. Rolls*, 1396-9, p. 522). Similarly, though the name of William Holme appears in the list of squires in 1379-83 (Reg. III, p. 11), there is no indenture for anyone of that name till 1397 (*ibid.*, p. 564).

[3] The duke of Exeter and Thomas Proudfoot esq. (above p. 206, n. 8).

tainer from service on an occasion when his own affairs urgently require his personal attention — as for a lawsuit; he may have latitude to decide for himself, in the case of any particular campaign or Crusade, if he will go or not;[1] or if, on the other hand, the lord decides not to go on some particular Crusade[2] or expedition,[3] or if he doesn't require the retainer for a particular tourney,[4] the retainer may, for that occasion, take service with some other lord. On the other hand, the retainer may have to seek the lord's permission to go abroad on his own affairs[5] and, in any case, the lord to whom he is indentured has always the first claim and, normally, the only claim on his services. Unlike the lawyer who may take retaining fees from many clients, or even the feudal tenant who may hold lands from many overlords, his allegiance, once pledged, is indivisible.[6]

And not only is it exclusive but, normally at any rate, it is also permanent. For though, in a few cases, as we have seen, the duration of the bond is limited to a short period of months or years or is left indefinite,[7] in the majority of cases the engagement is for life: and contracts frequently give very explicit safeguards to ensure the fulfilment of the bargain on both sides. In one extreme case the retainer is even protected by a clause laying down that he shall not be dismissed

[1] As in William Daventre's contract (*Pat. Roll, 1 Henry IV*, pt. v, m. 24).

[2] The earl of Hereford and Sir Bartholomew Denefeud (Bain, *op. cit.*, ii, no. 1899).

[3] John of Gaunt and Sir William Beauchamp (Reg. I, no. 832, p. 332). William Daventre also, apparently, is free to go to war with another leader if his lord gives permission (above, n. 1).

[4] The earl of Pembroke and John Darcy (*Cat. Anc. Deeds*, v, no. A. 11547).

[5] As in William Daventre's contract (above, n. 2).

[6] This is stated with particular explicitness in the very detailed and interesting contract of Sir John Segrave with the earl of Norfolk printed by Mr. Denholm-Young (*op. cit.*, p. 168) and referred to above (p. 208, n. 2): 'E il ne lyra james al avaunt dist sir Johan, taunt come le dist counte vist, a autre seignur demorer por nul fee ne bienfet ke em lui pusse doner saunz le gre e le volunte le Counte e ceo ad il premis e plein au Counte en sa bone leaute.'

[7] Above, p. 204, n. 2. Other examples are: Hugh le Despenser the elder and Sir Robert Fitzwalter for six months (Ancient Deed, A.S. 271); the earl of Pembroke and Sir Thomas Berkeley for an indefinite period (Bain, *op. cit.*, ii, no. 905).

except for reasonable cause: the reasonableness of the cause being judged by a tribunal of five independent arbitrators whose names are included in the contract, and who are also empowered to deal with any complaints which either the lord or his retainer may have against the other.[1] And it is quite common for the lord to give security to the retainer by submitting lands on which the retainer's fee is assigned to distraint if the fee is withheld or is in arrear for more than a limited period.[2]

The lord similarly is provided with safeguards against failure of service on the part of the retainer. Sometimes the retainer reinforces his written bond by a solemn oath on the Gospels to observe its terms;[3] in other cases he, like the lord, submits his lands and property to distraint or enters into recognisances for the payment of a substantial sum — sometimes as much as a thousand marks — if he is found at any time to have failed in loyalty to the lord.[4] And quite commonly the contract contains a clause explicitly entitling the lord to withhold payment of the retainer's fee or to cancel it altogether if he fails in the performance of his services.[5]

And the retainer had a further strong incentive, once he had engaged himself, to fulfil his obligations loyally. For the annual fee which was his principal reward was not only a payment for active service during the joint lives of himself and his lord, but was a pension which he continued to draw without further service if he had remained faithful to his engagements during the lord's life and survived him after his death. Contracts, in fact, sometimes explicitly submit the lands and property of the lord's heirs to distraint as security for the payment of these pensions;[6] and the number of retainers who sought confirmation of them

[1] Sir Ralph Hastings and John de Kirkby (Huntington Library, Hastings MS., no. 934: summarised in Hist. MSS. Comm., no. 78 (Hastings MSS.), vol. i, p. 198. [2] E.g., Reg. I, nos. 830, 832.

[3] The earl of Lancaster and Sir Philip Darcy (Ancient Deed, L. 3254).

[4] The younger Despenser and Sir Peter Ovedale (*Cat. Anc. Deeds*, iv. no. A. 8019); Sir Stephen Segrave and Sir Nicholas Cryel (Berkeley Castle, *Select charters*, no. 490). [5] See above, n. 3.

[6] Sir John Bluet and William Marcel (British Museum, Addit. Chart., no, 1531) and the earl of Hereford and William de Stapleton (*Pat. Roll, 47 Ed. III* pt. i, m. 23).

from the king after their lords' death,[1] shows not only how much importance was attached to them, but also how many retainers were enabled, by loyal service, to enjoy them. Although, therefore, the personal ties of the fourteenth century may not have been, in general, as stable as the tenurial ones of the feudal régime, the indentured retinue was certainly a steadying influence in a society where old institutional loyalties were breaking down and new ones had not yet fully developed to take their place. Its services in this respect were, perhaps, even greater than those it rendered in the military sphere: and the two forms of service together fully explain and justify the approval accorded to the indentured retinue by the constitutional mouthpiece of contemporary opinion.

N. B. Lewis

[1] Many of John Gaunt's retainers, for example, secured confirmation of their indentures after his death (*Cal. Pat. Rolls, 1396–9*, pp. 489–593), and the Black Prince's retainers, similarly, after his death, in the early months of Richard II's reign (*ibid., 1377–81*, pp. 155, 159, 161 and 209). Confirmation of the indentures of private persons are found from time to time on the patent rolls of Edward III's and Richard II's reigns.

11 The Use of French in England in the Later Middle Ages

The use of French in England during the later middle ages has frequently been discussed,[1] but rather surprisingly a large body of relevant documents has hitherto been almost entirely neglected. The documents in question throw much light both on the purposes for which French was used in this country in the fourteenth and fifteenth centuries and on the classes who employed it, and show that its use was more widespread and that it persisted longer than is generally supposed.

The categories of official documents in which French is to be found in the middle ages have long been known. The Chancery enrolments, in particular the Statute and Parliament Rolls, contain a fair proportion of French, though Latin was generally preferred for charters and letters under the great seal, as well as for most other public documents.[2] The first known letters patent in French are of the year 1258,[3] and from that date onwards until the beginning of the fifteenth century, French is to be found in documents relating to the general administration of the

[1] Among recent publications there may be noted: J. Vising, *Anglo-Norman language and literature*; E. Walberg, *Quelques aspects de la littérature anglo-normande*; M. D. Legge, 'Anglo-Norman and the Historian', *History*, xxvi. 163; R. M. Wilson, 'English and French in England, 1100–1300', *History*, xxviii. 37; G. E. Woodbine, 'The Language of English Law', *Speculum*, xviii. 395.

[2] H. C. Maxwell-Lyte, *The Great Seal*, p. 238.

[3] These are two proclamations in the form of letters patent dated 18 and 20 October 1258. They are enrolled on Patent Roll 42 Henry III, m. 1 (*Cal. Patent Rolls, 1247–58*, pp. 655–6) and are transcribed from other copies in the Annals of Burton (*Annales Monastici*, i. 453–6). The proclamation of 18 October is also in *Foedera*, i. 377–8. Other letters patent of 28 March 1259 communicating to the counties ordinances made by the council are on Patent Roll 43 Henry III, m. 10 (*Cal. Patent Rolls, 1258–66*, p. 19; *Foedera*, i. 381).

country, appointments, foreign negotiations and passports.[1] Letters patent were still occasionally written in French during the reign of Henry V, but only for formal business with foreign powers,[2] and French had not, in fact, been used for more general purposes since the beginning of the fifteenth century.[3] Similarly, French ceased to be employed for letters close at the same period, though French deeds continued to be enrolled upon the dorse of the Close Rolls until 1434.[4] Though Latin was the usual language of accounting, a good number of French entries, mainly letters by or to Exechequer officials, with an occasional inquisition or other exceptional document, are to be found on the Memoranda Rolls of the Exchequer.[5]

It was, however, from the Privy Seal Office that the largest number of official documents emanated. Though the first surviving warrants for the issue of letters under the great seal come from the reign of Henry III,[6] there is no evidence of the use of French for instruments under the privy seal until the closing years of Edward I. Under Edward II Latin and French were used in approximately equal proportions, while under Edward III Latin was noticeably less used.[7] English was not introduced in the Privy Seal Office until the very end of Henry V's reign, and the use of French for authorising the issue of instruments under the great seal was not abandoned until about 1437;[8] and though there exists a privy seal writ in French as late as the first year of Edward IV (1461), for some time previously French had rarely been used, except for communications to Gascony or the Channel Islands.[9] The earliest

[1] Numerous examples are to be found in Rymer's *Foedera*.

[2] *Foedera*, ix (1413-20).

[3] It may be added that at least two letters patent of James I concerning Jersey are in French, the warrants being in the same language (Maxwell-Lyte, *op. cit.*, p. 239).

[4] See Appendix V.

[5] For some examples of French documents on the Memoranda Rolls, see p. 226 below. For an inventory of 1419, see A. R. Myers, 'The captivity of a royal witch', *Bulletin of the John Rylands Library*, xxvi. 98–100.

[6] *Calendar of Chancery Warrants*, i. 1.

[7] E. Déprez, *Études de Diplomatique Anglaise*, p. 11.

[8] H. C. Maxwell-Lyte, *op. cit.*, p. 52 and note p. 53.

[9] *Ibid.*, p. 52.

surviving document under the privy seal written in English appears to be a safe conduct issued at Vincennes on 27 August 1422, four days before the death of Henry V.[1] There are, indeed, some grounds for taking the year 1422 as a definite turning-point. In that year the London Brewers' Guild decided to keep their records in English, one of their reasons being that the king had employed 'our mother tongue' for his letters missive[2] and it is true that the change from French to English had taken place in the Signet Office a few years earlier. In warrants under the signet English superseded French after 1417,[3] though French was and, of course, continued to be, used to some extent in correspondence with foreign courts. Such of the diplomatic correspondence under the signet as has survived is dispersed and fragmentary, but we know that much of it, in particular letters to the Curia, was in Latin.[4]

It has been necessary to review briefly the use of French for official purposes, but unofficial documents afford more useful data. We may begin with letters and, in the first place, the correspondence of members of the royal family, much of it connected with the administration of their households and estates. Eleanor of Provence, the wife of Henry III, is the first queen whose correspondence has come down to us. Among 144 originals in the Public Record Office, mostly written in the last quarter of the thirteenth century, after the king's death, the majority are in French.[5] Nearly every subsequent queen has left some letters behind her.[6] Most of them are of a semi-official or business

---

[1] Déprez, *op. cit.*, pp. 35–6.

[2] R. W. Chambers and M. Daunt, *A book of London English*, p. 139.

[3] Déprez, *op. cit.*, pp. 99–100.

[4] E. Perroy, *The diplomatic correspondence of Richard II* (Camden Third Series, xlviii).

[5] Ancient Correspondence, iii, vii, x, xi, xvi, xxii, xxiii, xxv, xxx, xlvii and xlviii.

[6] For Eleanor of Castile, see Ancient Correspondence, x. 52 and 55, xi. 25, xxiii. 45–51, xxx. 44–7, 50, 52, 53; Margaret of France, xxv. 198–204, xxvii. 96–7, xxviii. 27, 86–7, xxxv. 70, 131, 164, xlviii. 78; Isabella of France, xxxv. 62–5, 111–12; Philippa of Hainault, xxxvi. 107, xxxix. 15, 34, 35, 50, 163, 164, 175, xl. 30–2, 116, 137, xli. 80–7, xlii. 101–2, lvi. 26, 39, 40, 50, 78; Anne of Bohemia, li. 21.

character, but a few are of a more personal nature.[1] A portion of the correspondence of Philippa of Hainault supplies us with exceptionally valuable evidence. While the correspondence of other queens is fragmentary, a complete roll of Philippa's letters for the years 1330–6 has survived.[2] There are 331 entries in all, 128 French and 203 in Latin; French and Latin are frequently employed side by side and it is not always easy to conjecture what determined the use of either language. French is used to address the queen's stewards, her receivers, keepers of manors and castles, bailiffs and reeves, as well as persons unconnected with her estates such as sheriffs and widows in charge of children in ward. Among the Latin letters a good proportion were sent to bishops, the remainder being to estate officials to whom it was apparently immaterial whether they received instructions in Latin or French. The letters of appointment contained in the roll show the same parallel use of the two languages. It is difficult to understand why Latin should be used when appointing employees of such humble status as a messer and a doorkeeper at Rockingham castle, while French was employed in the case of receivers of the queen's gold and green-wax, stewards and constables. The last queen to use French in her correspondence seems to have been Joan, the second wife of Henry IV,[3] although some French petitions from Katherine of France, the queen of Henry V, survive for the period after her widowhood.[4] Margaret of Anjou, the wife of

---

[1] See, for example, the invitation from Margaret, the second wife of Edward I, to the abbot of Ramsey in 1301 to be the godfather of her child, Edmund of Woodstock (Register of Ramsey Abbey, Bodleian, MS. Ashmole 1524, fo. 10v–11r; printed by W. D. Macray, *Chronicon Abbatiae Ramesiensis*, Appendix, p. 373) and a letter from Philippa of Hainault asking the abbot of Glastonbury for a loan of a hundred pounds (Register of Glastonbury Abbey, Brit. Mus., MS. Arundel ii, fo. 35v).

[2] Public Record Office, C47/9/58. For analysis of contents see Appendix I.

[3] See Brit. Mus., MS. Julius B vi, fo. 54r (two letters written while she was still duchess of Brittany), MS. Vesp. F iii, fo. 5r, and Ancient Correspondence li. 41. For a letter written after her widowhood see Register of Lanthony Priory, Public Record Office, C115/A3, fo. 95v (1417).

[4] *Rot. Parl.*, iv. 183b and 186b–187a. Both petitions were made in 1422 after the death of Henry V. Two more petitions are also to be found in *Proceedings and Ordinances of the Privy Council of England*, iv. 48 and 179, dated 1420 and 1433.

Henry VI, appears not to have used French during her residence in England.[1]

A roll containing the correspondence of the prince of Wales for the year 1304–5 shows an extensive use of French.[2] Here out of a total of 719 letters sent out under the prince's privy seal, 676 appear to have been in French and 43 in Latin, the latter addressed exclusively to the pope, the papal nuncio and foreign prelates: letters from the prince to English ecclesiastics were never in Latin. French was used in addressing both government and local officials: the keeper and purveyor of the wardrobe, justices, the mayors of London and Northampton, the sheriffs of London, Essex and Wiltshire, the bailiffs of the manor of Windsor and of Woodstock, Boston and Salisbury, the constables of Carmarthen and Bristol, the baillis and commune of Brussels and the mayor and jurats of Bordeaux, as well as bankers and merchants such as Amerigo dei Frescobaldi and Baroncino of Lucca. Edward, of course, used the same language when corresponding with Prince Louis of France, the duke and duchess of Lorraine, the count of Savoy, with his stepmother, Margaret of France, his young step-brothers and his sisters.

The subject-matter of the letters is as varied as the range of correspondents and covers such trifles as the purchase of trumpets and a pair of kettle-drums and the provision of a gown for the prince's laundress as well as the grave issue of his quarrel with his father. That all the correspondents who received these letters were acquainted with French seems indisputable. And while many of them were of high social position — members of a French-speaking aristocracy for whom national boundaries were certainly not cultural boundaries — what is especially to be remarked is that local officials, in England and on the Continent, as well as Italian merchants, were expected to understand a common idiom.

Similar evidence of the use of French during the middle and latter part of the fourteenth century is afforded by registers of the Black

[1] C. Monro, *The letters of Margaret of Anjou* (Camden First Series, lxxvi).

[2] *The letters of Edward Prince of Wales, 1304–5*, ed. Hilda Johnstone (Roxburghe Club).

Prince[1] and John of Gaunt.[2] The 153 folios of the Black Prince's register for 1346–8 contain less than a hundred Latin documents, the great bulk of the business being conducted in French. In John of Gaunt's registers, which cover the years 1372–6 and 1379–83, nearly all the entries are in French. They are for the most part concerned with the administration of his English estates, the appointment of his officers and the purchase of provisions for his household. In the first register, out of a total of 1812 entries, 69 only are in Latin, that language being employed only for letters patent and for correspondence arising out of the Duke's extensive ecclesiastical patronage. In the second register the French entries number 1073 against 41 in Latin.[3]

From royal households we may conveniently turn to English religious houses, all of which, large and small, commonly used French for less formal documents. The majority of monastic registers contain some evidence,[4] but the most significant, because the most regularly kept, are the letter-book for the years 1351–66 of Walter Monyton, abbot of Glastonbury,[5] and the registers of Lanthony Priory[6] which cover not only the latter part of the fourteenth century but also most of the fifteenth century. The Glastonbury letter-book is especially valuable because a very large proportion of the letters which left the abbey were registered as well as a number of documents received from outside. Of

---

[1] *The Register of Edward the Black Prince* (Public Record Office). Four parts covering the periods July 1346–January 1348 and February 1351–November 1365.

[2] *John of Gaunt's Register, 1372–1376*, ed. S. Armitage-Smith (Camden Third Series, xx and xxi); *ibid., 1379–1383*, ed. E. C. Lodge and R. Somerville (Camden Third Series, lvi and lvii).

[3] For analysis of the second register, see Appendix II.

[4] The more important are those of Battle Abbey (Brit. Mus., MS. Harl. 3586), Bury St. Edmunds (Brit. Mus., MS. Harl. 230), Christ Church, Canterbury (Cambridge Univ., MS. Ee. v. 31), Ely (Brit. Mus., MS. Add. 41612), Evesham (Brit. Mus., MS. Titus C. ix), Langley (Bodleian, MS. Bodley 242), Merton (Bodleian, MS. Laud 723), Peterborough (Brit. Mus., MS. Vesp. E. xxi, xxii, Add. 25288), Rochester (Brit. Mus., MS. Faustina C. v), St. Albans (Brit. Mus., MS. Tiberius E. vi), Selby (Brit. Mus., MS. Cleop. D. iii; Public Record Office, D.L. 42/8), Thetford (Bodleian, MS. Gough Norfolk 18) and Whalley (Brit. Mus., MS. Add. 10374).   [5] Brit. Mus., MS. Arundel ii.

[6] Public Record Office C115/A3, A7 and A12.

the 439 letters it contains, half are in French and half in Latin.[1] Walter Monyton corresponded with people of all ranks: the king, the queen, the Black Prince, Princess Isabella, the earls of Salisbury and Stafford, Elizabeth de Burgh, William of Wykeham, the chancellor and barons of the Exchequer, the mayor of London, officials on the Glastonbury estates and many others. A good proportion of the Latin letters were, of course, addressed to ecclesiastics: archbishops, bishops, heads of monastic houses and individual monks, including two from Glastonbury studying at Oxford. Bailiffs and reeves appear to have received their orders mainly in Latin and, contrary to the practice observed on Queen Philippa's roll, all letters of appointment were in Latin. On the other hand, communications to higher officials, the chief baron of the Exchequer, the clerk of the Privy Seal, the king's secretary and Chancery clerks, were in French.[2] Normally, replies were in the same language as the letters they answered: for example, the reply to a summons to parliament was in Latin[3] while private correspondence with the Queen or her daughter, Isabella, was in French.[4]

Though the surviving registers of Lanthony Priory omit much of the correspondence that would have been preserved at Glastonbury, they are at least equally valuable by reason of their continuity. They contain relatively little official correspondence and few letters concerning the priory's estate, but a fairly complete record of correspondence with the patrons of the monastery appears to have been kept. In the fifteenth century the countess of Stafford seems to have been an exceptionally faithful correspondent, whether it was to give the prior first hand information of Henry V's campaigns in France,[5] the latest news about the peace negotiations and the king's proposed marriage,[6] or merely to thank the prior for a gift and say that she and her children were well.[7] The first English letters do not occur until 1424, when two were registered: one from the duke of Gloucester and the other from

---

[1] For analysis see Appendix III.

[2] When on one occasion letters in Latin were sent to all these officials it may have been merely a matter of convenience, since a letter in the same terms was being sent to the archbishop of York, then chancellor. Brit. Mus., MS. Arundel ii, fo. 19v.　　[3] *Ibid.*, fo. 14v.　　[4] *Ibid.*, fos. 35v–36r and fov. 65v–66r.

[5] Public Record Office, C115/A3, fo. 106v.

[6] *Ibid.*, fo. 130r.　　　　　　　　　　[7] *Ibid.*, fo. 129v.

the earl of March.[1] In 1426 there are two English letters from the countess of Stafford,[2] one from the duke of Bedford[3] and one from the
prior to members of the duke's council with their reply.[4] The countess
of Stafford, however, continued occasionally to use French for nearly
ten years longer, a warrant to one of her parkers being entered in 1429[5]
and two letters patent in 1435.[6]

More fragmentary sources afford similar evidence of the continued
use of French. Of particular importance is the French formulary
compiled by John Stevens, about the year 1420,[7] containing some 400
letters from the last years of the fourteenth century and early years of
the fifteenth until 1412. Stevens borrowed material from the files of
several government departments, including the correspondence of
Henry of Monmouth, and made use of the correspondence of two
archbishops of Canterbury, Henry Despencer, bishop of Norwich, the
Holland family and others. Not only does the formulary afford examples of French correspondence of extraordinary range and variety, but
it is clear that since Stevens intended his formulary to be used, he looked
forward to the continued currency of French for many years.

At the time, however, when the bulk of the letters in Stevens'
formulary were written, English was already beginning to supersede
French, and it may well be asked how far the use of French in correspondence had become conventional. Until the end of Richard II's reign
manuals of epistolography, such as those of Thomas Sampson who
taught at Oxford in the second half of the fourteenth century,[8] appear
to assume that French would be employed between all grades of society
for all purposes. They also assume that the writers would be conversant
with the language, for their object was not to teach the rudiments of
French but rather the refinements and, in particular, the proper address
for every rank. There is no doubt that these manuals were actually

[1] Public Record Office, C115/A3, fo. 166v.
[2] *Ibid.*, fo. 179r.   [3] *Ibid.*, fo. 188v.
[4] *Ibid.*, fo. 189r–189v.   [5] *Ibid.*, fo. 199r.   [6] *Ibid.*, fo. 247v.
[7] *Anglo-Norman letters and petitions from All Souls Ms. 182*, ed. M. Dominica
Legge (Anglo-Norman Text Society no. 3).
[8] Cf. H. G. Richardson, 'Business Training in Medieval Oxford', *American
Historical Review*, xlvi. 259.

employed as a guide in the composition of some of the original letters that have come down to us.

So far as government departments were concerned, convention played a large part in the choice of the language to be used on any particular occasion, and it was doubtless partly due to the force of tradition that French continued to be used in the offices of the Privy Seal and Signet until well into the fifteenth century. Official tradition was necessarily strong in the households of queens and princes — Philippa, Isabella, Edward of Caernarvon, the Black Prince, John of Gaunt — but it cannot be argued from this that French was not the language which unofficial correspondents instinctively preferred throughout the fourteenth century. Examples of private letters, in which the convention of an unfamiliar language would have been an absurdity, survive for the whole of that century and even beyond. It would be hard not to give the name familiar to some of Prince Edward's letters preserved in the roll of 1304–6,[1] or to such letters from the abbot of Glastonbury as those written to a knight inviting him to hunt,[2] to princess Isabella sending her fish to replenish her stewponds[3] and to Elizabeth de Burgh asking permission to send a carpenter to copy her horse-mill which had greatly impressed some of his monks,[4] or again to letters to the prior of Lanthony thanking him for his gifts of lampreys and cheese.[5]

By the turn of the century, however the use of French or English was becoming a matter of personal preference and, for some people,

---

[1] See in particular Edward's letter to Louis of France, accompanying gifts of a palfrey and greyhounds: 'Nous vous enveoms vn gros palefrai trottant . . . e vous enueoms de noz crocuz leurers de Gales que bien ateindroient vn leure sil le trouassent endormaunt . . . E, cher cosin, si vous volez dautres choses qui sont en nostre pais de Gales, vncore vous enverrom bien des gentz sauuages, si vous volez . . .' (*The letters of Edward Prince of Wales*, p. 11).

[2] Brit. Mus., M.S. Arundel ii, fo. 10r.

[3] *Ibid.*, fo. 27r.   [4] *Ibid.*, fo. 15r.

[5] Public Record Office, C115/A7, fo. 74v (from the earl of Buckingham) and fo. 180r (from the duchess of Gloucester); C115/A3, fo. 95v (from Henry IV's widow). In addition, C115/A3, fo. 129v, contains a letter from the prior to the countess of Stafford, dated 11 September 1419, thanking her for her gift of copes, and regretting that the hot, dry summer has prevented him from sending her cheese.

French was evidently a language of convention rather than of preference. At the close of Richard II's reign four letters from the Scottish earl of March were copied into the register of the prior of Durham. They dealt with the election of a new prior to Coldingham, Durham's most important dependency, the first two, dated 22 February and 17 April, being in French, and the remaining two written in English, dated 22 April and 23 May.[1] It was the same earl who wrote to Henry IV in 1400: 'And noble Prince mervaile yhe nocht that I write my letters in Englishe, fore that ys mare clere to myne understanding than Latyne or Fraunche'.[2] Richard Kingston, the dean of Windsor, experienced a similar difficulty in 1403, when he wrote to Henry IV, giving news of the success of the rebels at Hereford, in a curious mixture of French and English, his French failing him completely in the valediction.[3] A warning should perhaps be given against taking seriously the protest of the English ambassadors in 1404 that they understood French no more than Hebrew.[4] English diplomacy was commonly conducted in French; on this occasion the ambassadors evidently thought they should have been addressed in Latin.

The change from French to English in correspondence obviously took place less speedily in some circles and households than in others. Rather curiously the first known English letter was written from Florence in 1392–3 by the mercenary captain Sir John Hawkwood[5] and

---

[1] Brit. Mus., MS. Faustina A vi, fo. 90r–90v. It has unfortunately been impossible to ascertain the precise year in which these letters were written.

[2] F. C. Hingeston, *Royal and historical letters during the reign of Henry IV, 1399–1404*, i. 24. Another letter in English from a Scottish magnate, James Douglas, to Henry IV, written in 1405, has been erroneously dated 1384 in S. Bentley, *Excerpta Historica*, pp. 142–4: see J. H. Wylie, *History of England under Henry IV*, ii. 275–6, n. 1.

[3] Hingeston, *op. cit.*, p. 158. 'Jeo prie a la benost Trinitee que vous done bone vie, ove tresentier sauntee a treslonge duree, and send zowe sone to ows in helth and prosperitee . . .'

[4] *Ibid.*, Preface, pp. lxxxvii–lxxxviii, and p. 397. 'Vestras litteras scriptas in Gallico, nobis indoctis tanquam in idiomate Hebraico, apud Monstreueille xxmo die Octobris, recepimus Calisii eodem xxmo die de sero, inter cetera continentes qualiter . . .'

[5] C. L. Kingsford, *Prejudice and promise in fifteenth-century England*, pp. 22–3.

very few English letters are known before the fifteenth century.[1] On the whole, it seems safe to conclude that noble families and religious houses offered more resistance to the English vernacular than commercial circles and the lower ranks of society.

The evidence afforded by petitions and bills is less satisfactory than that of private correspondence and it need be but briefly reviewed. Very few petitions have been preserved before the reign of Edward I, and these few appear to be all in Latin, but from early in that reign petitions have survived in large numbers. Although Latin continued to be used on occasion, notably in some of the petitions put forward by churchmen, the vast bulk was written in French and continued to be so written until French gradually gave way to English, a process that began before the middle of the fourteenth century and was not completed until a hundred years later. Though Latin was the language usually associated with the clergy in the middle ages for their more formal documents, it is remarkable that in the thirteenth, fourteenth and early fifteenth centuries, their petitions were almost invariably framed in French, presumably because those who were to consider the petitions were familiar with that language.[2] The decline of French in parliamentary petitions appears to have been very rapid in the decade 1433–43. English was still comparatively rare in 1433, when French petitions which came before Parliament numbered 49 and English petitions 10. In 1439 the proportion was 24 French to 19 English, but in 1444 no French petitions were recorded, whereas those in English numbered 26. There was, however, one final flicker from the dying

[1] The next earliest English letter known appears to be that from Joan Pelham to her husband of 25 July 1399 (Laetitia Lyle, *A mediaeval post-bag*, pp. 267–8, from Collins' *Peerage*, viii. 95–6) though it is possible that the two letters from the earl of March mentioned above may be earlier.

[2] The earliest known English petition is an enclosure to a Privy Seal warrant to the chancellor: it is from John Drayton and Margery King, his wife, and is dated 5 February 1344. The next does not occur until twenty years later, it is from the abbot and convent of St. Mary Graces, 1364, and there is a third from the folk of the Mercerye dated 1386. After this last date a number of English petitions are to be found (R. W. Chambers and M. Daunt, *A book of London English, 1384–1425*, preface, p. 9 and pp. 272–3, 285, 288, 292–3, and *Rot. Parl.*, iv. 22, 57–61, 158–9).

embers in 1447 when two French petitions were presented.[1] A similar course can be traced for the petitions which were considered by the Privy Council.[2] No English petitions are known to have reached the Council during the reigns of Richard II, Henry IV and Henry V, and until 1436 English only occurred sporadically. The two last French petitions to come before the Council were written in the spring of 1441. We may fairly conclude that although convention delayed the substitution in petitions of English for French the time lag was not great, perhaps ten or a dozen years.

More instructive than petitions are French legal instruments. The conventional language of the law was Latin, and French was used not for show but for convenience. We could therefore have no better evidence of the widespread use of French in the fourteenth and fifteenth centuries than the French deeds which, in their original form, are to be found in the great public collections and in muniment rooms all over the country, and in greater numbers, in transcript in monastic cartularies and registers and endorsed on the Close Rolls. How soon after the Conquest French was used for legal instruments must remain in doubt, and if it was employed to any extent it has left practically no trace among the thousands of Latin deeds which have survived for the twelfth century. A Jewish 'starr' of the year 1215 is, in fact, the earliest known private deed in French[3] though some earlier official documents are known.[4] In spite of the great losses that have taken place it is evident that French was used for all kinds of transactions, though in certain categories, such as the bond, it was of rare occurrence, a fact which points to the truth, for which there is abundant evidence, that Latin was preferred for the more solemn and binding instruments.

[1] See Appendix IV for table covering the use of French and English in petitions from 1414 to 1447.

[2] *Proceedings and Ordinances of the Privy Council of England, 1386–1542*, ed. Sir H. Nicholas.

[3] *Starrs and Jewish Charters* (Jewish Historical Society), i. 12–20. An instrument by Stephen Langton of 29 January 1215 is endorsed on the Charter Roll of 16 John, but this is hardly a private deed (*Rotuli Chartarum*, p. 209).

[4] See H. Richardson, 'A twelfth-century Anglo-Norman charter', *Bulletin of the John Rylands Library*, xxiv. 168, and H. Suggett, 'An Anglo-Norman return to the Inquest of Sheriffs', *ibid.*, xxvii. 170.

French deeds connected with the sale and leasing of land are, how-ever, met with very frequently, and the lease of a tavern at the head of London Bridge in 1319,[1] and the sale of a Norfolk marsh in 1383[2] are typical examples. Still, it was more usual to employ French for sub-sidiary instruments and as many as three French documents relating to a single transaction may be found, as in the case of a grant, letters of attorney and a demise of October 1389 concerning the manor of Plait-ford.[3] The use of French for grants of office has already been mentioned: broadly speaking, the practice of royal and noble households was to use French and the practice of monastic houses to use Latin. Deeds granting pensions and other rewards were also drawn up in French, as were indentures of war, marriage contracts and marriage licences required by wards, deeds of manumission and pardons.[4] Contracts for the sale of goods and for undertaking specific services form one of the most interesting classes of French deeds. They include agreements with carpenters for the erection of shops,[5] weirs[6] and water-mills,[7] contracts for the construction of tombs and funeral herses,[8] for the provision of a clock,[9] for the painting of the great image of the apostle at St. Paul's Cathedral[10] and for the supply of tiles for Westminster Abbey.[11] In-ventories connected with the sale or transfer of goods were also frequently in French. Typical examples are an inventory of the contents

---

[1] H. T. Riley, *Memorials of London and London Life, 1276-1419*, pp. 131-2.

[2] Magdalen College, Oxford, Muniments, Beighton 114.

[3] Public Record Office, Ancient Deeds, E40/3233, 3234 and 3241.

[4] Examples of all these types of deeds are to be found in T. Madox, *Formulare Anglicanum*.

[5] Historical MSS. Commission, *Ninth Report*, Appendix, p. 20.

[6] Queen Philippa's Roll, Public Record Office, C47/9/58, m. 2.

[7] Magdalen College, Oxford, Muniments, Southwark 33.

[8] For the marble and metal work for the tomb of Richard II and Anne of Bohemia, see *Foedera*, vii. 795-6; for Anne of Bohemia's herses, see R. Gough, *Sepulchral Monuments*, i. 170*, and for an alabaster tomb for Katherine Green and her late husband, see R. Willis, *Architectural nomenclature of the Middle Ages*, p. 79.

[9] Brit. Mus., Cotton Charters xxi, 24. Printed in *Archæological Journal*, xii (1855), 173.

[10] Historical MSS. Commission, *Ninth Report*, Part 1, Appendix, p. 30.

[11] E. H. Pearce, *The Monks of Westminster*, p. 106.

(including books, vestments, plate, rings and seals) of coffers and baskets in the treasury of Wells Cathedral, once the property of bishop John Droxford;[1] a list and valuation of the stores belonging to the works at London Bridge and delivered to the new wardens in 1350 by the outgoing wardens;[2] an account of jewels sold to Master John Cambridge, executor of Michael Northburgh, late bishop of London, in 1363;[3] a list of jewels lost by the earl of Huntingdon in 1377;[4] and inventories of armour formerly belonging to the dukes of Gloucester and Arundel and passing to Richard II by reason of their forfeiture.[5] It has been said that bonds were almost invariably in Latin, but the defeasances, which were drawn up at the same time and represented the real engagement between the parties, were commonly in French, doubtless for the reason that the parties preferred to express their intentions in a manner they could readily understand. At the same time, it was necessary for the bonds to be carefully worded and based on approved, that is Latin, precedents since if they became operative they might need to be enforced by an action at law.[6] French was also extensively used for wills from the thirteenth century onwards and there have survived French wills of members of all classes of society who had sufficient property to make its disposal a matter of consequence, from princes of the blood to country squires.[7] The latest will known to me

[1] Public Record Office, L.T.R. Memoranda Roll, 4 Edward III, E368/102, m. 21. Also in K.R. Memoranda Roll 159/106, m. 154.

[2] H. T. Riley, *op. cit.*, pp. 261-2. It is interesting to note that a similar document drawn up on the same day, between the same people, namely, an inventory of the articles in the chapel of London Bridge, was in Latin. Cf. *ibid.*, pp. 263-4.

[3] *Ibid.*, p. 313.

[4] Public Record Office, Coram Rege Roll, Michaelmas 1377, K.B. 27/467, m. 36 schedule.

[5] Public Record Office, E163/6/13.

[6] A few examples of French bonds have survived, for example, one for the payment of forty shillings to the master of the hospital of St. John at Oxford in 1344 (Magdalen College, Oxford, Muniments, Willoughby 63).

[7] French wills are numerous and very scattered. Many are to be found in the following collections: J. Nichols, *A collection of all the wills of the kings and queens of England; Testamenta Eboracensia*, ed. J. Raine (Surtees Society, iv); *Testamenta Karleolensia (1353-1386)*, ed. R. S. Ferguson (Cumberland and Westmorland

is that of Philippa, duchess of York, dated 12 March 1431.[1] English wills had by then already begun to make their appearance in small numbers, the earliest one as yet discovered being of the year 1387.[2]

Since the survival of many French deeds seems to have largely depended on chance circumstances, it is not easy to estimate the relative proportion of French and Latin. However, it may be instructive to note that in the collections of thirteenth- and fourteenth-century deeds belonging to the Duchy of Lancaster the proportion of French deeds is as high as eleven per cent,[3] while in the *Formulare Anglicanum* compiled by Thomas Madox the proportion is about one in twenty.[4] Such figures probably convey a quite erroneous impression. Queen Philippa's clerks used Latin or French almost indifferently, with the result that grants, indentures and other deeds on the roll of 1330–6 number 85 in French as against 109 in Latin.[5] French is much more prominent in the second of John of Gaunt's registers, covering the years 1379–83, where there are only 27 legal instruments in Latin as against 253 French deeds.[6]

As far as is known the use of English for deeds did not begin until nearly the end of Edward III's reign, and though for many years English deeds are rare,[7] by 1440 they have become quite usual. On the

---

Antiquarian and Archaeological Society); *Calendar of wills proved and enrolled in the Court of Husting, London, 1258–1688*, ed. R. R. Sharpe; *The Register of Henry Chichele*, ed. E. F. Jacob (Canterbury and York Society), vol. ii.

[1] E. F. Jacob, *op. cit.*, ii. 457–9. Two wills of 1429 are also to be found in the same register; they are those of Thomas Colpeper (pp. 382–6) and John, duke of Norfolk (pp. 472–4).

[2] C. L. Kingsford, *op. cit.*, pp. 24–5.

[3] Public Record Office, Lists of Ancient Deeds, Series D.L.

[4] Further evidence is afforded by a series of 16 fourteenth-century (1316–32) French deeds relating to Norfolk preserved at Magdalen College, Oxford (Hickling 110–25) in which the same names recur as grantors, grantees and witnesses, and by a series of 36 deeds at Corpus Christi College, Oxford (Ca Kl Ev. 12–35 and 38–49), witnessing sales of land by one Simon Furneux, from 1334 to 1358. These two series point to the fact that losses must have been very great and that many documents considered of minor importance must have perished.

[5] See Appendix I.   [6] See Appendix II.

[7] A deed of 1376 is stated to be the oldest private legal instrument in Middle English (cf. J. E. Wells, *A manual of the writings in Middle English*, p. 442). In

other hand, legal instruments are still found in French in the 1430s: in 1434 one was entered on the Close Rolls[1] and another in Lanthony Priory register, the latter being an indenture between the countess of Stafford and the cellarer of Lanthony, notifying the receipt by him of a chalice and other silver vessels.[2] Furthermore, a fifteenth-century formulary[3] contains two surprisingly late examples, which are, without doubt, copies of actual documents. One is a grant of an annuity by William de la Pole, duke of Suffolk, dated 1450,[4] and the other a deed of John Arundel, concerning a debt of £26 due to a London skinner, dated 12 March 1456.[5] These are the latest French deeds that have so far come to light, but the fact that it was considered worth while copying them as models for future use, suggests that the compiler of the formulary expected other occasions to arise when French would be the language preferred by the parties.

The foregoing survey has shown the variety of uses to which French was put in the later middle ages, and something further may be said of the preference shown by the various classes of society for that language as opposed to English. It has already been remarked that, though the bulk of formal official documents were in Latin, certain categories were over a long period mainly written in French. The minutes of the council and the proceedings of parliament, the king's warrants to the chancery, the exchequer and other departments were normally in French: in other words, the less formal side of official business was transacted in French, as well as occasionally the more formal side. Indeed, it would have been difficult to proceed in any other fashion, for the executive work of government fell chiefly upon men

---

1397 an indenture in English was made at Dunfermline abbey, in 1398 two at Haudenstank and one at Clackmabanestane (Chambers and Daunt, *op. cit.*, pp. 278–9). In 1404 two more occur: a bond by John Stewart, knight, to Ralph, earl of Westmorland, and an indenture drawn up at Pontefract castle (*ibid.*, p. 283). No defeasance has been discovered earlier than 1422 (*ibid.*, p. 307).

[1] For table of French deeds endorsed on the Close Rolls, see Appendix V.

[2] Register of Lanthony Priory, Public Record Office, C115/A3, fo. 238v.

[3] Brit. Mus., MS. Royal 17 B xlvii.

[4] *Ibid.*, fos. 111v–112r. It can hardly be a coincidence that, as stated below, William de la Pole wrote poems in French.

[5] Brit. Mus., MS. Royal, 17 B fo. 21r.

who were, or had been, king's clerks; at the council itself, where decisions were taken, the clerks shared responsibility with nobles, who though well educated by the standards of their time and rank, were usually illiterate in the technical sense that they could not, with any fluency, speak, read or write Latin. Their ability to read and write French is difficult to estimate, but such fragments as are available suggest that this was not a rare accomplishment. Henry de Montfort wrote his father's will with his own hand,[1] a poem is credited to Edward II,[2] while his cousin Henry of Lancaster wrote a pious work of some length 'Le Livre de Seyntz Medecines'.[3] The poems of John de Montacute, earl of Salisbury, were praised by no less competent a critic than Christine de Pisan[4] and the tradition was continued until the middle of the fifteenth century by William de la Pole, who was also a poet.[5] Secretaries were, however, usually employed by persons of rank for writing both letters and legal instruments, though their employers doubtless dictated the substance when something more than the normal routine was involved. The level of culture reached by royal and noble ladies is more difficult to determine: in some cases it seems probable that they could read but perhaps not write. Queen Isabella possessed French romances and works of piety,[6] and from bequests of similar books in wills of the period, it would appear that some ladies could read for pleasure. It seems likely, too, that these ladies read some of the numerous letters and petitions addressed to them. As far as the higher ranks of the secular clergy were concerned, while Latin predominated in episcopal and other registers, this was the work of clerks and there is no reason to suppose that in their personal relations they differed from other members of the families from which they sprang.

[1] C. Bémont, *Simon de Montfort* (1930), pp. 276–8, with facsimile.

[2] It consists of 15 eight-line stanzas. Cf. P. Studer, *Modern Language Review*, xvi. 34 ff.

[3] Ed. E. J. Arnould (Anglo-Norman Text Society, no. 2).

[4] *Lavision-Christine*, ed. Sister M. L. Towner (Catholic University of America), p. 165. The poems do not seem to have survived.

[5] His poems in English and French have been edited by H. W. MacCracken in *Publications of the Modern Language Association of America*, xxvi. 141–80.

[6] T. F. Tout, *Chapters in the Administrative History of Medieval England*, v. 249.

Some private letters of one prelate, Henry Despencer, bishop of Norwich, are known to us, and they are among the best examples of French as it was written in England in the closing years of the fourteenth century and the beginning of Henry IV's reign.[1]

It has already been said that the contents of monastic registers indicate that replies from religious houses to the king were generally determined by the language in which the official communications were couched. It is plain, moreover, from a formulary drawn up for the Cistercian abbey of Combe about the year 1340, that monks normally expected to conduct correspondence with secular persons in French, for the formulary comprises model letters for use in writing not only to the king but to sheriffs, judges, relatives and friends.[2] Other sources make it clear that correspondence between religious foundations and noblemen and ladies was almost invariably in French and that, when the change came in the fifteenth century, it was to English. It may be remarked also that while letters in French from one ecclesiastic to another might be hard to find, deeds to which all parties were clergy were not uniformly drawn up in Latin. Three surviving examples in French are an agreement between the prior of Merton and one of his canons, about the year 1390,[3] another between the bishop of Lichfield and the abbot of Leicester in 1403,[4] and an indenture of arbitration drawn up between the abbot of St. Peter's, Gloucester, and the prior of Lanthony in 1417.[5] In our period nuns generally were unfamiliar with Latin and their learning was similar to that of laymen of their

[1] M. D. Legge, *op. cit.*, prints seven of his letters (Nos. 44, 55, 58, 62, 64, 297 and 318), the most remarkable of which is his letter of condolence to his niece, Lady Despencer, after the execution of her husband in 1400 (no. 62). Other scattered letters show the bishop of Durham corresponding in French with his chancellor in 1430 (Letter book of Thomas Langley, bishop of Durham, Brit. Mus., MS. Add. 27401, fo. 2r) and the bishop of Hereford's vicar-general writing in the same language to a noble about some tithes due to the prior of Lanthony, c. 1371 (Register of Lanthony Priory, Public Record Office, C115/A12, fo. 63r).

[2] Marquess of Bath, MS. Longleat 37, fos. 114r–114v.

[3] Register of Merton Priory, Bodleian, MS. Laud 723, fo. 30r.

[4] Register of Lichfield Cathedral, Bodleian, MS. Ashmole 1527, fo. 79v.

[5] Register of Lanthony Priory, Public Record Office, C115/A3, fos. 109v–111v. It is interesting to note that an English version follows on fos. 111v–114r.

class.[1] They, therefore, used French for their correspondence, though the number of surviving letters from nunneries is comparatively small.[2] They also used French for other purposes and, as we should expect, the trousseau to be provided by a novice entering Blackborough priory in the fourteenth century was set out in French,[3] whereas the list of a young man's requirements on entering Tonbridge priory was in Latin.[4]

It is hardly necessary to show that the language of the law was French, a French that in the earlier fifteenth century had not yet degenerated into a mere technical jargon, nor to repeat that the king's clerks, until well into that century, were necessarily proficient in French. These are commonplaces which have been regarded as consistent with the disappearance of French in social intercourse, at some time in the fourteenth century, in all circles below that of the Court. But the truth seems to be that country gentlemen, and the middle classes generally, used French whenever all but the most formal writing was to be done. Some examples have already been given,[5] and little need be added. Husbands wrote to their wives during absences from home, giving instructions regarding payments and the management of their estates.[6] Wives — unless their letters were invariably written for them[7] — were equally capable of expressing themselves in French and their

---

[1] E. Power, *Medieval English nunneries*, pp. 247–9.

[2] See, for example, in the register of Blackborough Priory, a letter from the sub-prioress and convent to Roger Scales, asking permission to elect a new prioress (Brit. Mus., MS. Egerton 3137, fo. 167v).

[3] Brit. Mus., MS. Egerton 3137, penultimate flyleaf, dorse. Printed in *B.M. Quarterly*, xi. 65.

[4] Bodleian, MS. Kent Roll 6 (w). Printed in Preface to *Calendar of Charters and Rolls preserved in the Bodleian Library*, ed. W. H. Turner, p. x.

[5] See above, p. 221.

[6] An interesting example of this type is preserved in Magdalen College, Oxford, Muniments (Multon 71a). It is a farewell letter from John Multon to his wife in 1367, before his departure to Prussia. The final words are in English: 'Here have my lovee and keppe it well.'

[7] The earl of Kent stated in 1330 that a letter was written for him by his wife: 'fut escripte de la meyn sa femme' (A. Murimuth, *Continuatio Chronicarum* (Rolls Series), p. 255). Agnes, the wife of John the Organist *Gallicus*, who taught the Scottish orphan Tomlin his letters (literatura) in 1311–12, was also presumably able to write (Bentley, *Excerpta historica*, p. 278).

letters gave details of estate management and domestic matters, and sometimes contained intimate touches which could have been plain only to the recipient.[1] Other letters such as one from a stepfather to his stepson promising to send a cloak, providing the boy will specify the kind he wants,[2] and another to John of Gaunt from his daughter Philippa's nurse, warning him of the hostility of certain Franciscans and Dominicans at Cambridge,[3] show that the writers could express their thoughts in French without difficulty and were by no means content to string together a number of conventional phrases.

What is true of the gentry seems also to be true of the commercial classes. Mention has already been made of contracts with skilled artisans: carpenters, builders, masons, clockmakers and painters. In most of the contracts every detail to be performed was minutely described, doubtless to enable each item to be checked as the work progressed. It is therefore to be expected that the official correspondence of towns was conducted in the language that townsmen understood. Our best evidence comes from London. The mayor and aldermen used French not only when writing to large towns such as Bristol,[4] Winchester,[5] York,[6] Edinburgh[7] and Dublin,[8] but also when corresponding with the bailiffs of small communities such as Alton,[9] Erith,[10] Horsham,[11] Maidenhead[12] and Woburn.[13] Similar testimony to the use of French

---

[1] One such letter, in the muniments of Corpus Christi College, Oxford (Surrey Gl. cap. 8(1) 11), ends thus: 'A Deu, tresdouté sire, qe vous sauve et gard et vous defend de mortele peché, et vous salue par celuy enseigne qe le surcote fust detray sur nostre lit mes puys savey pur quey ceo fust.'

[2] Public Record Office, Ancient Correspondence SC1/51/67.

[3] *Ibid.*, SC1/43/81: printed by F. J. Tanquerey, *Recueil de lettres anglo-françaises*, pp. 168–9. It is not perhaps due to chance alone that this letter quotes rather formally a proverb: 'Et pur ce, tresnoble seignur, qe l'anxien proverbe dit en ceste maner qe "celui qu'est avant garnys n'est pas honys"', when a model letter by Thomas Sampson, conveying a warning about an ambush, begins in a similar manner: 'Nesqedent pensant q'il est par temps garny n'est pas hony' (Cambridge Univ., MS. Ee. iv. 20, fo. 159r).

[4] R. R. Sharpe, *Calendar of letters from the mayor and corporation of the city of London, A.D. 1350–70*, pp. 3–4, 7–8, 11–12, 22, 50–51, 54, 61, 171.

[5] *Ibid.*, p. 68.	[6] *Ibid.*, p. 56.	[7] *Ibid.*, p. 155.
[8] *Ibid.*, p. 63.	[9] *Ibid.*, p. 154.	[10] *Ibid.*, p. 111.
[11] *Ibid.*, pp. 32–3.	[12] *Ibid.*, p. 124.	[13] *Ibid.*, p. 59.

by the commercial classes lies in its employment for proclamations to the citizens of London until the close of the fourteenth century,[1] and pointing in the same direction are the lengthy ordinances of 1389, written in French, for the government of the town of Shrewsbury, which were directed to be read on days when elections took place,[2] while at Southampton the water-bailiffs' accounts were kept in French as late as 1428.[3]

Nor must another important class be forgotten. On large estates, whether belonging to secular magnates or to ecclesiastics, the actual management of a manor or a group of manors was in the hands of a steward, who was normally a layman. Before occupying such a post he would have received a training, very possibly at Oxford, to enable him to write letters, draw up deeds, hold manorial courts, keep accounts and control subordinate officers.[4] Correspondence with his lord and with other persons with whom he came into contact was in French, as were many of the other documents which he found it necessary to read or write. Men of this type were of much the same class as royal officers of similar status, receivers, parkers and foresters, who were expected to understand instructions in French and to send replies if necessity arose.

French was, in fact, associated with all the phases of daily life of fourteenth-century society which had to find expression in writing. Not only was it the means of registering grievances and recording legal transactions, it was also the medium of correspondence of all classes above the humblest, including the clergy, while news letters in French, of happenings at home and abroad, were widely circulated among them up to the end of Henry V's reign.[5] French followed them

---

[1] A proclamation in English occurs in 1387; cf. H. T. Riley, *op. cit.*, p. 500.

[2] *Calendar of Patent Rolls, 1396–9*, pp. 472–5.

[3] P. Studer, *Supplement to the Oak Book of Southampton*, ii. 9. Professor Studer concluded that French was the language of the seafaring classes generally at this period. Professor Tanquerey came to a similar conclusion regarding the use of French by the commercial classes, but his evidence was drawn from the earlier fourteenth century and particularly from the *Literae Cantuarienses* (*Recueil de lettres anglo-françaises*, pp. xxvi–xxvii).

[4] See H. G. Richardson, *ut supra*.

[5] Typical of such letters are one from the Parliament of Carlisle, 1307

even in death. From the early years of Henry III, until nearly two hundred years later, many of those who could afford to be commemorated by a tomb or a monumental brass preferred the inscription to be in French rather than Latin. Indeed, the evidence of these inscriptions tallies exactly with other written evidence. While six lines of English verse commemorated Henry Notingham and his wife at Holme-next-the-Sea, Norfolk, about the year 1405,[1] a memorial in Stoke-sub-Hamdon church in Somerset recalled in French the valiant deeds in battle of Matthew Gourney, who died in 1406, at the advanced age of ninety-six.[2] Matthew was perhaps old-fashioned, but there are later French inscriptions, though very simple and demanding little knowledge of the language.[3] The latest known to me bears the date 1427 and commemorates John Beaufitz and Isabelle his wife who lie in Gillingham Church: *Christ-Jesu nostre saveour de sa graunde pite de lour almes eit mercy.*[4]

What, then, were the characteristics of this French language which was still used for correspondence and to commemorate the dead in the early years of Henry VI, and lingered on in petitions and deeds until the middle of the century? Was it a Norman dialect which, cut off from its parent stem, suffered progressive debasement or did it bear

---

(printed by H. G. Richardson and G. O. Sayles, *English Historical Review*, liii. 436–7), another giving news of Edward III's campaign, 1339–40 (printed by H. Richardson, *Medium Aevum*, x. 20–1), a long letter from a courtier to a noble describing Richard II's reception by the City of London in 1392 (printed by H. Suggett, *English Historical Review*, lxii. 209–213) and two letters from the countess of Stafford to the prior of Lanthony giving news of Henry V's campaigns in 1418 and 1419 (Public Record Office, C115/A3, fo. 106v and 139r).

[1] Victoria and Albert Museum, *Catalogue of rubbings of brasses and incised slabs*, p. 12.

[2] *The Itinerary of John Leland*, ed. L. Toulmin Smith, i. 297.

[3] At Cople (Beds.) are the brasses of Nicholas Roland and Pernelle, his wife, c. 1410, and of Walter Roland, c. 1415: see G. Isherwood, *Monumental brasses in the Bedfordshire churches*, pp. 20–1. For a more elaborate inscription at Little Horkesley (Essex), commemorating Sir Thomas Swinburne, see Gough, *Sepulchral Monuments*, i. 152: the date should, however, be 1412 and not 1415.

[4] R. Griffin and Mill Stephenson, *A list of monumental brasses remaining in the county of Kent in 1922*, plate xxii.

comparison with the tongue of France? In spite of certain peculiarities of spelling and some uncertainty as regards genders and conjugations, which, together with the introduction of English words, often make the language recognisable as French written in England, gross lapses are less frequently found than might be expected. Though the style may sometimes appear stilted and the construction of sentences involved, contemporary documents written on the other side of the Channel display a similar tendency, which indeed was that of the age. Every piece of information available seems to show that the French used in England was no mere accomplishment, but that it was a true vernacular whose roots had penetrated deeply into all classes of English society who could read and write. To express quantitively the decline in the use of French in England is obviously a matter of difficulty. Records are incomplete, and the rate of decline must have differed considerably among different classes of writers. But perhaps as good an idea as it is possible to get may be obtained from the deeds endorsed on the Close Rolls. In the sixteen years from 1369 to 1384, when French was as extensively used in England as at any period, the number of French deeds so enrolled was 463, an average of 29 a year. In the sixteen years from 1403 to 1418 the number of French deeds was 60, an average of less than four a year. In the sixteen years from 1419 to 1434 the total number is 15, an average of one a year. Thereafter they cease entirely.[1] This evidence is not inconsistent with the testimony of such writers as Trevisa[2] and William of Nassington[3] to the displacement of French by English. The mistake has been to base too sweeping generalisations upon utterances which represent but a narrow circle of experience or which illustrate but a part of a complicated and developing linguistic pattern.

[1] See Appendix V.
[2] Higden, *Polychronicon* (Rolls Series), ii. 159 ff.
[3] 'Speculum Vitae' in Historical MSS. Commission, *Report on the Manuscripts of Lord Middleton*, p. 239.

APPENDIX I

QUEEN PHILIPPA'S ROLL

(PUBLIC RECORD OFFICE, C47/9/58)
DATED LETTERS AND DEEDS

Year	Letters		Deeds	
	French	Latin	French	Latin
1330 . . .	1	8	14	16
1331 . . .	17	9	28	31
1332 . . .	9	6	11	8
1333 . . .	4	4	7	8
1334 . . .	2	5	9	5
1335 . . .	3	16	6	23
1336 . . .	2	8	10	16
1337 . . .		2		1
1338 . . .				
1339 . . .				1
Totals . . .	38	58	85	109

The total number of French and Latin documents, including those of which only a note is given, undated documents and illegible items is, as stated above (p. 216), 128 and 203 respectively.

APPENDIX II

JOHN OF GAUNT'S REGISTER, 1379–83

(Camden Third Series, nos. lvi and lvii)

Year	Letters and warrants		Deeds	
	French	Latin	French	Latin
1376 . . .			1	
1377 . . .		2		
1378 . . .	1		1	1
1379 . . .	78		24	1
1380 . . .	340	2	68	13
1381 . . .	208	8	78	9
1382 . . .	153		40	3
1383 . . .	129	2	41	
1384 . . .	11			
Totals . . .	920	14	253	27

APPENDIX III

GLASTONBURY REGISTER. BRIT. MUS., MS. ARUNDEL II

Year			Out-letters		In-letters	
			French	Latin	French	Latin
1351	.	.	.	30	23	2	5
1352	.	.	.	9	6	2	3
1353	.	.	.	20	28	6	2
1354	.	.	.	6	14		3
1355	.	.	.	17	6		1
1356	.	.	.	12	8	5	9
1357	.	.	.	31	11	3	1
1358	.	.	.	3	10	2	5
1359	.	.	.	12	15		2
1360	.	.	.	27	3	5	4
1361	.	.	.	9	12	4	1
1362	.	.	.	7	18		1
1363	.	.	.	7	17		1
1364	.	.	.	2	5	2	2
Totals	.	.	.	192	176	31	40

APPENDIX IV

FRENCH PETITIONS, 1414–47

Year	Rotuli Parliamentorum, vol. iv				Proceedings and Ordinances of the Privy Council, vol. v	
	Private Petitions		Common Petitions			
	French	English	French	English	French	English
1414	32	1	26	1	3	
1415	23		35		4	
1416	7		9			
1417	2		8		1	
1418					1	
1419	2		8			
1420			16			
1421	23	2	30		11	
1422	15	1	6		2	1
1423	18	1	12	5	16	5
1424					4	3
1425	12		12	3	1	
1426	18	1	9	4	4	1
1427	6		22	2	3	
1428					3	
1429	2	2	26	8	1	
1430					6	
1431	12	5	17	1	2	1
1432	16	4	13	4		
1433	24	6	25	4	2	
1434						1
1435	1	1	8	4		1
1436	1	6	12	8	2	1
1437					1	1
1438						2
1439	6	7	18	12		2
1440						2
1441					2	9
1442	1	3	12	13		1
1443						
1444		4		22		3
1445						
1446						
1447	1	3	1	8		

APPENDIX V

FRENCH DEEDS ENDORSED ON CLOSE ROLLS

1369–1406				1407–34			
1369	.	.	. 23	1407	.	.	. 1
1370	.	.	. 25	1408	.	.	. 4
1371	.	.	. 17	1409	.	.	. 3
1372	.	.	. 22	1410	.	.	. 2
1373	.	.	. 41	1411	.	.	. 2
1374	.	.	. 26	1412	.	.	. 5
1375	.	.	. 36	1413	.	.	. 5
1376	.	.	. 46	1414	.	.	. 4
1377	.	.	. 35	1415	.	.	. 1
1378	.	.	. 24	1416	.	.	. 2
1379	.	.	. 31	1417	.	.	. 1
1380	.	.	. 36	1418	.	.	. 1
1381	.	.	. 21	1419	.	.	.
1382	.	.	. 34	1420	.	.	.
1383	.	.	. 27	1421	.	.	. 1
1384	.	.	. 19	1422	.	.	. 2
				1423	.	.	. 3
				1424	.	.	. 3
				1425	.	.	.
1398	.	.	. 2	1426	.	.	. 3
1399	.	.	. 9	1427	.	.	.
1400	.	.	. 10	1428	.	.	.
1401	.	.	. 3	1429	.	.	.
1402	.	.	. 1	1430	.	.	. 1
1403	.	.	. 7	1431	.	.	. 1
1404	.	.	. 8	1432	.	.	.
1405	.	.	. 7	1433	.	.	.
1406	.	.	. 7	1434	.	.	. 1

HELEN SUGGETT

12 Parliament and 'Bastard Feudalism'

'Edward I,' said Stubbs, 'had made his parliament the concentration of the three estates of his people; under Edward II, Edward III and Richard II, the third estate claimed and won its place as the foremost of the three.'[1] While the resounding emphasis is Stubbs's own — his common sense was of the kind called robust — the sentiment expressed was then and for long afterwards the traditional one. It is only of late years that opinion has swung to the opposite pole and maintained with an equal want of compromise the absolute insignificance of the commons in the political struggles of the later middle ages. The first open challenge to tradition came, I think, from Professor J. E. Neale in 1924.[2] Mainly concerned to trace the growth of free speech in parliament under the Tudors, he found himself confronted with a medieval background to his subject which seemed to him at variance with the course of its later development. The prologue, as it were, anticipated too much of his play. In a bold attempt to refashion it, he outlined a theory which did not at first attract much attention from medievalists, but which has recently, thanks to Mr. H. G. Richardson, begun to enjoy a considerable vogue among them.

As stated by Mr. Neale, this theory was at least simple. While admitting that attacks on the crown in Henry IV's reign, and to some extent in Richard II's, 'were seemingly launched by the commons', he argued that this had only a formal significance. So long as procedure by petition lasted, the commons were bound to be 'the petitioners *par excellence*'; but that did not mean that they spoke only, or even primarily, for themselves. They were inspired and sustained by the lords. They were 'the initiating organ of parliament', they 'were necessarily

---

[1] *Constitutional history of England*, ii (1906 edn.), 320.

[2] 'The commons' privilege of free speech in parliament', in *Tudor studies*, ed. R. W. Seton-Watson, pp. 257 *et seq.*

saddled with the task of petitioning', but when they presumed to oppose the king's will, it was because the magnates were in the saddle and had a firm hold on the reins. As evidence of this there could be adduced the custom, followed repeatedly between 1373 and 1407, of assigning a number of lords to assist the commons in their deliberations. 'True, we do not find the entry in every parliament', but after all the clerks were probably careless and omitted to record every instance upon the rolls.[1] Therefore, 'we need no longer conclude that the real test of strength in parliament was between the king and the commons. In all likelihood it was between the king and the lords.'[2]

In adopting this theory of the relations of the two houses, Mr. Richardson wisely preferred to underline the importance of the territorial and personal ties which attached many members of the commons to the magnates of their shires.[3] There is no question that these

[1] Generous use has to be made of this assumption. There were thirty-four parliaments in the period 1373-1407; in only ten of these do the rolls record that lords were either asked for or assigned to confer with the commons (1373; 1376; January and October 1377; 1378; 1381-2; February 1383; April 1384; 1402 and 1407; *Rotuli Parliamentorum*, ii. 316, 322, 363, and iii. 5, 36, 100, 145, 167, 486 and 610). To presume clerical negligence on this scale is surely a desperate course. It should be noticed that nearly all the recorded conferences of this type belong to the period 1373-84 and the rest to the reign of Henry IV. Nor is it without interest that in 1378 the commons' request for one was refused *by the lords themselves*, a fact which makes it difficult to believe that the procedure was designed to enable the magnates to influence opinion and direct action in the other house. In 1383 the king asserted his right, though he did not exercise it, to choose other lords than those named in the commons' petition. In 1402 Henry IV took much the same line, protesting 'q'il ne le vorroit faire de deuete ne de custume, mais de sa grace especiale a ceste foitz' and not only ordered this protestation to be put on record in the rolls, but sent his secretary and the steward of his household to the commons to make his position clear to them. The signs are that the initiative in this as in other matters came from the commons and that the lords were hardly more enthusiastic than the king in welcoming the novelty. It should also be observed that in January 1404 the commons asked that some of their own body should be allowed to go and confer with the lords and that this was granted (*Rot. Parl.*, iii. 523). [2] Neale, *op. cit.*, pp. 261-3.

[3] *John of Gaunt and the parliamentary representation of Lancashire*, reprinted from the *Bulletin of the John Rylands Library*, xxii (1938).

ties were often close. 'To suggest', therefore, 'that the knights should have been able to provide an independent opposition to the lords appears, in regard to the circumstances of the time, to be little short of fantastic'; rather 'the strength of the commons in parliament was not their own but the lords''.[1] And this was echoed more recently by Miss Helen Cam, after a re-examination of the poem generally known as *Richard the Redeles*: 'the leadership and direction of policy came from the lords, who, by getting their dependents elected members and by the device of sending members of their own order to discuss plans with the representatives, were able effectively to exploit the economic and political resources of the commons'.[2] This, then, is the conclusion,

[1] *Op. cit.*, pp. 27 and 46.

[2] H. M. Cam, 'The relation of English members of parliament to their constituencies in the fourteenth century: a neglected text' in *L'Organisation corporative du Moyen Age à la fin de l'Ancien Régime. Études présentées à la Commission Internationale pour l'Histoire des Assemblées d'États*, Louvain, iii (1939), 152. I am at a loss to understand how the passage in 'Richard the Redeles' (*Mum and the Sothsegger*, ed. M. Day and R. Steele, Early Eng. Text Soc., 24-6) helps Dr. Cam's argument. Until I read her article, I had supposed it to give some slight support to the exactly opposite view, and that still seems to me the more satisfactory interpretation. One does not expect a medieval satirist to weaken his case by admitting any merit in his victims; but this one does — by accident. For he attacks those who

> '. . . to þe kyng wente,
> And formed him of foos þat good frendis weren,
> Þat bablid for þe best and no blame serued
> Of kynge ne conceyll ne of þe comunes, noþer,
> Ho-so toke good kepe to þe culorum' (iv, ll. 57-61).

So there were good men in the commons! Then first place is given to those who only *pretended* to guard the interests of those they represented (iv, ll. 44-52). If that was the worst they could be accused of, their constituents were not badly served. Medieval satire generally tries to prove too much, and the present example seems no exception. The author should have stopped short after accusing the members of ineffectiveness and pusillanimity. But he goes on to describe (iv, ll. 71-82) some as hotheads whose intemperance has to be restrained by the influence of the lords. What is meant to be a bitterly scornful description of Richard II's 'privy parliament' suggests — to me at any rate — that an apologist for the commons would have had an easy task. And after all what parliament from that day to this has not contained men of the types satirised by our anonymous poet?

reached — as we are told[1] — 'by converging lines of investigation', and damaging alike to Stubbs and Tout. But before we set about the task of rewriting the political history of two centuries in obedience to the new formula, it would be wise to make sure that it is sound.

It has at least one obvious merit, that it takes account of certain facts which were far too lightly set aside by earlier scholars. Such a fact, for example, as that in the first half of the fifteenth century the attorneys of the great lords of the franchises, to whom suit of the county-court was still, it seems, confined, were primarily, if not solely, responsible for the choice of the knights of the shire for York. This was well known to Stubbs, but he does not appear to have regarded it as a stumbling-block to his reading of the Lancastrian constitution.[2] Again the theory derives strength from the discovery, made by Mr. Richardson, that the representatives for the county of Lancaster were returned to parliament more than once by the order of John of Gaunt alone. It would, nevertheless, be dangerous to generalise upon the basis of evidence from such exceptional counties as those of Lancaster and York without unmistakable confirmation from elsewhere. On the other hand, even when allowance has been made for the special conditions of the palatinate and for the tenacious conservation of the 'highland zone', the existence of such practices cannot but arouse suspicion about the elections in the less atavistic south and east. For, after all, many of the knights returned were, like Sir Peter de la Mare himself, the tenants, retainers or servants of their baronial neighbours, and it would be in the last degree unrealistic to deny considerable influence at elections to the great ones of the shire. Disagreement is only likely when we attempt to decide how much and to assess its effect upon the independence of the commons. The evidence for elections is admittedly slight, but I doubt whether full use has yet been made of the *Paston Letters*. Certain passages have, it is true, been quoted often enough, some to bolster one thesis, others another. Yet, perhaps there is something to be said for considering together all the references to electioneering scattered through the many pages of this Norfolk family's papers.

[1] H. G. Richardson, reviewing the *Études* cited above: *Eng. Hist. Rev.*, lvi (1941), 125.

[2] Stubbs, *op. cit.*, iii (1903 edn.), 424-5.

In all, the *Paston Letters* make mention of five county elections.[1] These belong exclusively to the third quarter of the fifteenth century, namely, to the most disturbed period in late medieval times in England; and, as it happens, to some of its most disturbed years. Such being the case, it would be unreasonable to assume that their conduct was absolutely typical of the century as a whole. Yet whatever abnormalities the wars may have produced, it is not in the least likely that they had the effect of reducing aristocratic influence; rather then did the over-mighty subject enjoy his brief eventful fling. If, therefore, the part played by the great East Anglian houses was not decisive in these years, it is most improbable that it was so in more orderly times.

In September 1450, when writs were issued for a parliament to meet at Westminster on 6 November, the country was already preparing for civil war. Before the ministers could recover from the fall and death of Suffolk, rapidly followed by Cade's rebellion, they were threatened anew by the duke of York's landing in arms from Ireland. Three letters written to John Paston in October were concerned with the election. The first, dated 6 October, was from a friend in London informing him of York's arrival and the panic this had caused in the royal household.[2] It contained a great deal of practical advice about how to obtain the boon of York's 'good lordship' and then continued as follows:

> Sir, labour ye for to be knight of the shire and speak to my master Stapleton also that he be it. Sir, all Swaffham, an they be warned, will give you their voices. . . . Sir, labour ye to the mayor that John Damme or William Jenny be burgess for the city of Norwich. . . . Also, sir, think on Yarmouth that ye ordain that John Jenny, or Limnour, or some good man be burgess for Yarmouth. Ordain ye that Jennys must be in the parliament, for they can say well. Sir, it were wisdom that my lord of Oxford wait on my lord of York. In good faith, good sir, think on all these matters.[3]

It is not known whether Paston heeded this advice; but Sir Miles Stapleton was certainly a candidate, and Oxford, with whom the Pastons seem then to have been acting, was not slow to court the friend-

---

[1] References are to pages in J. Gairdner's library edn. of 1904.
[2] *Paston Letters*, ii. 174.   [3] *Ibid.*, ii. 176.

ship of York, at that time expected in the shire.[1] The removal of Suffolk had released the pent-up discontents of his oppressed East Anglian neighbours and it was said that a strong sheriff would be needed to restore the peace.[2] The new head of the de la Pole family was a minor, the lawless Lord Moleyns was rumoured to be out of grace with the duke of York,[3] and the way was therefore open for the pretensions of the duke of Norfolk. On 16 October, after a meeting with his kinsman York at Bury St. Edmunds, he wrote to Paston to tell him whom they had decided were to be knights of the shire, 'convenient and necessary' for its welfare, and to ask him as he valued their favour to 'make no labour contrary' to their desire.[4] Two days later the earl of Oxford wrote to say that he had received from York 'a token and a shedule of my lord's intent whom he would have knights of the shire' and enclosed the names of Sir William Chamberlain and Henry Grey.[5] In spite of these efforts, only the latter was returned, the other successful candidate being Sir Miles Stapleton. But one of York's council and a future servant of the Mowbrays were elected in Suffolk. John Damme represented Norwich and, though neither of the eloquent Jennys secured a Norfolk seat, William got in for the borough of Dunwich.[6]

Mowbray influence was exercised more effectively in 1455, when a parliament was summoned immediately after the Yorkist victory at St. Albans. As the duchess of Norfolk told Paston, it was 'thought right necessary for divers causes that my lord have at this time in the parliament such persons as belong unto him and be of his menial servants'.[7] She therefore asked him to give his voice for John Howard and Sir Roger Chamberlain and to exhort others to do the same. It is

---

[1] James Gresham to John Paston, *circa* October 1450 (*Paston Letters*, ii. 180–1): 'it was told me that my master Calthorpe had writing from my lord of York to await on him at his coming into Norfolk to be one of his men, and that no gentleman of Norfolk had writing to await on him but he; and some folk ween that it is to the intent that he should be either sheriff or knight of the shire, to the furthering of other folks &c.' William Calthorp was neither sheriff nor M.P. in 1450. But it is interesting to find that the greatest duke in England was believed to be paying compliments to a mere esquire.

[2] *Ibid.*, ii. 182.   [3] *Ibid.*, ii. 176.   [4] *Ibid.*, ii. 184.   [5] *Ibid.*, ii. 184–5.

[6] *Return of members of parliament* (Parl. Papers, 1878, vol. lxii), pt. i, p. 345.

[7] *Paston Letters*, iii. 34. 'Menial' has not here acquired its modern meaning.

difficult to judge from the civil tone of this letter whether the duchess expected, or merely hoped, that it would be obeyed, but the civility should be remarked. Its effect upon Paston was not to make him give up all hope of being returned himself. He still pressed his claims cautiously, and for a time it looked as if he might prevail. Two letters written him by John Jenny a fortnight later reveal more of the mind of a fifteenth-century election-agent than any other in this series. 'I told my lord of Norfolk at London,' Jenny wrote, 'that I laboured divers men for Sir Roger Chamberlain and they said to me they would have him; but not Howard, inasmuch as he had no livelihood in the shire nor conversement; and I asked them whom they would have and they said they would have you; and thus I told him.'[1] Next day he expanded his first report:

> My servant told me ye desired to know what my lord of Norfolk said when I spake of you. And he said, inasmuch as Howard might not be, he would write a letter to the under-sheriff that the shire should have free election, so that Sir Thomas Tuddenham were not nor none that were toward the duke of Suffolk; he said he knew that ye were never to himward. Ye may send to the under-sheriff and see my lord's letter. Howard was as wood as a wild bullock; God send him such worship as he deserveth. It is an evil precedent for the shire that a strange man should be chosen, and no worship to my lord of York nor to my lord of Norfolk to write for him; for if the gentlemen of the shire will suffer such inconvenience, in good faith the shire shall not be called of such worship as it hath been.[2]

That after this both Chamberlain and Howard were returned says much for the weight of the duke's authority; but it is also obvious from Jenny's comments that there were limits beyond which it was not wise to go.

That Norfolk's men were not altogether approved of became evident at the next election of which we have any knowledge, that held after Edward IV's conquest of the throne in 1461. In the interval John Paston had at length sat for Norfolk in the parliament of 1460, with the good wishes of the common people — or so his wife assured him — and,

[1] *Paston Letters*, iii. 38; 24 June 1455.   [2] *Ibid.*, iii. 39.

what was perhaps more useful, the approval of the mayor of Norwich.[1]
When he decided to stand again for the first Yorkist parliament, it was
in opposition to the Mowbray candidates. His old rival, Sir John
Howard, was now Sheriff. The shire met at Norwich on 15 June,
William Pryce, the under-sheriff, presiding. According to a return
afterwards made to the king by Howard, his deputy was prevented by
the threats of John Berney, who was one of the candidates, backed by
a crowd of armed men, from holding the election and only escaped
unharmed by the help of three of Norfolk's servants.[2] But the exaggeration in Howard's story is proved by a letter from the under-sheriff
himself to John Paston, written on 18 June 1461, but wrongly supposed
by Gairdner to belong to 1455.[3] In this Pryce says: 'Sir, as for the election of the knights of the shire here in Norfolk, in good faith there hath
been much to-do; neverthelatter to let you have knowledge of the
demeaning, my master Berney, my master Grey, and ye had greatest
voice; and I purpose me, as I will answer God, to return the due election, that is after the sufficiency,[4] you and master Grey. Neverthelatter
I have a master.' Shortly afterwards Margaret Paston was sent a letter
of advice by her husband's servant, Thomas Dennis: 'it were expedient
that the king were informed of the demeaning of the shire.[5] Therefore
I send to you a testimonial, which is made by a great assent of great
multitude of commons, to send to the king.'[6] He urges her to have it
sent post-haste. 'Beside forth, that ye vouchsafe to let diligent labour be
made to a sufficient number to seal [the indenture of election] for my
master Paston alone; for if both hold not, I would one held. . . . For on
the adversary part Judas sleepeth not. Berney promised to have sent, but

[1] *Paston Letters*, iii. 239–40.

[2] 'A Norfolk parliamentary election, 1461' by C. H. Williams, *Eng. Hist.
Rev.*, xl (1925), 79–86, where the sheriff's return is printed. The opportune
presence of Norfolk's servants is significant.

[3] *Paston Letters*, iii. 36.

[4] I.e., in accordance with the votes of those qualified to take part in the
election.

[5] I.e., of the shire-court of 15 June.

[6] *Ibid.*, iii. 284. It is dated Sunday only, but it must have been written after
the meeting of the shire on Monday 15 June and before Dennis's murder on
4 July, that is on either 21 or 28 June.

for our Lord's love trust not that; for I see his sloth and silly labour, which is no labour.'[1] Evidently his fellow candidate was an embarrassment to John Paston, for on 12 July, by which time the meeting of parliament had been put off until 4 November, he instructed his wife to 'tell the said Berney that the sheriff is in a doubt whether he shall make a new election of knights of the shire, because of him and Grey; wherein it were better for him to have the sheriff's goodwill. Item me thinketh for quiet of the country it were most worshipful that as well Berney as Grey should get a record of all such that might spend forty shillings a year that were at the day of election, which of them that had the fewest to give it up as reason would.'[2] So far it is clear that Paston had no anxiety about his own return; he confidently assumed that he had been and would remain at the head of the poll.[3] Even later, on 1 August, when he knew that the postponement of parliament might occasion a fresh election and had observed for himself some shiftiness in the under-sheriff's manner, his optimism was unshaken; Pryce had evidently deserted Berney, but then Berney's chances had never been good, since he had not had a majority of the 'sufficienty'; the other seat at least was safely his own. So he wrote to his wife from London: 'I hear say the people is disposed to be at the shire at Norwich on St. Laurence's day [11 August] for the affirming of that they have done afore, whereof I hold me well content, if they do it of their own disposition, but I will not be the cause of the labour of them, nor bear no cost of them at this time, for by the law I am sure before, but I am well apaid it shall be on a holiday for letting of the people's work.'[4] He did not retain this aloofness for long. Unfortunately his arrival in Norfolk soon afterwards meant an end of correspondence and we have only Howard's *ex parte* statement of what happened next;[5] Paston's rejoin-

[1] *Paston Letters*, iii. 284.   [2] *Ibid.*, iii. 290.

[3] In view of his remarks about a contest and a count, the phrase is not inappropriate.

[4] *Ibid.*, iii. 297.

[5] It is necessary to emphasise its *ex parte* character as compared with the familiar letters of the Pastons, since Mr. Williams seems inclined to regard them as of equal value. Howard was making a case against an enemy in the king's court; the Pastons had no motive for deceiving one another and were not writing 'for posterity'.

der, if he made one, was not enrolled. But we do know that he was arrested on going to London in October and then released; and this was followed by rumours in Norfolk that Howard in his turn had been imprisoned.[1] In his petition, Howard alleged that Paston swamped the shire-meeting with 'insufficient' [i.e. unqualified] persons, heavily armed and intent on violence, who prevented the return of the duly elected candidates, Sir William Chamberlain and Henry Grey the younger, and forced the sheriff in fear of his life to seal the indenture in the names of Paston and Berney. This neither squares with the previous correspondence already quoted nor with what happened in the sequel. Paston was without any doubt capable of chicanery, but there was no need to throw dust in the eyes of his own wife. It is more likely that he was led to intervene violently in response to a last-minute attempt by the sheriff to set aside the earlier election and to substitute candidates of his own. But whatever happened at Norwich on 11 August, it was Paston and Berney who were returned and no action was taken by the king's court as a result of Howard's information.[2] According to Margaret Paston, they were acclaimed as popular heroes by their countrymen, and eventually at a shire-court, held under a new sheriff in January 1462, their election seems to have been peacefully confirmed.[3]

The Pastons had by now established themselves as people of consequence in Norfolk. John Paston, it is more than likely, sat again in the parliament of 1463–5;[4] but he died in 1466 and his son, Sir John, who succeeded to his claims and ambitions, represented Norfolk in the next parliament of 1467–8. It is not, however, until we come to Henry VI's 'readeption parliament' of 1470 that electioneering is once more clearly mentioned in the *Letters*. Sir John was now anxious to be returned again. The restoration of Henry VI had brought the earl of Oxford into

[1] *Paston Letters*, iv. 2. He received a pardon on 6 February 1462 (C. L. Scofield, *The life and reign of Edward the Fourth*, ii. 380 n., citing Pardon Roll 1–6 Edw. IV, m. 43).

[2] According to Mr. Williams (*op. cit.*, 86 n.) the case reappears on the Coram Rege Roll of Michaelmas Term, 4 Henry VII.

[3] *Paston Letters*, iv. 25 and 27.

[4] See *ibid.*, iv. 66, for evidence that he was being considered as a candidate and *ibid.*, pp. 74–6 and 121–8, for evidence that his visits to London coincided with the sessions of parliament.

power in East Anglia and it was therefore necessary to impress him with the Pastons' importance. As Sir John told his younger brother on 15 November, if he and his friends 'hold as one body' at the meeting of the shire, the earl might realise 'that some strength resteth thereby'. He urged him, therefore, to let the earl know 'that the love of the country and city resteth on our side and that other folks be not beloved nor never were.'[1] How the contest went is not definitely known, but what evidence there is indicates that the result was acceptable both to Oxford and the Pastons. For on 22 November, Margaret Paston wrote to her sons in London to warn them that since the shire-day 'the other part' had been trying to get the returns upset: 'there was made labour and like to be concluded that the election of knights of the shire should be changed and new certificate made and John Jenny [no longer a friend evidently] set therein; therefore do your devoir to understand the truth as soon as ye can, for the said Jenny this day rideth up to Londonward and I suppose because of the same'. In a postscript she advised them to get 'my lord' — probably of Oxford — to send for the sheriff's deputy on the day before parliament met to make quite sure that the certificate had not been tampered with. For on that evening or the following morning 'it shall be put in and if it is put in, there is no remedy. Jenny saith he will attempt the law therein.'[2] And that is all we hear.

By 1472, when the next election was held, Edward IV was king again and his friends had matters all their own way in Norfolk. Mowbray and de la Pole were acting in concert and Sir John Paston failed to secure their nomination. As his brother told him on 21 Sep-

[1] *Paston Letters*, v. 89.

[2] This letter (*ibid.*, v. 159–61) is dated 'Thursday next before St. Katherine' and is assigned by Gairdner to 19 November 1472. But the parliament of that year began on 6 October (*Interim report of the Committee on House of Commons personnel and politics, 1264–1832*, 1932, pp. 86–7) and it was obviously written before the opening of the first session. On the other hand a reference to the manor of Gresham connects it with letter no. 792 (v. 126–7) which in view of its mentioning Sir Robert Harcourt's recent murder, can be dated 1 December 1470; for Harcourt was slain 14 November of that year (J. C. Wedgwood, 'Harcourt of Ellenhall' in *Staffordshire Collections*, William Salt Archaeological Soc. (1914), 203).

tember: 'your desire as for the knights of the shire was an impossible to be brought about. For my lord of Norfolk and my lord of Suffolk were agreed amore than a fornight ago to have Sir Robert Wingfield and Sir Richard Harcourt, and that knew I not till it was Friday last past.' A complication was that he had sent to their friends to be at Norwich 'to serve your intent' and he had therefore great difficulty in avoiding loss of face. However, he pretended that his brother after all would not be in England for parliament. 'So they came not at the shire-house; for if they had, it was thought by such as be your friends here that your adversaries would have reported that ye had made labour to have been one and that ye could not bring your purpose about.' He had been too late also for Yarmouth, but he had procured a recommendation to the bailiff of Malden in Essex for his brother's return there.[1] Yet although this letter was in the most fulsome terms and declared Sir John to be one of the duchess of Norfolk's counsel and 'to stand greatly in favour with my lord chamberlain', it produced no effect.[2] The returns for East Anglia and indeed for all England except Cornwall are extant, but Paston's name does not appear in them.[3] The dukes' nominees were duly elected for Norfolk. Nevertheless John Paston the younger wrote to his brother on 26 March 1473: 'I pray God send you the Holy Ghost among you in the parliament house, and rather the Devil, we say, than ye should grant any more taxes.'[4] So he got there somehow in the end.

Now, many valuable lessons can be drawn from the Pastons' electoral adventures, but one so simple as that the great lords *controlled* the suffrage of the county, I dare assert, cannot. Even at the height of a civil war in which the landed classes at least were risking their lives and fortunes, when the country swarmed with armed men fresh from victories in the field of battle and when the sheriff was a notorious partisan, the winning side could not be sure of returning its own men. Those to whom the electors 'gave their voices' were not necessarily the candidates for whom a duke had 'written'. On the other hand there were a large number of voters who were willing to follow the lead of those

---

[1] *Paston Letters*, v. 149–51.   [2] *Ibid.*, v. 148–9.

[3] *Returns*, pt. i, pp. 360–2.

[4] *Paston Letters*, v. 178. This letter is fully dated.

powerful enough to maintain and protect them, and when two such local potentates as the dukes of Norfolk and Suffolk joined forces and had announced their choice, they could carry sufficient numbers with them to decide the election; to pursue the contest against them then was to court a humiliating defeat. These combines were, nevertheless, a confession of weakness, since their object could only be to secure one seat for each partner. Even so, the alliance of York and Norfolk was only half successful in 1450. In 1461 the Mowbray influence, used too high-handedly and without Yorkist backing, overreached itself altogether. The right deduction seems to be that the opinion of the gentlemen of the shire counted for much. These men would take, as they would give, advice; they appreciated the value of 'good lordship'; and they were willing to be guided by those who had claims on their support; but it was foolish to attempt to drive them with too tight a rein. 'Management' was already a necessary art for those who wished to influence elections.

John Jenny's remarks about Howard's candidature in 1455 are particularly interesting. The objection that Howard had no livelihood or conversement in the shire, although he was the duke of Norfolk's cousin and ultimate heir and, what is more, a considerable landowner in the linked county of Suffolk, proves that the statutable property qualification had its roots firmly planted in local sentiment. All the other ducal candidates, and indeed all those elected for Norfolk in these years, were substantial men in the shire.[1] So substantial indeed as to raise an even more interesting question: how far were they at the disposal of their magnate backers when they arrived at Westminster? Is it really justifiable, for example, to speak of them — the phrase is Mr. Richardson's[2] — as 'credulous and willing to be led' once they had met together in the common house? I very much doubt it. It seems to

[1] Sir Richard Harcourt might be counted an exception, since his lands lay for the most part elsewhere; but he had recently married a de la Pole who was the widow of Sir Miles Stapleton (M.P., Suffolk 1439–40, Norfolk 1442, 1449–50 and 1450–1; *Returns*, pt. i, pp. 333, 339 and 345; J. C. Wedgwood, *History of Parliament, Biographies of the Members of the Commons House, 1439–1509*, pp. 804–5) and was in possession of the Stapleton place at Ingham at the time of his election (Wedgwood, *op. cit.*, p. 419).

[2] *John of Gaunt*, &c., p. 33.

me to assume a degree of subordination and a want of political training which nothing in their careers would lead one to expect. It is true that they were labelled feeble and hesitant by more whole-hogging chroniclers and satirists, but this was because they had the sense to come to terms with the king. Their critics would have been content with nothing less than a refusal to vote taxation altogether. If the knights preferred to bargain for such safeguards as the appropriation of their grants, only a monastic doctrinaire would have ascribed this to weakness. After all, were they not taxpayers themselves?

If there is any tendency to underrate the capacity of these early M.P.s it can be corrected by a study of their lives. Experienced administrators, rising lawyers and prosperous men of business were from at least the reign of Edward III onwards collected in the commons. Some were old parliamentary hands with half a dozen elections and more to their credit.[1] It is difficult to believe that these still felt any great awe in the presence of the king and lords. Though few, they preserved continuity in the frequent and short-lived parliaments of the fourteenth century. But experience gained elsewhere was commoner and could be just as valuable. Sir Peter de la Mare, whose sagacity and eloquence won him the admiration of all, was actually a newcomer to the house when he was chosen to speak for the commons in 1376. Anyone who showed fewer signs of being credulous and willing to be led, it would be difficult to imagine. He had served his apprenticeship at the council-table of the earl of March. There were many such training-grounds, and to others of less repute than de la Mare long lives of service brought opportunities for knowledge and for practice in debate. Few knights were not actively employed most of their lives in local government, and some, especially such early speakers as Sir James Pickering,[2] Sir

[1] For example, in the parliament of 1399, four knights were sitting for the 6th time, two for the 7th, three for the 8th, one for the 9th, one for the 10th, two for the 12th (Sir Robert Neville of Hornby and Robert Urswyk) and one for the 19th (Sir William Bonville). These figures are derived from the *Return*, pt. i, *passim*.

[2] Speaker in the parliaments of 1378 and February 1383, he was M.P. for Westmorland in 1362, 1365, October 1377, 1378, 1379 and October 1382, for Cumberland in 1368 and for Yorkshire in February 1383, November 1384, September 1388, November 1390 and 1397–8 (here and elsewhere, unless

William Sturmy[1] and Thomas Chaucer,[2] had quite outstanding and varied records in affairs of state. These were professional administrators. But they and their fellow knights were for the most part also well-to-do country gentlemen, whose social position as much as their width of experience marked them out for leadership in the commons house.

What that position often was is clearly brought home to us by the records of two graduated taxes on incomes from land voted in the parliaments of 1411 and 1435. Each necessitated an *ad hoc* assessment and parts of both sets of returns have survived. Those made in 1436 were analysed a few years ago by Professor H. L. Gray. They reveal the existence of some ten commoners whose landed wealth was not much less than that of the average baron and of many more who were entitled

---

otherwise stated, the elections are taken from the Public Record Office copy of the *Return*). He accompanied William of Windsor to Ireland in 1369 and was, as 'chief justice of the pleas following the lieutenant and the principal person of his secret council' accused by the Irish of corruption, extortion and malversation (M. V. Clarke, *Fourteenth-century studies*, 186, 206, 220–9 and 231–2). Thereafter until the end of the century the Chancery rolls abound with his commissions and appointments. See also the *D.N.B.* and N. B. Lewis, 'Re-election to parliament in the reign of Richard II', *Eng. Hist. Rev.*, xlviii (1933), 394.

[1] Sturmy or Esturmy (J. H. Wylie, *History of England under Henry the Fourth*, ii. 71, n. 1) is not in the *D.N.B.* Speaker in the parliament of October 1404, he was M.P. for Hampshire in April 1384 and November 1390, for Wiltshire in January 1390, 1393, 1399, 1401, May 1413, November 1414, 1417 and 1422, and for Devon in November 1391 and October 1404. He was frequently Henry IV's envoy to the German princes between 1401 and 1407. For information about him and about all others who sat in the parliament of 1422 I am deeply indebted to Mr. J. S. Roskell. [See, for further details about Sturmy and other M.P.s mentioned in this paper, J. S. Roskell, *The Commons in the Parliament of 1422* (1954) and *The Commons and their Speakers, 1376–1523* (1965).]

[2] Speaker in the parliaments of 1407, 1410, 1411, November 1414 and May 1421, he sat for Oxfordshire in 1401, 1402, 1406, 1407, 1410, 1411, May 1413, November 1414, May 1421, 1422, 1426, 1427, 1429–30 and 1431. He was chief butler to Henry IV, Henry V and Henry VI, and after various employments was appointed a councillor in 1423 (*Rot. Parl.*, iv. 201). He died in 1434 (*D.N.B.*; see also R. Krauss, 'Chaucerian problems: especially the Petherton Forestership and the question of Thomas Chaucer' in *Three Chaucer studies* by R. Krauss, H. Braddy and C. R. Kase).

to be classed in this respect with the lesser baronage.[1] The returns made in 1412 tell the same story in rather a different way.[2] It appears, for example, that there were in all fourteen Dorset landowners — excluding the house of Lancaster, ecclesiastics and religious houses — whose estates in that and one or more of the adjacent counties of Hampshire, Wiltshire, Somerset and Devon were assessed at more than £200 a year (it is advisable to include the adjacent districts in the reckoning, since a county boundary was itself no barrier to the exercise of territorial influence; only great distances were). Of these fourteen eight were peers and six were commoners. The comparable figures for Sussex (taking account of lands in Kent, Surrey and Hampshire) were four in all, two peers and two commoners.[3]

That is to say that there were in Dorset and Sussex together eight non-baronial landlords entitled to be classed high among the great ones of their shires. It is interesting, therefore, to find that all eight sat as knights in parliament. At their head for wealth stood Sir Humphrey Stafford the elder of Hooke in Dorset.[4] He was a cadet of the family which was soon to be granted the dukedom of Buckingham and his connection with the south-west was recent. He had married the widow of one Sir John Mautravers, who had sat for Dorset in eight consecutive parliaments at the beginning of Richard II's reign.[5] This match had brought him the custody of large estates in Somerset and Dorset, which he further secured to his descendants by marrying his wife's daughter by Mautravers to his own son and heir. Along with Sir John's manors, the Staffords can be said to have inherited his seat in parliament. Sir Humphrey the elder was a knight of the shire at least fifteen times,

---

[1] 'Incomes from land in England in 1436', *Eng. Hist. Rev.*, xlix (1934), 620–1.

[2] *Rot. Parl.*, iii. 648–9; *Inquisitions and assessments relating to feudal aids, 1284–1431*, vi. 391–501 and 503–51. These returns may not give us the real value of a man's lands to him, but so long as they are only made a basis of comparison between one landowner and another, their absolute trustworthiness is immaterial. [3] For a list, see Appendix, pages 264–9 below.

[4] S. W. Bates Harbin, *M.P.s for the county of Somerset*, 71–2; *Register of Henry Chichele*, ed. E. F. Jacob, ii. 677.

[5] Bates Harbin, *op. cit.*, pp. 65–6. M.P. for Dorset, 1368, 1381, May 1382 and October 1382; for Somerset, February 1383; for Dorset, October 1383, April 1384, November 1384 and 1385. *Ob.* 1385 or '86.

mostly for Dorset, between 1383 and 1410, sitting in all but four of the parliaments for which the returns are known between 1388 and his death in 1413.[1] Thereafter his heir, who had already represented Staffordshire in the 'long parliament' of 1406, was elected ten times for Dorset before 1432.[2] The grandson of this Sir Humphrey the younger was summoned as a baron to Edward IV's first parliament and eventually created earl of Devon.[3] For more than a century before this the Staffords had had the means to support at least the humbler dignity. Exclusive of their lands in the midlands, they were assessed at close on £600 a year in 1412.[4]

Sir John Pelham, who was treasurer of England at the time, was said to be in possession of even more than £600 a year in 1412, but some of this may not have been his own.[5] An old supporter of the house of Lancaster, he owed his position to the king's favour. As the second largest non-ecclesiastical landowner in Sussex, he represented it in every parliament but one of Henry IV's reign for which returns survive, and at least twice afterwards.[6] Sir Thomas Brooke the elder, whose lands were mainly in Somerset, sat thirteen times or more for that county between 1386 and 1413, in all the most eventful parliaments of Richard II's majority.[7] His son, Sir Thomas the younger, was elected for Dorset in the first parliament of Henry V's reign and four times for Somerset between 1417 and 1427.[8] He had married the Cobham heiress,

---

[1] M.P. for Warwickshire, October 1383; for Wiltshire, November 1384; for Dorset, September 1388, January 1390, 1391 and 1393; for Somerset, 1394; for Dorset, 1395, January 1397, 1399, 1401, January 1404, 1406, 1407 and 1410.

[2] April 1414, November 1414, 1417, 1419, 1420, May 1421, 1422, 1426, 1427 and 1432. *Ob.* 1442 (*Chichele Reg.*, ii. 620–4 and 677; J. C. Wedgwood, *Staffordshire parliamentary history*, William Salt Archaeological Soc., i. (1917), 165–6).   [3] G. E. C., *Complete Peerage*, iv (1916), 327–8.

[4] £596 exclusive of Staffordshire lands made over to Sir Humphrey the younger (*Feudal Aids*, vi, *passim*).   [5] £618–6–8 (*Ib.*).

[6] 1399, 1401, January 1404, October 1404, 1406 and 1407; 1422 and 1427. *Ob.* 1429 (*Cal. Fine Rolls*, xv. 236; *Cal. Inq. post mortem*, iv. 121; *Chichele Reg.*, ii. 408–9 and 669).

[7] Bates Harbin, *op. cit.*, 67–8: 1386, February 1388, 1391, 1393, 1395, January 1397, 1397–8, 1399, 1402, January 1404, 1407, 1410 and May 1413. *Ob.* 1417 (*Cal. Fine Rolls*, xiv. 196).

[8] 1417, May 1421, 1422 and 1427. Bates Harbin, *op. cit.*, pp. 84–5.

Sir John Oldcastle's stepdaughter, and his son, Edward, after sitting for
Somerset in 1442, was summoned to the lords in 1445.[1] Sir John Tiptoft, scarcely if at all less wealthy than Stafford and Pelham, was the
heir of Sir Pain Tiptoft, M.P. for Cambridgeshire in 1399 and January
1404. Sir John had been in Bolingbroke's service before Richard's
deposition and was one of the many gentlemen who profited largely
from the change of dynasty.[2] He sat for the county of Huntingdon in
both the parliaments of 1404 and, as speaker, in that of 1406. From 1406
to 1408 he was treasurer of the king's household and from 1408 to 1410
was treasurer of England. He represented Somerset in the Leicester
parliament of 1414 and, after serving for most of Henry V's reign in
France, returned in 1422 to become a member of the minority council
and to sit from 1426 onwards among the lords.

Not all knights of the shire were as rich or as eminent as these. But
in every parliament there was a nucleus of such men, often with one,
two or even three ex-speakers among them,[3] not only skilled in business
and ripe in counsel, but with a backing of landed wealth and influence
to give that counsel weight even among the lords. Such outstanding
parliamentarians as Sir Walter Hungerford[4] and William Burley of
Broncroft[5] immediately spring to mind; or such families as the Bonvilles

---

[1] G. E. C., *Complete Peerage*, iii (1913), 346; *Hist. of Parl.*, *Biogs.*, pp. 115–16.

[2] *D.N.B.*

[3] The parliament of May 1382 had at least three (de la Mare, Hungerford
and Waldegrave); so did those of October 1382 (de la Mare, Pickering and
Waldegrave), February 1383 (de la Mare, Gildesborough and Waldegrave)
and September 1388 (Hungerford, Pickering and Waldegrave).

[4] Son of Sir Thomas Hungerford (speaker, January 1377, M.P. for Wiltshire, 1357, 1360, 1362 and January 1377; for Somerset, 1378; for Wiltshire,
1379, January 1380 and November 1380; for Somerset, May 1382; for Wiltshire, October 1383; for Somerset and Wiltshire, April 1384; for Wiltshire,
1386; for Somerset, September 1388; for Somerset and Wiltshire, January
1390; for Somerset, November 1390; and for Wiltshire, 1393. *Ob.* 1397 (*Cal.
Fine Rolls*, xi. 268; *Cal. Inq. post mortem*, iii. 217).) M.P. for Wiltshire, 1401,
October 1404 and 1407; for Somerset, 1410; for Wiltshire, May 1413 and
April 1414 (speaker). Summoned to the lords, 1426. Treasurer of England,
1426–32. *Ob.* 1449 (*D.N.B.*).

[5] M.P. for Salop, 1417, 1419, 1420, May 1421, 1422, 1425, 1427–8, 1429–30,
1431, 1432, 1433, 1435, 1437 (speaker), 1429–40, 1442, 1445–6 (speaker),

of Shute,[1] the Montforts of Coleshill,[2] the Arundells of Lanherne,[3] the Tyrells of Heron,[4] the Stourtons of Stourton,[5] the Stanleys of

---

1449–50, 1450–1 and 1455–6. *Ob.* 1458. His great-uncle was Sir Simon Burley, victim of the Lords Appellant in 1388. His father, John Burley, was M.P. for Salop, 1399, 1401, January 1404, October 1404, 1410 and 1411. (W. T. Weyman, 'Shropshire members of parliament (1325–1584)' in *Trans. Shropshire Archaeol. and Nat. Hist. Soc.*, x and xi, nos. 89 and 98; *Hist. of Parl., Biogs.*, pp. 139–40; *D.N.B.*).

[1] Sir William Bonville (*c.* 1340–1408), M.P. for Somerset, 1366; for Devon, 1371, 1376, 1378, 1379, November 1380, 1381–2, May 1382 and October 1382; for Somerset, October 1383; for Devon and Somerset, April 1384; for Somerset, November 1384, 1386, February 1388, 1393 and 1395; for Devon, January 1397 and 1397–8; for Somerset, 1399; and for Devon, 1402. (Bates Harbin, *op. cit.*, pp. 54–5).) His grandson and heir, Sir William, was M.P. for Somerset, May 1421; for Devon, 1422, 1425 and 1427–8. Afterwards Lord Bonville (1449). *Ob.* 1461. (Bates Harbin, *op. cit.*, pp. 87–9.) His brother, Thomas, was M.P. for Cornwall, 1439–40. (*Hist. of Parl., Biogs.*, p. 92.)

[2] Sir John Montfort, M.P. for Warwickshire, 1361. His grandson and heir, Sir William (1385–1452), M.P. for Warwickshire, 1422, 1423–4, 1427–8, 1429–30, 1437, 1445–6 and 1450–1. He married the daughter of Sir John Pecche, M.P. for Warwickshire, August 1352, 1354, 1358 and 1373. Sir William's younger son, Sir Edmund, was M.P. for Warwickshire, 1447 and 1459; for Gloucestershire, 1491–2. Sir Simon, son and heir of Sir William's eldest son, Sir Baldwin, was M.P. for Warwickshire, 1463–5, 1478 and 1491–2. (W. Dugdale, *Antiquities of Warwickshire* (1656), pp. 728–32; *Hist. of Parl., Biogs.*, pp. 602–4.)

[3] Sir John Arundell, M.P. for Cornwall, January 1397, 1397–8, January 1404, October 1404, 1406, 1411, April 1414, March 1416, 1417, May 1421, 1422 and 1423–4. *Ob.* 1435. His son and heir, John (*ob. v. p.* 1423) was M.P. for Devon, November 1414; for Cornwall, 1419, December 1421 and 1422. Sir John's younger son, Sir Remfrey, was M.P. for Cornwall, 1431, 1433 and 1442. (*Hist. of Parl., Biogs.*, pp. 19–20.)

[4] Sir Thomas Tyrell, M.P. for Essex, 1365, 1366, 1369, 1372 and 1373. His grandson, Sir John Tyrell, M.P. for Essex, 1411, May 1413, March 1416, 1417, 1419, May 1421, 1422 and 1425; for Hertfordshire, 1427–8; and for Essex, 1429, 1431, 1433 and 1437 (speaker, 1427, 1431 and 1437). (*D.N.B.*) His son and heir, Sir Thomas, M.P. for Essex, 1442, 1447, February 1449 and 1459. Sir John's 2nd son, William, was M.P. for Suffolk, 1447 and 1459 and *his* son and heir, Sir James, was M.P. for Cornwall, 1478. Sir John's fifth son, Sir William, was M.P. for Weymouth, February 1449; for Essex, 1449–50, 1450–1 and 1455–6. (*Hist. of Parl., Biogs.*, pp. 889–94).

[5] See Appendix, Table A below, pp. 264–5.

Knowsley[1] and the Harringtons of Farleton and Hornby,[2] to name but a few whose members often sat in the lower house. If these men were independent and outspoken in criticism, and swayed their fellow knights and burgesses, it is surely no matter for surprise. They represented a powerful and respected element in the community of every shire, and there was no need for them to stand in dread of the great, for they were not small themselves. Their existence forbids us to divide that society into powerful barons on the one hand and humble commoners on the other, into leaders among the peers and led among the knights. Even the greater magnates were not a class apart; they had their place, if they could keep it, at the forefront only of a larger body of men, landed and gently born, in the middle ranks of whom peer and commoner jostled together. The recipient of a personal summons to parliament was expected to have the means to support his rank, but the means alone were not sufficient to earn it; that required military and political services. The Staffords and the Stourtons, in spite of their wealth, had to wait, while the Hungerfords and the Tiptofts moved up rapidly; not, however, across some social gulf dividing masters from men; only higher in the same class. It is this community of aim and outlook which made it difficult for lords and commons to disagree violently or for long in parliament; not the ties of service by which some have set so much

---

[1] Sir John Stanley, M.P. for Lancashire, May 1413 and November 1414. *Ob.* 1437. His son and heir, Sir Thomas Stanley, M.P. for Lancashire, 1427–28, 1433, 1439–40, 1442, 1447, February 1449, 1449–50, 1450–1, 1453–4, 1455–6. Lord Stanley 1456. *Ob.* 1459. His grandson, Sir George, was M.P. for Lancashire, 1478. Lord Strange 1482. *Ob.* 1503. (J. S. Roskell, *Knights of the shire for Lancashire*, Chetham Soc., pp. 123–8 and 162–72; *Hist. of Parl., Biogs.*, pp. 796–7 and 800).

[2] Sir Nicholas Harrington of Farleton (second son of Sir John, M.P. for Lancashire, 1343, 1352 and 1357), M.P. for Lancashire, 1372, October, 1377, 1379, 1386 and 1402. *Ob. c.* 1403. His second son, James, M.P. for Lancashire, October 1404, was the father of Sir Richard, M.P. for Lancashire, 1450–1, 1453–4 and 1459. Sir Nicholas's grandson and ultimate heir, Sir Thomas, was M.P. for Lancashire, 1432, 1437, 1442, 1447 and February 1449; and for Yorkshire, 1455–6. His son and heir, Sir James, was M.P. for Lancashire, 1467–8 and 1478. Sir Thomas's second son, Sir Robert, was M.P. for Lancashire, 1472–5. (J. S. Roskell, *op. cit.*, pp. 33–8, 103–6, 179–86 and 195–8; *Hist. of Parl., Biogs.*, pp. 423–7).

store. Without such a community, the ties would not have held, for they had very little strength.

Late medieval lordship, indeed, has not much in common with feudal *dominium*.[1] When a man asked another to be his 'good lord', he was not commending himself and his land; nor did he become anything remotely like a vassal. Rather he was acquiring a temporary patron. In this loosely-knit and shamelessly competitive society, it was the ambition of every thrusting gentleman — and also of anyone who aspired to gentility — to attach himself for as long as suited him to such as were in a position to further his interests. For those who wished to rise in the world, good lordship was essential. A successful man, therefore, gathered about him what was sometimes called his 'affinity'; those who staked their hopes on a share of his good fortune. And since *his* chances of winning his desires increased as his following grew, he in his turn used all the arts at his command to attract useful men to his service. It was a partnership to their mutual advantage, a contract from which both sides expected to benefit. And so around the hard core of household and estate officials there accumulated a vast but indefinite mass of councillors, retainers and servants, tailing off into those who were believed to be well-wishers. These were the 'bastard feudatories'.

All this is familiar enough. But it is still necessary to emphasise the political consequences which followed from the impermanence of these associations. Lordship lasted only so long as it was found to be *good* lordship or until it was ousted by a better. As John Paston the younger told his brother in 1475, 'I have given my lady [of Norfolk] warning that I will do my lord no more service; but ere we parted she made me to make her promise that I should let her have knowledge ere I fastened myself in any other service; and so I departed.'[2] A few years earlier he had given his mother no thanks for obtaining for him Lord Scales's good lordship, 'whereof I am nothing proud'.[3] Many instances could be collected from the *Paston Letters* to illustrate the want of settled loyalty which marked these contracts of service. Those changes of allegiance which have been noted by Tout in the careers of Bushy,

---

[1] On this subject, see H. M. Cam, 'The decline and fall of English feudalism' in *History*, xxv (1940), 216–33.

[2] *Paston Letters*, v. 240. [3] *Ibid.*, v. 106.

Bagot and Green, Richard II's notorious agents, do not seem to have been exceptional.[1] There is not even much sign, though it may perhaps be glimpsed in Paston's promise to the duchess, that any sense of the decencies of public life had yet developed to replace the feudal oath. There were few who in that period clung to one family through good and bad fortune. They might fight for their lords in the gamble for power, but desertion often followed defeat. Watching which way to jump, most, like the Pastons themselves, cultivated friends in every camp and turned the least change in the balance of forces to immediate account.[2] It is, therefore, to the last degree unlikely that when they came to parliament, they were more reliable.

Some have jibbed, and, I think, rightly jibbed, at the use of the word 'party' to describe these political groups. The 'affinity' had little in common with the modern party; but it did, it seems to me, in many ways resemble the eighteenth-century 'connection', so fully anatomised by Professor Namier. There was the same element of voluntary interdependence, the same competition for 'place' and the same absence of any separate fund of political principle. Held together by little else than the hope of gain, these affinities swelled with success and dwindled in adversity. Their management must have called for the exercise of considerable art, knowledge and force of character. The tactful handling of many different types of men came easily no doubt to some magnates. But is it likely that the gift of political leadership was possessed by all or even by most? I should be reluctant to go so far with Professor Galbraith as to think that 'the members of the ruling class were *in general* men of arrested intellectual development, who looked to those below them in the social scale for the intelligence necessary to order and govern society'.[3] One can exaggerate the political immaturity

---

[1] T. F. Tout, *Chapters in Administrative History of Medieval England*, iv. 12–14.

[2] *Paston Letters*, ii. 80 contains an amusing account of one Steward's predicament: 'He enquired me', wrote Edmund Paston, 'of the rule of my master Daniel and my lord of Suffolk, and asked which I thought should rule in this shire; and I said, both, as I trow, and he that surviveth to hold by virtue of the survivor, and he to thank his friends and to acquit his enemies. So I feel by him he would forsake his master and get him a new, if he wist he should rule; and so, ween I, much of all the country is so disposed.'

[3] 'A new life of Richard II', *History*, xxvi (1942), 227. My italics.

of this warrior class. As Mr. Galbraith himself reminds us in another connection, a chronicler could say that 'the temporal lords always feared John of Gaunt because of his power, his prudence and his extraordinary ability'.[1] Nevertheless I believe it to be true that the directing brain behind the activities of a baronial household and its extensive connections was not always that of its nominal head. As Pecock remarks in his *Repressor*, there were great lords and ladies who 'could not reckon a sum into a hundred shillings' and who for that reason had to find 'officers under them for to attend sufficiently to all the worldly needs of their lands.'[2] Such men were bound to be to some extent in the hands of their councillors and civil servants for more important matters than estates management and some would be so entirely. Edward IV is reported to have said to Sir William Brandon, one of the duke of Norfolk's council: 'Brandon, though thou can beguile the duke of Norfolk and bring him about the thumb as thou list, I let thee weet thou shalt not do me so, for I understand thy false dealing well enough'; and the account of the interview continues, 'for he told him that he knew well enough that he might rule my lord of Norfolk as he would; and if my lord did anything that were contrary to his laws, the king told him he knew well enough that it was by nobody's means but by his'.[3] Like other members of Norfolk's council, Sir William Brandon sat in the house of commons. The Brandons of that world usually did. Is it therefore certain that the chroniclers were mistaken when they gave the credit for leadership in the 'good parliament' to speaker de la Mare and not to the earl of March, a young and not particularly distinguished soldier, who in the event showed himself something of a coward?[4] Even the sagacious Gaunt is said to have planned his campaign against the commons in 1376 with the advice of his *privati homines*; and when he railed furiously at the presumptuousness of the knights, it was one of his own esquires who is credited with the rebuke which brought him to his senses.[5] To argue in such circum-

---

[1] *History*, xxvi (1942), 229.

[2] Reginald Pecock's *Repressor of over-much blaming of the clergy*, ed. C. Babington (Rolls Series), ii. 306.

[3] *Paston Letters*, v. 31.

[4] *Chronicon Angliae*, ed. E. M. Thompson (Rolls Series), pp. 107–8.

[5] *Ibid.*, pp. 74–5.

stances that the initiative always came from the lords is surely to enter the world of fantasy indeed.

The interdependence of magnates and gentry meant that the English body politic in the later middle ages was a complex organism and it would be doing no service to truth to emphasise the share of any one part in the working of the whole. Power was not concentrated in the hands of a few. It was distributed among king, magnates and commons in various and varying degrees, according to each man's wealth, affiliations and political capacity. A baron inherited rank and great possessions to do with what he could. They gave him vast opportunities had he the wits to use them. But he was dependent upon the goodwill, the confidence and the co-operation of his less rich but still substantial neighbours, many of whom were better educated, more experienced and more prudent than he was himself. Politics were a joint-stock enterprise and he and his advisers had got to make them pay. If they failed, there were always keen competitors ready to enlist the services of those who thought themselves ill-rewarded, slighted or badly led. These are the circumstances in the light of which the evidence for the Norfolk elections must be read. The ramifications of that intricate network of personal relationships, constantly changing and forming fresh patterns, will never be fully traced, but as we make ourselves familiar with the lives and achievements of the country gentry, and especially of those who sat in the commons, the main outlines of local and central politics may be expected to emerge.

K. B. McFarlane

APPENDIX

ANALYSIS OF THE RETURNS OF THE COMMISSIONERS, 1412[1]

TABLE A

Dorset landowners with lands in Dorset, Devon, Hampshire, Somerset and Wiltshire assessed at £100 p.a. and more[2]

No.	Name of landowner	Annual value in pounds sterling of lands in Dorset and adjacent counties					Total	Family[3] total
		Dorset	Devon	Hants	Somerset	Wilts		
1. a.	Thomas, earl of Salisbury[4]	60	—	235	90	120[5]	505	929
b.	Maud, countess of Salisbury[6]		100				100	
c.	Elizabeth, countess of Salisbury[7]	23			301		324	
2.	Edward, duke of York[8]	11		261	116[9]	231[10]	618	618
3. a.	Edward, earl of Devon[11]	60	400		40		500	600
b.	Sir Edward Courtenay[12]			40	60	—	100	
4.	Queen Joan[13]	67		281	40[14]	158	546	546
5.	Sir Humphrey Stafford[15]	237		?[16]	155	12	405+	405+
6. a.	William, Lord Botreaux[17]	20		27	168	28	243	355
b.	Elizabeth, Lady Botreaux[18]	—	40		72		112	
7.	Sir John Tiptoft[19]	51			232	50	333	333
8. a.	Sir Thomas Brooke[20]	20	40		189	20	269	313
b.	Thomas Brooke junior[21]	44			—		44	
9.	Duchy of Lancaster[22]	200		85	—	—	285	285
10.	Sir Hugh Mortimer[23]	110[24]		3	84[25]	80	277	277
11. a.	William Stourton[26]	64		20	40	70	194	275
b.	John Stourton[27]	4	10		67		81	
12. a.	John, Lord Lovel[28]	—				20	20	275
b.	Maud, Lady Lovel[29]	20				145	165	
c.	Robert Lovel[30]	50	40				90	
13.	Margaret, countess of Somerset[31]	15[32]	40	12	200	—	267	267
14.	Sir John Arundel, styled Lord Maltravers[33]	149	—	—	60	48	257	257

1 See above, p. 255.

2 In addition to the other sources mentioned in the notes, use has been made of the *Dictionary of National Biography* (those whose lives are noticed therein are marked by asterisks) and both editions of G.E.C.'s *Complete Peerage*.

3 'Family' is here taken to include only its head, his sons and brothers and the widows of his ancestors enjoying dower lands.

4* 4th earl (1388–1428) (*Register of Henry Chichele*, ed. E. F. Jacob, ii. 390–400 and 664–5).

5 £20 p.a. from issues of the county included.

6 Widow of John*, 3rd earl (1350?–1400), and mother of last-named. *Ob.* 1424 (*Cal. Fine Rolls*, xv. 52).

7 Widow of William*, 2nd earl (1328–97), and aunt by marriage of the 4th earl; daughter and co-heir of John, Lord Mohun* (1320–75). Her assessment includes that of her Mohun lands to which the Montagu earls were not heirs. *Ob.* 1415 (*Chichele Reg.*, ii. 14–18 and 664; *Cal. Inq. post mortem*, iv. 27 and 33).

8* 2nd Duke (1373?–1415) (*Chichele Reg.*, ii. 63–6 and 670–1).

9 During the minority of William Bonville the younger.

10 £66 13s. 4d. p.a. from issues of the county included.

11 3rd earl (1357–1419) (*Chichele Reg.*, ii. 178 and 649).

12 Son and heir of last-named. *Ob. s.p.* 1418.

13* Second wife of Henry IV (1370?–1437).

14 During the minority of John Daubeny.

15 See above, pp. 255–6.

16 He is said in his Dorset return (*Feudal Aids*, vi. 428) to have lands in Hampshire, but these were not assessed by the commissioners for that county.

17 (1380–1462.)

18 Widow of William, Lord Botreaux (1367?–1395) and mother of last-named. *Ob.* 1433 (*Cal. Fine Rolls*, xvi. 104).

19 See above, p. 257.

20 See above, p. 256.

21 See above, pp. 256–7.

22 In the king's hands since 1399.

23 M.P. for Gloucestershire, September 1397. *Ob.* 1416 (*Chichele Reg.*, ii. 86–7 and 666).

24 Including £40 p.a. during minority of Alice Seymour.

25 Including £60 p.a. during minority of Alice Seymour.

26 M.P. for Somerset, 1401, 1402 and January 1404; for Wiltshire, 1407; and for Dorset, 1410 and May 1413. Speaker, May 1413. *Ob.* 1413. (*Cal. Fine Rolls*, xiv. 30; *Cal. Inq. post mortem*, iv. 5.) His son and heir, Sir John, afterwards 1st Lord Stourton (1403–62), was M.P. for Wiltshire, December 1421; for Dorset, 1423; and for Wiltshire, 1425 and 1432.

27 Brother of last-named. M.P. for Somerset, 1419, 1420, December 1421, 1423–4, 1426, 1429–30 and 1435. *Ob.* 1439 (*Cal. Fine Rolls*, xvii. 52; *Cal. Inq. post mortem*, iv. 186).

28 (c. 1375–1414.)

29 Widow of John, Lord Lovel (c. 1342–1408) and mother of last-named. *Ob.* 1423.

30 Brother of 12a. M.P. for Dorset, May 1421 and 1422. *Ob.* 1428.

31 Widow of John, earl of Somerset* (1373?–1410), whose son and heir, Henry (1401–18), was a minor. She had already married, 1411, Thomas of Lancaster* (1389–1421), the king's second son. *Ob.* 1439.

32 During the minority of her son Henry.

33 (1385–1421.) Cousin and heir male of Thomas, earl of Arundel* (1381–1415). Never summoned to the house of lords, though his son and heir, John* (1408–35), afterwards was. (*Chichele Reg.*, ii. 322, 381–2, 541–4 and 637–8.)

TABLE A—continued

No.	Name of landowner	Annual value in pounds sterling of lands in Dorset and adjacent counties					Total	Family total
		Dorset	Devon	Hants	Somerset	Wilts		
15.	Henry, prince of Wales	140[1]	100	—	—	—	240	240
16.	Sir Maurice Russell[2]	122	—	40	40	—	202	202
17.	John Chidiok[3]	118	—	40	—	43	201	201
18. a.	Henry Popham[4]	8	—	60	—	90	158	191
b.	Sir John Popham[5]	—	—	20	—	13	33	
19. a.	John Lisle[6]	—	—	86	—	40	126	188
b.	Elizabeth, Lady Lisle[7]	35	—	26	—	—	61	
20.	Robert More[8]	108	—	20	—	60	188	188
21.	Robert, Lord Poynings[9]	60	—	—	123	—	183	183
22.	John Roger(s)[10]	56	—	27	100	—	183	183
23.	John Kirkby[11]	76[12]	—	33	—	53	162	162
24.	Mr. Richard Courtenay[13]	40	100	—	21	—	161	161
25.	Edward, Lord Cherleton[14] of Powys	125[15]	—	20	—	—	145	145
26.	Sir Ivo Fitzwaryn[16]	86	—	—	44	13	143	143
27.	Sir William Cheyne[17]	20	20	—	44	52	136	136
28.	John Kaynes[18]	60	20	10	40	—	130	130
29.	William Filoll[19]	124	—	—	—	—	124	124
30. a.	Robert Derby[20]	40	—	—	—	—	40	104
b.	Anice, Lady Derby[21]	43	—	—	21	—	64	
31.	Walter Beauchamp[22]	10	—	—	—	90	100	100
32.	Sir John Moigne[23]	50	?[24]	5	—	—	55+	55+

[1] During the minority of Edmund, earl of March.

[2] M.P. for Gloucestershire, 1402 and January 1404. Ob. 1416 (Cal. Fine Rolls, xiv. 143).

[3] Son and heir of Sir John Chidiok (M.P. for Dorset, 1369). M.P. for Dorset, November 1414. Ob. 1415 (Ibid., xiv. 104). He had married Eleanor, daughter and co-heir of Sir Ivo Fitzwaryn (see below, no. 26) and had succeeded to the latter's estate just before his own death (Ibid., xiv. 89). His son and heir, Sir John, was M.P. for Dorset, 1433.

⁴ Son and heir of Sir John Popham (M.P. for Hampshire, 1352). M.P. for Hampshire, February 1383, 1385, February 1388, September 1388, November 1390, 1394 and October 1404. *Ob.* 1418 (*Chichele Reg.*, ii. 137–9 and 671). His son and heir, Sir Stephen Popham (*ob.* 1444) was M.P. for Hampshire, 1420, 1423–4, 1425, 1431, 1442 (*Hist. of Parl., Biogs.*, p. 693). Sir Philip Popham (*ob.* 1397), M.P. for Hampshire, 1369, 1371, 1372, 1378 and November 1384, was a kinsman, possibly his father's younger brother.

⁵ Younger brother of last-named. M.P. for Hampshire, January 1397, 1402, January 1404 and 1407. *Ob. c.* 1415. His son and heir (and ultimately heir to Henry Popham's entailed lands), Sir John Popham★ (*ob.* 1463), was M.P. for Hampshire, 1439–40 and 1449–50 (speaker-elect). (*Hist. of Parl., Biogs.*, pp. 692–3.)

⁶ Son and heir of Sir John Lisle (M.P. for Hampshire, 1401 and January 1404. *Ob.* 1408). M.P. for Hampshire, 1417 and 1422. *Ob.* 1429 (*Cal. Fine Rolls*, xv. 236; *Cal. Inq. post mortem*, iv. 121). His son, Sir John Lisle (*ob.* 1471) was M.P. for Hampshire in 1433 and February 1449 (*Hist. of Parl., Biogs.*, 546).

⁷ Widow of Sir John Lisle and mother of last-named. *Ob.* 1435 (*Cal. Fine Rolls*, xvi. 216; *Cal. Inq. post mortem*, iv. 158).

⁸ M.P. for Dorset, 1417. *Ob. c.* 1426 (*Cal. Inq. post mortem*, iv. 101).

¹⁰ M.P. for Bridport, 1395, 1410 and May 1413; for Dorset, December 1421. *Ob.* 1441 (*Chichele Reg.*, ii. 589 and 674).

¹¹ M.P. for Hampshire, 1420. *Ob.* 1424 (*Cal. Fine Rolls*, xv. 51).

¹² £5 6s. 8d. during minority of Thomas, son of Thomas West, included.

¹³★ Son and heir of Sir Philip Courtenay of Powderham (M.P. for Devon, February 1383, 1386, February 1388, January 1390, 1393, 1395, 1399 and 1401. *Ob.* 1406). Chancellor of the university of Oxford, 1407–12; bishop of Norwich, 1413–15. *Ob.* 1415. His nephew and heir, Sir Philip Courtenay, was M.P. for Devon, 1427 and 1455. *Ob.* 1463 (*Hist. of Parl., Biogs.*, pp. 229–30).

¹⁴★ (c. 1371–1421.)

¹⁵ During the minority of his stepson, Edmund, earl of March★ (1391–1425). His 1st wife, Eleanor, dowager countess of March, *ob.* 1405.

¹⁶ M.P. for Dorset, 1378; for Devon, February 1383; for Somerset, 1397–8; for Dorset, 1406 and 1407. *Ob.* 1414 (*Chichele Reg.*, ii. 18–22, 32 and 653; *Cal. Inq. post mortem*, iv. 9).

¹⁷ M.P. for Dorset, 1402. *Ob.* 1420 (*Cal. Fine Rolls*, xiv. 334–5; *Cal. Inq. post mortem*, iv. 48).

¹⁸ *Ob.* 1419 or 1420 (*Cal. Fine Rolls*, xiv. 275; *Cal. Inq. post mortem*, iv. 44).

¹⁹ M.P. for Dorset, April 1414. *Ob.* 1415. His son, John Filoll (*ob.* 1467), was M.P. for Dorset, 1437, 1442, 1447, 1449–50, 1450–1, 1455–6 and 1467 (*Hist. of Parl., Biogs.*, pp. 325–6).

²⁰ *Ob.* 1421 (*Cal. Fine Rolls*, xiv. 377; *Cal. Inq. post mortem*, iv. 60). Son of Sir Stephen Derby (M.P. for Dorset, 1372, 1379, January 1380, November 1380, 1381–2, May 1382, October 1382, February 1383, October 1383, April 1384, November 1384, 1385 and 1386; for Somerset, January 1390; and for Dorset, November 1390 and 1394).

²¹ Widow of Sir Stephen Derby and mother of Robert. *Ob.* 1420 (*Cal. Fine Rolls*, xiv. 331; *Cal. Inq. post mortem*, iv. 51).

²²★ M.P. for Wiltshire, March 1416, speaker.

²³ M.P. for Dorset, September 1388, 1393 and January 1397. *Ob.* 1429 (*Cal. Fine Rolls*, xv. 236; *Cal. Inq. post mortem*, iv. 125).

²⁴ He is said in his Dorset return (*Feudal Aids*, vi. 425) to have lands in Devon, but these are omitted from the returns for that county.

TABLE B

Sussex landowners with lands in Sussex, Hampshire, Kent and Surrey assessed at £100 p.a. and more

No.	Name of landowner	Sussex	Hants	Kent	Surrey	Total	Family total
1. a.	Thomas, earl of Arundel[1]	546[2]	4	35	60	645	} 745
b.	Margaret, Lady Lenthale[3]	100[4]	—	—	—	100	
2.	Sir John Pelham[5]	497[6]	8	—	—	505	505
3. a.	Thomas, Lord St. John[7]	60	70	149	—	279	} 303
b.	Thomas Poynings[8]	20	4	—	—	24	
4.	Nicholas Carew[9]	80	9	45	80	214	214
5.	Richard, Lord Grey of Codnor[10]	100[11]	12	83	—	195	195
6.	John Norbury[12]	120	—	66	—	186	186
7.	John Bohun[13]	151[14]	2	—	—	153	153
8.	Thomas, Lord Camoys[15]	100	30	—	20	150	150
9.	Alice, countess of Kent[16]	8[17]	10[18]	110	20	148	148
10.	Robert, Lord Poynings[19]	144	—	—	—	144	144
11.	Sir Thomas Skelton[20]	30	107	—	—	137	137
12. a.	William Kyriell[21]	—	—	109	—	109	} 129
b.	Elizabeth, Lady Kyriell[22]	20	—	—	—	20	
13.	Sir John Arundel, styled Lord Mautravers[23]	70	—	35	20	125	125
14.	Prince Thomas[24]	100	—	—	20	120	120
15.	Thomas, Lord de la Warr[25]	100	—	—	—	100	100
16.	Joan, Lady Dallingridge[26]	100	—	—	—	100	100

Annual value in pounds sterling of lands in Sussex and adjacent counties

1* 5th earl (1381–1415) (*Chichele Reg.*, ii. 71–8 and 652).

2 £56 of this from lands held by feoffees *'ad usum domini comitis Arundellie'*.

3 3rd sister of last-named and ultimately his co-heir, wife of Sir Rowland Lenthale.

4 *'Ex assignacione predicti comitis [Arundellie]'.*

5* See above, p. 256.

6 £138 of this from manors of the Earl Marshal in Pelham's keeping by royal grant during the earl's minority, which did not end until 1413; £53 in addition by reason of the minority of John St. Clair; and a further £148 for which he had to pay annuities of that value to others. For a 'rent-roll' of Pelham's estates and offices, 1403, see Collins's *Peerage of England*, ed. Sir E. Brydges, 1812, iv. 494–5

7 (c. 1357–1429) (*Chichele Reg.*, ii. 387–90, 432 and 672).

8 Son of last-named.

9 Son of Nicholas Carew (keeper of the privy seal, 1371–7; M.P. for Surrey, 1360 and October 1377. Ob. 1390 (T. F. Tout, *Chapters in the Administr. History of Medieval England*, v. 44–5; *Cal. Fine Rolls*, x. 329 and 359; *Cal. Inq. post mortem*, iii. 124 and 131).). M.P. for Surrey, 1394, 1395, January 1397, 1397–8 and 1417. Ob. 1432 (*Cal. Fine Rolls*, xvi. 102). His son, Nicholas (1405?–58), was M.P. for Surrey, 1439–40.

10* (c. 1371–1418.) The Sussex returns have *Thomas*, Lord Grey of Codnor. This must be an error.

11 The manor of Rotherfield, formerly Lord Despenser's, Lord Grey's *'ex concessione domini regis'*, he paying Joan, widow of Sir John Dallingridge (see no. 16 below), £40 p.a.

12 M.P. for Hertfordshire, 1391. In Henry IV's service as earl of Derby. Treasurer of England, 1399–1401. Alive 27 March 1414 (*Cal. Close Rolls, Henry V*, i. 179), but seems to have died soon afterwards. (J. H. Wylie, *History of England under Henry the Fourth*, i. 28 and iii. 43, n. 12).

13 Ob. 1432 or 33 (*Cal. Fine Rolls*, xvi. 103; *Cal. Inq. post mortem*, iv. 140).

14 £41 *'de iure uxoris'*.

15* (c. 1360–1421.)

16 Widow of Thomas*, 2nd earl (c. 1350–97). Ob. 1416. There were two other dowager countesses living, Joan, widow of Thomas, 3rd earl* (c. 1371–1400, *s.p.*) and Lucia, widow of Edmund*, 4th earl (1383?–1408, *s.p.l.*, when the lands of the family were divided between co-heiresses).

17 Annuity paid by Richard Prat from manor of Iden to 'the countess of Kent'; probably the Countess Alice.

18 During the minority of the son and heir of William Audley.

19* (1380–1446.)

20 M.P. for Cambridgeshire, January 1397; for Hampshire, 1399 and 1406. Ob. ?

21 Son of Sir Nicholas Kyriell. Ob. 1413 (*Cal. Fine Rolls*, xiv. 2; *Cal. Inq. post mortem*, iv. 2). His son, Sir Thomas Kyriell (c. 1399–1461), was M.P. for Kent, 1455–6 and 1460–1 (*Cal. Fine Rolls*, xiv. 328–9; *Hist. of Parl., Biogs.*, pp. 521–2).

22 Widow of Sir Nicholas Kyriell and mother of last-named. Ob. 1419 (*Cal. Fine Rolls*, xiv. 274).

23 See above, p. 265, n. 33.

24* The King's second son (1389–1421) (*Chichele Reg.*, ii. 293–6 and 647).

25 (c. 1346–1427.)

26 Widow of Sir John Dallingridge (M.P. for Sussex, 1402, October 1404, 1406 and 1407. Ob. 1408 (*Cal. Fine Rolls*, xiii. 122; *Cal. Inq. post mortem*, iii. 321), whose father, Sir Edward Dallingridge, was the builder of Bodiam Castle, councillor to Richard II and M.P. for Sussex, 1379, January 1380, November 1380, 1381–2, May 1382, April 1384 (*Cal. Close Rolls, Richard II*, ii. 453; the *Returns* have 'Edmund'), November 1384, 1385, 1386 and February 1388).

Index